Yusuf Agherdien AmbroseC George Shaheed Hendricks

SOUTH END
- *AS WE KNEW IT*

Edited and Annotated
by
ROY H DU PRÉ

Port Elizabeth 1997

SOUTH END A

THE STORY OF SOUTH END, AS TOLD BY SOUTH ENDERS:

YUSUF AGHERDIEN,

AMBROSE C GEORGE

SHAHEED HENDRICKS

(EDITOR - PROF. ROY DU PRÉ, DEPARTMENT OF HISTROY, UNIVERSITY OF TRANSKEI)

S WE KNEW IT

P.E. Municipality

©Western Research Group, P.O.Box 17093, Saltville 6059

ISBN 0-620-20415-X

Typesetting, Layout and Design: Rahod Publishing Services, East London
Proofreading: B. Jeffery, Vista University, Port Elizabeth
Printed and bound by: Kohler Carton and Print, Port Elizabeth
Set in 11 point Times Roman
Printed on Sappi Dukuza Art.   Cover on 230gsm Dukuza Gloss
                                Text on 130gsm Dukuza Matt

Cover Picture: Eastern Province Herald, Times Media Library
Back Cover Picture: Port Elizabeth Museum

TABLE OF CONTENTS

PREFACE

Ambrose C.George and Shaheed Hendricks, school principal and teacher respectively, were toying with the idea of writing a story of SOUTH END, the suburb near the centre of the city of Port Elizabeth, where they were born and grew up. Unbeknown to them, Yusuf Agherdien, living just a few streets away, was sitting with the same idea. He, too, had been born and grew up in South End. Samiega Davids, a teacher at Arcadia High School and colleague of Shaheed, heard about the project, and brought Shaheed and Yusuf together. All the parties involved met in October 1994, and out of that meeting came the collaboration which produced this book.

The motivation for this book grew out of the desire to leave for their children the story of South End, the suburb in which their forefathers were born and grew up. It is a story which their parents had mixed feelings about repeating: On one level, the story was one of nostalgia - about the `good old days', the cameraderie, the community spirit, the happy times; about playing, living and going to school in South End. On another level, the story was too painful to recount: the trauma of forced removals in the 1960s and 1970s; the Group Areas Act and the dreaded evictions; the destruction of their houses, of the community, of their churches and their schools; banishment to the dreary and soulless northern areas; the old folks who died of broken hearts before they could moved; the friends who chose rather to emigrate.

Today, South End as they knew it, is no more. Its heart was ripped out. The suburb was bulldozed and rebuilt; streets were obliterated and others were changed and renamed. Today, it is just another upper-class white suburb of Port Elizabeth - rows upon rows of faceless townhouses; yuppie pads and uninspiring simplexes: in the words of a well-known song, `little boxes on the hill'.

Before they pass on, before they get too old, before the memory fades, the authors want to leave for their children the memory of South End as it was - the South End they knew; the South End they remembered - before the little bureaucrats came in and destroyed it all. However, while they had a burning desire to leave something for posterity, putting it into print was another matter, and a unique story on its own. This book began as a combined effort with Yusuf, Ambrose and Shaheed each bringing something valuable to the project - their memories. But this was not always going to be enough. Time plays havoc with the memory. To supplement and substantiate what they remembered, they scoured the archives and conducted interviews. Ambrose wrote up much of the information thus obtained; Shaheed conducted interviews, wrote up some of the information, and proofread early drafts. Yusuf organised the typing of the various drafts of the earlier manuscripts, put the tables and other details on computer, hunted for maps and photographs and sought out many bits of information needed to fill in the gaps. After this task was completed, the next hurdle was getting the book prepared for publication and getting it printed. In this they were very fortunate to have a number of people come to their aid.

While calling on printers to establish the cost of printing a book, Yusuf met Jimmy Fields, Publishing Manager of Kohler Carton and Print. Jimmy immediately stepped in with an offer for his company to print the book. He unselfishly gave of his private time and expert advice in organizing the printing of a sample copy of this book, and offered to find sponsors to assist with the costs of printing. Jimmy stuck with the project right to the end. This book owes much to his tenacity and loyalty.

The involvement of Roy du Pré, a History Professor at the University of Transkei, in this project was another amazing coincidence. He had come across an article, quite by chance, in an old newspaper about a `forthcoming book' on South End, and phoned Yusuf to enquire about its availability. When he found out that the process had bogged down, he offered his professional expertise as a historian and a writer; made recommendations for improvement in the content; plunged into the task of editing and annotating the manuscript; liaised on technical matters with the printers: in short, took on the role of publisher. Without the co-operation, sacrifice and interest of the many friends, colleagues and family, this book would not have been published. A huge debt of gratitude is owed all of them, as well as the many well-wishers who constantly encouraged the writers to keep going until the project was completed.

The Editor

ACKNOWLEDGEMENTS

A number of people, in a variety of ways, made this book possible. We would be remiss if we did not express our heartfelt thanks to all those who contributed in their own little ways, and to those who gave encouragement throughout the period of research.

To our mothers Galiema Agherdien, Sarah Rosaline George and Maaida Hendricks for encouragement throughout the period of research, and whose fortitude and inspiration got us to where we are today; Awaatif Agherdien, Shamiela Rasdien, Pumla Masemola and Nazley Madatt for the tedious and time-consuming task of typing the various manuscripts and (many) `final' drafts; Faizal Felix, for a highly-skilled and monumental effort photographing places of interest relevant to the study of the South End; re-shooting and developing old photographs and for providing expert advice on the quality and type of pictures which should be placed in the book; Ivan Du Plessis for developing the photographs; Margaret Harridene, Historian at the Africana Library (Main Library), Port Elizabeth for her expert guidance and valuable suggestions to expedite the research; Mrs O'Brian, librarian, Times Media, Port Elizabeth, for making available relevant material; Mr E Pike for sharing his expertise in photography; the Staff at the Intermediate Archives for extracting and making available relevant material; the library staff at the University of Port Elizabeth for making available relevant material; Jenny Benny, curator of the Port Elizabeth Museum, for her encouragement and moral support; Mr R Ball of Times Media, Port Elizabeth, for permission to use photos in the Times Media Library; Mrs B Jeffery, lecturer at Vista University (PE), for proof-reading various drafts; Mr M Dana, principal of St Thomas High School, for proof-reading the very first draft; our colleagues for their moral support and encouragement; all Ex-South Enders who so willingly shared their experiences; Fuaad Abrahams for compiling the map on South End; Tim Boddil, for guidance; Jimmy Fields for assisting in all spheres of the task of printing this book, organising the first mock-up copies, and for getting assistance from sponsors; Roy du Pré for coming to our aid with valuable advice, historical input, and for the thankless task of editing, annotating and preparing the book for publication. Lastly, but by no means the least, to our wives and family for sacrificing private time and understanding the significance of the many absences and moments of preoccupation. Without their support and encouragement, this book would never have emerged.

We would particularly like to express our gratitude to Mr S. Kleinhans and Mrs Z. Peracek for finalising the maps and Mr Shun Pillay for valuable advice.

Our heartfelt thanks to everyone
Yusuf Agherdien, Ambrose George, Shaheed Hendricks
Port Elizabeth, 1997

YUSUF AGHERDIEN was born and grew up in South End. His great-grandfather moved to Port Elizabeth in the 1800s and was a mason by trade. Yusuf was born in the same home in 10 Armstrong Street in South End, where his father and grandfather were born..

He began his schooling at Dower Primary School, continued at Hindu Primary, South End High and finally Bethelsdorp High; obtained his tertiary education at the Bethelsdorp Technical College; and currently works for the Port Elizabeth Municipality as a Plumbing and Drainage Inspector.

Agherdien has a keen interest in History and Photography and took some of the photographs in this book. He was also instrumental in the formation of the South End Museum Foundation.

AMBROSE C GEORGE was born and grew up in South End, as did his father and grandfather. He matriculated at South End High in 1961 and completed his undergraduate studies at the Universities of the Western Cape, South Africa and London. Dr George holds the B.Sc, B.Ed. Degrees from UNISA, the Secondary Teachers Diploma (postgraduate) from the University of the Western Cape, and an Associateship of the University of London Institute of Education. He completed a MEd degree with Rhodes University, Grahamstown in 1983 (dissertation:`The London Missionary Society: a study of the Eastern Cape to 1852'). In 1989 he completed a Doctor of Philosophy degree at the same university (Thesis: `A Mission and Five Commissions: A Study of Some Aspects of the Educational Work of the American Zulu Mission 1835-1910'.) Throughout his career, Dr George has been active in the community. He started his teaching career in 1965 at South End High, and spent 31 years as an educationist .He was the principal of Gelvandale High School, and also became an Educational Development Officer in 1993, retiring at the end of 1996. He suffered the wrath of the Nationalist Government during the 1960s as a student activist at the Bush University (UWC) for Coloured students. He still carries the scars, exacerbated by teaching as an unqualified teacher, and by the forced removals from South End. He retired in 1996.

SHAHEED HENDRICKS was born and grew up in South End. His parents, grand-parents and great- grandparents were born in South End. Shaheed began his education at Dower Primary in South End. He holds a teacher's diploma from the University of the Western Cape and BA degree and BA (Honours) in English at Vista University, Port Elizabeth. He is currently studying for a B.Comm degree at Vista University. Besides being a member of the South End Museum Foundation, Hendricks is also a member of the executive of the Eastern Cape Islamic Congress and convenor of the Education Committee which is a sub-department of the Eastern Cape Islamic Congress. He is an English teacher at Arcadia Senior Secondary School, Port Elizabeth.

ROY DU PRE is a History Professor at the University of Transkei. He came to the Eastern Cape in 1991, and

has lived in East London since 1992. His involvement in the South End story came after many years of research and writing on the apartheid era and its effects on various communities and individuals. In the past few years he has conducted research in the United States on the reaction and response of African-Americans to discrimination and segregation. Du Pré holds a BA in History and Sociology, BA(Hons) in History, MA in History, Higher Education Diploma (Postgraduate), and a Doctor of Philosphy degree, the latter obtained from Rhodes University, Grahamstown. (Thesis: `Confrontation, Co-optation and Collaboration: The Reaction and Response of the Labour Party of South Africa to Government Policy, 1965- 1984'). Prof du Pré has written and co-authored a number of books on South African history such as: *The Making of Racial Conflict in South Africa (1990 and 1992); Strangers in their Own Country (1992); The Rape of the Coloured People (1993); Separate but Unequal: The `Coloured' People of South Africa (1994); MZ Cornelius: A Biography (1994); A Century of Good Hope: A History of the Good Conference (1995); Hercules des Prez and his Thirty-Seven Grandchildren (1996); Against the Odds: The Life and Times of Dr IF du Preez (1996).* His latest works are *The Compromise of the Powerless, a History of the Labour Party of South Africa* (1997), and *An Introduction to American History* (due 1998). He has written chapters in books such as `One Nation, Many Afrikaners: The Identity Crisis of Brown Afrikaners in the New South Africa', in *Nasiebou in `n Multikulturele Samelewing,* by the Afrikaner Bond (1996) and `Historical Positioning' in *Wakker, Wakker en aan did Brand* by Dr C Thomas (1997). Prof du Pré also writes articles for historical journals; presents conference papers and contributes letters and articles to various newspapers.

INTRODUCTION

South End today is a quiet suburb of Port Elizabeth, most notably identified by two mosques on the way to the Airport. Despite the constant traffic on the busy freeways it looks peaceful and quiet. Yet, only thirty years ago it was a bustling suburb, brimming with activity, and populated by a very cosmopolitan community. Were it not for the Group Areas Act, it might not have been necessary to tell this story.

The story of South End is long overdue. In essence this suburb was a forerunner of South Africa's `Rainbow Nation' of the 1990s. A variety of communities and nationalities such as Indians, Malays, English, Afrikaners, Chinese, Greeks, Portuguese, St Helenians, Khoikhoin, Xhosa and Fingoes lived in harmony with one another, respecting one other's culture, language and way of life. After more than a century, the government of the day decreed that people of different colours and cultures could not live together any longer. And so came the Group Areas Act in 1950, which set aside separate residential areas for each population group as provided for by the Population Registration Act of 1950. The Group Areas Act aimed at restricting each population group to defined places as far as ownership, occupancy and trading were concerned. The ultimate goal of the Group Areas Act, however, was to extend restrictions in order to establish residential racial purity by shifting groups from one place to another.

The story of the destruction of South End is also the story of the Shame of Port Elizabeth. It is a sad fact that the Municipality of Port Elizabeth closely conspired with the National Party government of the day to evict `non-whites' from South End and other areas close to the city. Many Port Elizabeth citizens of prominent standing today, were diligent agents of the government at the time and conspired in back rooms and in secret meetings with government officials to drive people of colour out of South End, and other areas close to the city centre, and declare them residential areas for whites only.

The first sign for the South End community that it was earmarked for removal was the proclamation in 1963 which declared South End a Group Area. Then followed two years of agony and tension while the `non-white' inhabitants of the suburb waited to hear their fate. A bold headline in the newspapers on 1 May 1965 confirmed their worst fears. Soon after came eviction notices, ordering residents to move from their homes by a certain date. These notices heralded a period of extreme anguish and wrought havoc in the South End community. For many months and years, people waited in anguish for the impending removals. The agonising went on day after day - they knew they were not going to get much for their houses - which white family would want to live in their humble homes? - they would probably be compensated for the land only - that meant they would not have enough money to buy property in another (group) area, much less to even be able to build a house. Thus, many realised with a sinking feeling that they would have to move into rented houses or cramped housing schemes. How would their furniture fit into those little matchboxes? After living for generations in their own, rent-free homes, how were they now going to cope in terms of rent money, space and environment, away from their churches, schools, sports fields and clubs? They would now have to travel by bus to get to work, to school, to church. Or they would have to buy a car when they had never needed one. Would their meagre budgets be able to cope with this extra expense? The community would also be broken up as people moved piece-meal and to different areas. Would they see their friends and neighbours again? What of other members of their family?

As the axe dangled over their heads, the people of South End became obsessed with the impending removals. In many instances, the eviction notice was a death notice. Many died of a broken heart long before the bulldozers and removal trucks arrived. The pain, anguish and worry took its toll long before the move was made. Most South Africans who did not undergo this experience will never even begin to understand the consternation in the earmarked communities, nor appreciate the mental and physical anguish that accompanied forced removals. To be thrown out of your home where you and your forefathers have lived all your life was an extremely traumatic experience. If one law could be singled out as the one which caused the most anguish, the most suffering and the most deprivation, and the one which the affected people still talk about today with hatred and bitterness - then it was the Group Areas Act. The Group Areas Act dealt people a crippling economic blow and caused the death of many of the old folk. This Act will go down in history as one of the most odious and devastating of the apartheid laws. And it is this law which signalled the destruction of South End.

South End, Port Elizabeth has often been compared to District Six in Cape Town where freed slaves had started living in 1834. In the 1960s a vibrant and cosmopolitan community of 40 000 people was moved out and their homes bulldozed. However, this is where the similarity ends. District Six stood virtually empty right up to 1991, grass growing over the ruins of the homes. Although the area had been declared a white suburb, few construction companies or property developers wished to incur the wrath of the coloured people by building or investing there. That was however not the case in South End. The Port Elizabeth Municipality and property developers had no such scruples. Once the people had moved, South End was razed; churches torn down, schools demolished, the well-known streets obliterated, changed or renamed. In its place came rows and rows of identical little townhouses.

In the case of District Six, when the Group Areas Act was repealed in 1991, moves were made to return the original inhabitants to the area. As the area had remained largely undeveloped, the local authorities, property developers and former inhabitants could sit down together and plan the redevelopment of the area and the return of former residents. Unfortunately that is not the case in South End. After the inhabitants were evicted, the area was developed in indecent haste so that today, there is hardly an original house left; hardly an open stand available. The Land Claims court has now made provision for former owners to reclaim their property. But what is there to reclaim in South End? This is the Shame of Port Elizabeth.

Government bureaucrats, municipal officials, and the many whites who had been witnesses and parties to the forced removals in, and the destruction of South End, will probably shrug their shoulders and say that South End was a `slum, an eyesore and a blight on the Port Elizabeth landscape'. To them, the Group Areas Act was a welcome mechanism which enabled people to move from `unhappy, run-down surroundings to a more comfortable and civilised existence'. Many rationalised, and blindly accepted government assurances, that people would be better off living `with their own' in brick houses, with their `own churches, own schools, own community centres and own sports clubs'. While many blissfully accepted such propaganda to salve their consciences, the truth of the matter is that the Group Areas Act was not intrinsically altruistic, and the welfare and happiness of `non-whites' was furthest from the minds of the race-conscious social engineers in the National Party. The Group Areas Act had only one aim in mind, and that was racial separation.

Thus, the `non-whites' of South End had to go. But it was not merely a matter of moving people out of one area to another area. Churches had to close and church buildings had to be deconsecrated; most of them were demolished. Members of congregations were scattered all over the Northern Areas and had to start up all over again - in their homes, in little back-rooms, in community halls - until they had saved enough to build a new church building. Schools had to close; pupils had to start all over again - in strange surroundings, with strange children. Sports clubs had to close down; members had to find new facilities, in new areas, with new challenges. Businesses and shops closed down; their proprietors made destitute.

The Group Areas Act did not just move people from South End - it destroyed a community; scattered families and friends. This Act also had unfortunate and little-known consequences. Besides the old people who never made it out of South End, many residents refused to move to their designated group area and chose instead to emigrate. It might comes as a surprise to Port Elizabethans that a number of `coloured' and Indian families in South End chose to leave the country in the 1960s and 1970s, rather than become a `Group Areas Act statistic'. This phenomenon was repeated in other parts of South Africa, as well. These were the middle-class, the intelligentsia, the professionals - people with skills much-needed by this country. They emigrated to Canada, the USA, England, Australia and New Zealand. This `non-white' brain drain has seldom been mentioned, nor its cost calculated. Lastly, the Group Areas crippled its victims because many had to start all over again, with crippling mortgages.

The story of South End is a bitter-sweet story. While it might offend those whose culpability might be laid bare; while it might prove upsetting to the many who silently stood by while the Nationalist government of the day, and its willing supporters in local government, proceeded to destroy an entire community; while it might also bring back many bitter memories to former residents who might have tried to forget, it is the hope of the authors that this story might also bring hope and joy to the hearts of the thousands of powerless and voiceless South Africans who see `their' story and their `lives' revealed at last.

Because this book started out as the reminiscences of the writers - the distant childhood memories, the hazy recollections of teenage years, the hardened attitudes of young adults bitter at having been wrenched from their homes by an unfair law - it could never, nor was it intended to be the definitive history of South End. To have included everything, and everyone ever connected with old South End would have been a task so monumental that this book would never even have got off the ground. Hopefully, this humble effort will spur others to take up where this book has left off.

While this book might have started out as a casual desire on the part of the writers to let their children know something of the place where their parents and grandparents came from, it has graduated into a something more - a fairly substantial history of the area which former residents, schools, religious organisations, researchers and others could use as reference work, a source book. Because of the paucity of literature on South End, this book traverses uncharted territory. Undoubtedly, its shortcomings and inadequacies as a substantive history of the area will be corrected and improved upon by future historians and researchers. In addition, besides its contribution as a valuable historical record, this book also makes available to the public many rare and valuable photographs which have lent an air of immediacy and humanity to some of the narratives, while others will ensure that faces and places will be preserved forever for posterity. This book is therefore far being the ramblings of three raconteurs, swathed in a mist of romantic visions of a long gone era. However, while it has been the task of the editor to bring a professional historical approach to the subject matter, and provide substance to memories, it is hoped that this has not in any way interfered with the original brief, which was merely `to write a story which provides former residents of South End with the opportunity to give their children a little glimpse of how it was in South End, long, long ago.........'

SOUTH END, PORT ELIZABETH
HISTORICAL BACKGROUND

THE DEVELOPMENT OF A SEGREGATED CITY

The site of the future city of Port Elizabeth was guarded by Fort Frederick since 1799, and it was only in 1815 that a formal city was laid out. In 1820 it received its name, that of the wife of Sir Rufane Donkin, Elizabeth Donkin. One of the main features of the city was that it was British from its inception and was administered by Colonial officials. The early township was characterized by the settlement of European, Cape Malay and immigrant communities according to economic and social status, rather than on an ethnic basis as was the case in later years.[1] The British were to implement the policy of divide and rule which had been used with devastating effect in countries like India, Malaysia, and most countries in Africa.

 The presence of indigenous persons such as the Khoikhoi and Fingo in the vicinity of the town, and the influx of new settlers resulted in the introduction of a formal arrangement of segregation. The first settlement of this kind was the establishment of the segregated mission of Bethelsdorp for the Khoikhoi in 1804 by the London Missionary Society. From its inception, Bethelsdorp Mission Station provided spiritual ministry to the garrison at Fort Frederick. In 1820 work in Port Elizabeth was started in earnest for the new citizens (the 1820 settlers) who immigrated from Britain. The close association between the Bethelsdorp Mission Station and the 1820 settlers is indicated by the fact that the marriage and baptismal register of the Union Church has a number of entries of the early settler families.[2] The Union Church built in 1828 was one of the first churches built in Port Elizabeth under the aegis of the London Missionary Society. In those early years it served as a place of worship for Anglicans, Presbyterians, Baptists, Methodists as well as Congregationalists.[3] As early as 1847 the Municipality of Port Elizabeth was encouraged by the Cape Colonial Government to set aside distinct `Native Locations' some distance from the center of the town in order to ensure greater control over the indigenous inhabitants. The first location established by the Municipality was the `Native Stranger Location'. This was clearly indicative of the Colonial Government's policy that the indigenous people were only to be a temporary part of the urban population. In later years new municipal locations were established west of the city as the population increased in numbers and the existing accommodation became overcrowded. One private location called Gubb's location was established and run independently of the Municipality. Here, Africans[4] were allowed to build `traditional-style' houses and brew beer - activities not allowed in municipal locations. Gubb's location at the end of the 19th century was by far the most densely-

---

[1] AJ Christopher `Formal Segregation and Population Distribution in Port Elizabeth', *Contree,* No 24 (September 1988), 5.

[2] *Eastern Province Herald*, 28 April 1961.

[3] Union Congregational Church, *150th Anniversary Brochure, 1830-1980* (1980), 11.

[4] As is now common practice, the term `African' is used in this book in reference to those South Africans who were labelled and described as `blacks', `natives', `indigenous people', etc. The term `black' will be used in reference to all those who were victims of government discrimination. The term `non-white' is unacceptable and will not be generally used in this book. Where it has been used in the context of the time, it is placed in quotation marks.

populated location, and demands were made by white settlers for the removal of Africans to locations even further away from the city. Mainly as a result of the on-going frontier wars of the time, the attitudes of whites to racial separation hardened. his was evidenced to great effect in what Christopher calls the `sanitation syndrome. This related the mixing of the races to the prevalence of disease, while segregation, it was to be believed, would leave both whites and blacks less liable to its incidence.[5]

The crunch came in 1901 when the bubonic plague broke out in the city. This gave the Municipality the opportunity to obtain government finance to remove Africans from centrally-situated locations. Inhabitants from these locations now had two options: they could either move to a new government location at New Brighton which was situated eight kilometers north of the town, or they could buy or rent property outside the boundary of the municipality at Korsten. Korsten subsequently became the site of speculative ventures. Plots were available at low cost and the area was not subject to municipal bye-laws.[6] The Municipality succeeded in the resettlement of Africans at Korsten and New Brighton and by 1910 all Africans who could not be housed by their employers or purchase property, were settled in these two areas. Almost half of them were accommodated in barrack-style housing in New Brighton, erected by the Harbour Board, while 30% stayed in Korsten. By 1911 the African population of Port Elizabeth was highly segregated and subjected to a number of legal restraints on residential options.[7]

After the formation of the Union of South Africa in 1910, there was tremendous growth in Port Elizabeth. The population increased from 42000 in 1911 to 200 000 in 1951 due to a massive influx of people who were attracted by opportunities which developed from a broad industrial base. This resulted in rapid expansion in the size of the city as new, formal suburbs were laid out, and many populous shanty towns were erected during and immediately after the Second World War. However, this expansion of the city also resulted in new legislative measures by the government which restricted the residential options of Port Elizabeth's growing population.

Firstly, laws which governed African residence and occupation were tightened, particularly under the Natives Urban Act of 1923. The Municipality was given the responsibility for establishing and maintaining African townships which were subject to strict control. The aim was to limit the influx of migrants from the rural areas. Under the Native Trust and Land Act of 1936 restrictions were placed on the purchasing of property outside demarcated African Locations. It also prevented the establishment of new independent African residential areas. African political rights, which enabled them to purchase property in Korsten, were extinguished with the removal of the African voters from the common roll in the same year. Any new housing for Africans was confined entirely within officially-designated areas adjacent to New Brighton and Walmer Location.

Secondly, the housing of the poor, better known as slum clearance, had become the responsibility of the Municipality under the Housing Act of 1920. In order to qualify for government loans for the purpose of erecting sub-economic and economic housing schemes, the Municipality was forced to build separate housing schemes for each of the different race groups in what was known as their `own areas.' Unfortunately, no master plan was adopted in Port Elizabeth to define `own areas'. This resulted in coloured[8] and white housing schemes often being sited adjacent to one another on municipal land. These housing schemes were however separated by buffer strips and, initially, there were no road links between the townships of different groups. This resulted in single race areas for whites and coloureds

---

[5] Christopher, 'Formal Segregation' 6.
[6] Ibid.
[7] Ibid. See figure 1, 'Distribution of population, 1911'.
[8] The term `Coloured' was a creation of the Population Registration Act of 1950 and used in reference to all South Africans not classified as `European' (white) or `Native' (African). Prior to 1950, many of the people so classified had been variously referred to as `Mixed', `coloured',`St Helenian', `Malay', `Griqua', etc. At the time, Chinese and Indians were also classified `Coloured'. The former were allowed to reclassify to white and the latter were later placed in the `Asiatic' Population Group. However, for purposes of identification in this book, the term `coloured' will be used in reference to people classified or referred to as `Coloured'. See R.H.du Pre, `Racial Classification in South Africa, 1950-1991: Implementation, Implications and Consequences.' Paper presented at the biennial Conference of the South African Historical Society, Rhodes University, Grahamstown, July 1995.

being built for the first time in the 1920s. By 1940, houses for 1402 whites, 2038 coloured people and 2648 Africans had been approved by the Municipality.[9]

Thirdly, private township developers included racially-restrictive clauses in their title deeds to prevent ownership of plots by people other than those regarded as the desired race group. In most cases ownership and occupation were confined to whites. One example of this was when properties in Newton Park were sold to the Fairview Suburban Estate Company. Included was a clause which prohibited ownership or occupation by any `Coolie, Chinaman, Arab, Kaffir or any such Coloured persons.' Other developers indicated that only `fully blooded Europeans' would be allowed to occupy or purchase property. However, a fairly standard form of clause was formulated:

> This erf or any portion thereof shall not be transferred, leased or in any other manner assigned or disposed of to any Asiatic, African, Native, Cape Malay, or any other person who is manifestly a `Coloured' person, as also any partnership or company (whether incorporated or otherwise) in which the management or control is directly or indirectly held or vested in any such person. Nor may any such person other than the domestic servant of the registered owner or his tenant reside on this erf or in any other manner occupy the same.[10]

Open areas which did not have any racial restrictions attracted coloured and Asian residents, as this was the only option available to them. South End, which fell under the Walmer Municipality, a municipality with a more rural and less industrial character,adjacent to the Port Elizabeth Municipality, was one such suburb. The result was an increase in segregation as all-white suburbs such as Newton Park, Algoa Park and Humewood came into existence. In the period from 1910 to 1950, although the Port Elizabeth Municipality, like other municipalities of cities all over South Africa, had no overall segregationist philosophy, the various population groups became more separated from one another until many of the features of segregation noted elsewhere in the world became apparent. Christopher points out that although African suburbs, referred to as locations, originated in the 19th century already, only white and coloured suburbs have their origins in the 1920s.[11] Mixed suburbs like South End continued to exist, although the proportion of the population that lived there decreased, as most of the new extensions to the city grew.

It is in the light of the above development and distribution of different population groups in Port Elizabeth that we can more clearly view the South End story, and understand the broad framework in which its `cosmopolitan' make-up fitted.

ORIGINS OF SOUTH END

Originally South End consisted of four portions of land. The first portion, known as the farm Paapenbietjesfontien, was the land south of Walmer Road as far as the Shark River. The second portion of land was the section along the foreshore. The third portion of land was the section given to Captain Moreby of the 1820 British Settlers, situated all along the south side of the Baakens River. The fourth section was the section bordering Walmer in the west. The farm Paapenbietjesfontien was allocated on 21 October 1820 by Governor Lord Charles Somerset to Mynheer Gerhardus Oosthuizen. After his death his daughter, Johanna Magdalena Oosthuizen, bought the estate for 135 pounds sterling. She married a tall bearded Hollander, Jacobus Andreas Roedeloff, whose name was abbreviated to Rudolph (which became a well-known street name in South End). Roedeloff's surviving spouse became the wife of William Gardner. After the death of Johanna Magdalena Gardner, her sons acquired the estate but were not keen to look after it. A portion of the land north of Walmer Road was given to the Municipality, upon which the present Port Elizabeth Town Hall was built. In 1859, the estate of the late

[9]Christopher, `Formal Segregation', 7.
[10]Port Elizabeth Municipality: Terms and conditions of township establishment, Algoa Park.
[11]Christopher, `Formal Segregation', 7

Johanna Magdalena Gardner was divided into building plots.[12] This was the first time that South End started to develop in an orderly fashion. Up until then South End was merely a farm. Although building plots were now available in South End very few of them were purchased or developed. The cost of building and hence renting of houses was very expensive. It was not yet the responsibility of the Town Council to build houses for its inhabitants.

According to Redgrave `the development of South End was very slow and even in the late 1860s there were still very few dwellings in that part of town'.The dwellings which existed were of primitive architecture, which included 'the wattle and daub huts and tin shanties of the Malay Fishermen dotted all along the Foreshore'[13] He also mentions the `ancient red and yellow tenement that stood for many years in Thomas Street [and which] denoted the early domicile of the Rudolph family whose family graveyard was at the top of Rudolph street'[14] Prominently situated along Scott Street was a collection of tin shanties. Situated on the site where the Tyrone Hotel was later built, stood a large kraal where people kept their cattle, sheep, goats, and horses at night, and where they could allow them to graze on the commonage every morning. Firewood was gathered by the neighbours in the area, while `natives' gathered bundles of wood which they sold from door to door. From the nearby quarry, large quantities of stone was acquired to be used as ballast in unloaded ships, in order to give weight when they traversed the high seas.[15] From Rock Street on the West, to Duin farm to the South, and 1st Ave Walmer, there were no streets.

Malays played an integral, important role in the development of South End, having settled in the vicinity of Port Elizabeth from the time of the founding of the city. They were from the Cape Town area and had moved east for a number of reasons. These ranged from escaping from military duty in the face of the imminent British occupation of the Cape in 1795, to travellers with the Trekboers in the late 1700s, etc. What is certain is that the main body of Malays arrived in Port Elizabeth in 1846 when a number of those who fought for the Colonial Army against the Xhosas, decided to establish themselves in Port Elizabeth and Uitenhage after the war on the Eastern Frontier.[16] In the first directory of the inhabitants of Port Elizabeth drawn up in 1849, seventeen Malays and their families were mentioned, of which eleven lived in the so-called Malay Quarter. The presence of Malays between Main and Strand Street was established when a mosque was built in Grace Street with financial assistance from a Turkish sultan, Abdul Majid. On 7 December 1855 land was granted south of the Baakens River to the Malay community. A portion of this land was to be used as a cemetery. The Malay community had increased to such an extent that a second mosque was built in 1866 in Strand Street.[17]

In the area now called South End, Malay fisherman had already lived for a long time along the coast, south of the Baakens River. The Malays also bought some of the first plots which were offered for sale in 1859. According to Nel, `Maleiers het ook aanvanklik erwe in die nuwe woonbuurt gekoop, wat toe `n permanente Maleier teenwoordigheid van die staanspoor af in Suideinde verteenwoordig het`[18] The Malay Quarter consisted of an area between Strand Street and Main Street.(see map p.6). All the Malay families, except for three, would have been unaffected by the expansion program of the Railways at the time. One can deduce however that the later removal of Malays from the Malay Quarter to South End was a forced one. The central area of the city was being developed and Malays, regarded an 'non-whites' had to move. "Met die gedeeltelike sloping van die Maleier buurt wat as 'n kernwoongebied

---

[12]J.J.Redgrave, *Port Elizabeth in Bygone Days* (Wynberg: Rustica Press, 1947), 71.
[13]*Ibid*, 72.
[14]*Ibid,* 73.
[15]*Ibid,* 72.
[16]J.G.Nel, `Die Geografiese impak van die Wet op Groepgebiede en verwante wetgewing op Port Elizabeth.' (MA dissertation, University of Port Elizabeth, 1987).
[17]Ibid, 19.
[18]Ibid.

Port Elizabeth (1830) taken from where South End was later established.
(Cape Archives)

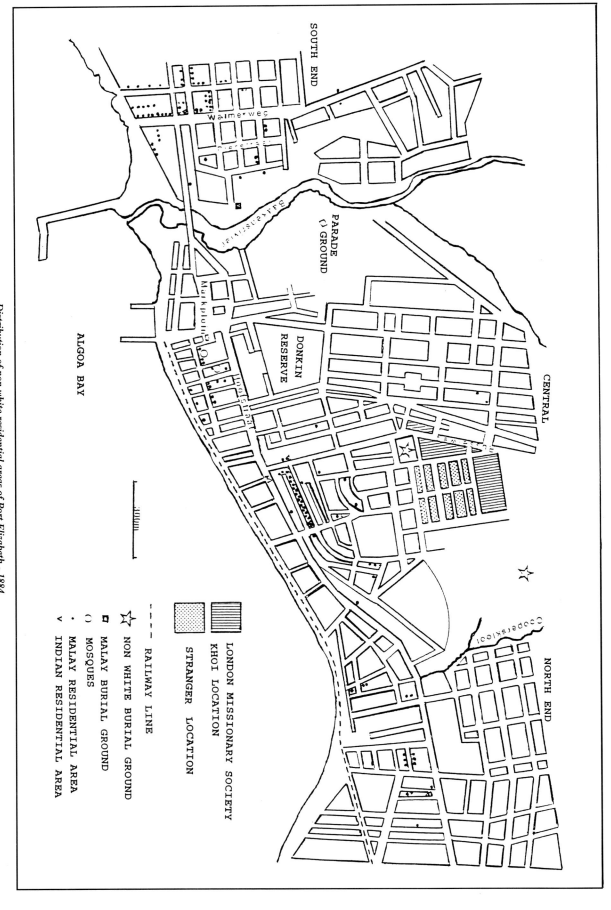

Distribution of non white residential areas of Port Elizabeth - 1884

(Source G.I. Nel, M.A. dissertation, UPE, 1987)

gedien het, is die groep se teenwoordigheid suid van die Baakensrivier numeries versterk'.[19]

The area called South End was, in the early years of its existence, referred to as `the place over the river', since access to it could only be gained by wading across the shallow part of the Baakens River, or by getting a lift on passing wagons. First erected for the use of pedestrians was a narrow wooden footbridge. However it did not last long and the whole structure was swept away by a great storm in 1847. The Malays plied the trade of using ferry boats to convey people at a penny per crossing. However this proved to be unsatisfactory and the populace began to agitate for a new bridge, to be sturdier than the previous one. The new bridge was built in 1852 by public funds and convict labour. It was renamed the `Union Bridge', since it united the town proper with `the place over the river' (South End). The newly-built thoroughfare had two names, namely North Union Street and South Union Street; streets which existed up to the demolition of South End in the 1960s and 1970s.[20]

In October 1857 there was a heavy downpour of rain which resulted in the Baakens River coming down in flood. One Sunday morning a large part of the bridge was swept into the sea. Shortly after the collapse of the bridge, ferry boats were again used to transport people across the river. The wooden part of the bridge was rescued and moored in as safe as possible a recess next to the South End breakwater, which was then in the course of construction. There was a great amount of agitation amongst the ratepayers for the building of a solid and substantial bridge in the place of the one which had been badly damaged. A new bridge was subsequently constructed for pedestrians and traffic alike.[21]

The advent of the Harbour Board, and the construction of the old South End breakwater, brought great improvements to South End. Houses of every shape and size were built, `including the humble cottages of the Malay Fishermen, and shops and stores that catered for their humble needs'. The area was progressively improved until it was almost completely devastated by a terrible storm which swept over the bay during 20 and 21 November 1867.

Apart from the Malays who lived in South End, other groups also moved into the area: Indians, Chinese, Europeans, `non-Europeans' (St Helenians), Portuguese, Greeks, Khoikhoi, Fingoes and Xhosa.

Indians - During the last three centuries large numbers of Indians set sail from the shores of India to settle in various parts of the world in countries such as Indonesia, Malaysia and Singapore; the South Seas as well as Fiji; and East and South Africa. In the latter country, British settlers in Natal in the 1800s, as in other British colonies around the world, sought agricultural labourers from India. It came to their notice that sugar cultivation in Mauritius had developed into a prosperous industry, using Indian labour. So, Natal which was known for its favourable sugar-growing potential, followed the example of Mauritius by importing indentured labour from India. The first group of labourers, who came from Madras, went ashore in Durban on the morning of 17 November 1860. Although, Madras and Calcutta were the main ports of embarkation, emigrants came from almost every part of India. They spoke a variety of languages and most of them belonging to the Hindu faith. They set foot in a strange land, bringing with them only their labour potential and cultural heritage. Twenty years later a group of professional and trading class Indians arrived in the country from Mauritius[22]. The immigrant Indian community, within a period of forty years, represented a broad spectrum of the peoples of India. Indians who belonged to various language groups, and several groups professing different faiths, lived in harmony with each other.

The indentured labour system came to an end in 1911 and the majority of Indians, who had already

---

[19]Ibid, 23

[20]Redgrave, *Port Elizabeth in Bygone Days*, 72.

[21]*Ibid*, 74.

[22]These referred to themselves as the `Passenger Class', in order to distinguish themselves from those who came as `indentured' labourers.

served their five-year terms of contract, remained in South Africa, rather than return to India.[23] Exactly when the first Indians arrived in Port Elizabeth is uncertain but it has been established that by 1890 Indians were already living in Port Elizabeth.

St Helenians - As far back as 1878 immigrants from the island of St Helena in the South Atlantic came to settle in South Africa. Those who came to Port Elizabeth settled in North End, South End, and the Hill area. They were mainly tradesmen, such as shoemakers, bakers, confectioners, etc. Some of the well-known family names include George, Benjamin, Maggot, Johns, Barth, Bowers, Joshua, Jacobs, Barry and Allison.

Chinese - The first Chinese to arrive in Port Elizabeth came on the *Norfolk* in the service of J O Smith in 1849. This was the first direct vessel to come to Port Elizabeth from China. The dates November 1881 and December 1882 are mentioned in research documents. Chinese immigrants traveled in 1881 on ships bringing tea and, in 1882 bringing artisans from Hong Kong.

In 1899 a number of Chinese refugees arrived from the Transvaal, where they had worked in the mines, at the out-break of the South African (Anglo-Boer) War. The 1905 voters' roll contained the names of 11 men, all of them general dealers and shop assistants. At the turn of the century several market gardens existed and were known as 'Chinaman's Gardens'. Of these the best known one was a large site in Princess Street between Elizabeth and Myrtle Streets. Today Port Elizabeth has the second largest Chinese community in South Africa.

Khoikhoin - The Eastern Cape was originally inhabited by Khoikhoi. Later Xhosa tribes and Fingoes formed one continuous belt from the Natal border, to the Fish River. Early contact with Port Elizabeth was made through the Bethelsdorp Mission Station, north of Port Elizabeth, which at first served mainly the Khoikhoi. The latter soon established themselves in Port Elizabeth and South End.

Africans - At the outset Africans were thinly-spread over Port Elizabeth in general and South End in particular. They contributed to the welfare and development of South End, but gradually moved to other parts of Port Elizabeth. Some of the family names in South End were Parley, Pemba and Zondi. Africans settled in South End mainly to work on the harbour.

English - The pioneering white families in South End were mainly 1820 British Settlers. Most of the streets were named after them.

Afrikaners - The origin of the Afrikaner stock can be traced to 1834 trekkers who came to settle in the vicinity of South End.

Portuguese and Greeks - Portuguese and Greeks were mainly sailors who came to settle in South End. Both of these groups tended to be business people.

Jews - During the very early years of South End, Jews were not actually resident there. They only established businesses in the area.

The mingling of the different cultural groups created a cosmopolitan South End community, characterised by a generally harmonious co-existence and cultural and religious tolerance. While many of the original inhabitants left South End, some as individuals and others as cultural groupings, others continued to arrive, maintaining the cosmopolitican nature of South End. All of this came to an abrupt end when the old South End was destroyed in the 1960s and 1970s .

---

[23]See K Harris, `Accepting the Group, but not the Area: The South African Chinese and the Group Areas Act'. Paper presented at the South African Historical Society Conference, Pretoria (6-9 July 1997), 3.

*South End
in early days.
(Africana Library)*

*Rudolph Street
after floods in 1867
(Bob Binnell
Collection)*

*North Union Street
looking into
South Union Street
(Africana Library)*

*Tram at the top end
of Walmer Road
(Bob Binnell
Collection)*

A view of South End looking towards the harbour
(Bob Binnell Collection)

Looking up South Union Street
(Bob Binnell Collection)

2

CULTURAL DIVERSITY

One of the outstanding characteristics of the old South End community was the respect for the cultural diversity of its residents. Feast days such as Eid (Muslims), Diwali (Hindus and Tamils) and Christmas (Christians) were celebrated by all the inhabitants, in the sense that they shared in the joy of the respective cultural groups. Cultural intolerance was largely absent in old South End. However, the aim of this chapter is not to discuss the culture of each group, but to concentrate on the religions. The churches, temples and mosques are discussed in the order that they were established.

ST. PETERS CHURCH

By 1860 many people were living over the Baakens River (South End) and Rev Samuel Brook of the Anglican Church in Port Elizabeth saw the need to establish a church and an elementary school. A congregation of Anglicans at South End, which was a daughter church of St. Mary's in the city, was initiated in 1871. This was done under the auspices of a missionary, Rev William Greenstock, in temporary premises. Part of the St Mary's cemetery ground was obtained to erect a church building, designed by Rev George Smith. He later became the first resident minister of the church. The foundation stone was laid on 30 October 1875 by Bishop Merriman and on 29 July 1877 a permanent structure was opened. It became an independent parish in 1878.[1] Father Paddy served as minister and principal of St. Peters Church and school respectively. He was `a legend in his own right in the history of the church'[2] and took an active part in sport. He was instrumental in the formation of Paladins Soccer Club and St Peters Hockey Club.

Other priests who followed over the years also made their mark on this church. For instance, Rev Saeger, who followed Rev Harrison in 1954 as minister of the parish, established the Sea Scouts. This organisation was not confined to boys of St Peters church only, but was open to all interested youth. St Peters made its mark as a church, school and sports centre. However a tragic chapter in its history unfolded after the wave of Group Areas removals forced congregants out of the area by the 1970s. The church was vandalised after most of the congregants had left South End. Eventually the church was deconsecrated in 1972, bringing to an end a century of witnessing in old South End. The scattered congregation was dispersed all over the Northern Areas. Groups of former congregants came together and organized religious worship services in homes, school halls, and community centres in different parts of the suburbs. The majority joined up with Anglicans from other areas in Port Elizabeth who had also been affected by the Act. These were later instrumental in forming Christ the King Church in Gelvandale, St Mark and St John's in Parkside and St Mary Magdalene in West End.[3]

PIER STREET METHODIST CHURCH

Rev James Fish of the Russell Road Methodist Church started Methodism in South End in 1872. He held regular services in a chapel in South Union Street. The early years were difficult, but at a meeting

---

[1] Margaret Harridene, *Port Elizabeth* (Port Elizabeth: EH Walton Group, 1996).
[2] Danny Barth, interview with authors, Port Elizabeth, 18 July 1996. Danny Barth was a church member and youth leader at St Peter's.
[3] Ibid.

held on 15 July 1881 it was decided to build a church. Plans were drawn and building operations started. On 3 May 1882, two foundation stones were laid by Mr R King and Mr H Bisseker.

The church was built on the corner of Upper Pier and Mitchell Streets and was to serve the community for nearly ninety years. On Friday 5 January 1883, an announcement appeared in the *Herald*: `To-morrow (Sunday) 7 January 1883, the Dedicatory Services will be held, when the Rev J Walton, M.A., President-Designate of the Wesleyan Conference, will preach Morning and Evening.' In the *Herald* of 8 January 1883, the church was described as follows: `The new church is situated in a commanding position and though without much architectural ornament is light, strong, comfortable and splendidly ventilated'.[4] Thus the church was consecrated on 7 January 1883. Thereafter, the congregation grew rapidly.

This church was affected by the Group Areas Act in the 1960s and had to be expropriated. The 30th Minister of Pier Street Methodist Church, Rev R Davies, had to see to the implementation of a resolution of the Church, namely that it be closed down. It was not an easy task to undertake, especially as he had chaired some difficult meetings which had to decide on the procedure of how the closure of the church should be undertaken. The last christening service at Pier Street was conducted on the morning of 30 January 1970. On Sunday morning 20 February 1972 he administered the sacrament of Holy Communion for the last time to the congregation. The church was deconsecrated after more than 90 years of Christian witness in South End.[5]

WALMER ROAD BAPTIST CHURCH

Walmer Road Baptist Church in South End was the first extension of the Queen Street Church, the first Baptist Church established in Port Elizabeth in 1854. The first church building was in the vicinity of a blacksmith's shop of which Kenhall remarked: `Where fire moulded stubborn iron, superior fires were lit to mould young lives in the South End Sunday School'.[6]

The children in the Sunday School were from the Baptist families which had emigrated from St Helena. The minister of the Queen Street Baptist Church, Rev HJ Batts reported: `South End Mission was begun in 1881 with encouraging results'. However, it was only in 1888 that a church was established with twenty-five members. Its first minister was Rev HJ Cousins. The next minister was Rev JH Buchanan who in the two periods of his ministry saw the church emerge from its infancy into adolescence[7] It was in 1898 that a church was built, and it remained a prominent landmark on the brow of Walmer Road hill for three quarters of a century.[8]

The church showed rapid development and in 1912 the membership doubled. Sunday School membership reached the record number of 264. However in 1913 the inter-racial character of the church ended with the exodus of the larger European section of the congregation to form the Victoria Park Baptist Church on the corner of Walmer Road and First Avenue, Walmer. The Walmer Road Baptist Church subsequently went through a difficult period of development under successive pastors. During the second period of Rev Buchanan's ministry, he took up the task of encouraging his congregants to accumulate funds for the building of a hall. Enough money was collected and the hall was built, named the Buchanan Hall. The hall was used by the whole South End community as classrooms, as well as a meeting place for sports bodies. The Church developed rapidly under Rev LJ Larson and it experienced a renewed upsurge in interest and membership.

The work of the Church was consolidated under Rev Waterson who took over the ministry in 1951. He was succeeded by Rev Kinsman, who presided when the church was deconsecrated about 1970.

---

[4] C. Derbyshire, Brochure, *South End Methodist* (n.d.), 19.
[5] *Ibid.*
[6] Kenhall, *Walmer Road Baptist Church, Port Elizabeth, 75th Jubilee* (1988), 23.
[7] *Ibid,* 25.
[8] *Ibid.*

13

St Peter'xs Church Wardens
L-R Mr Isaacs, Mr J. Muller, Mr Oosthuizen, ... Mr D. Macbean, Mr J. Dorothy, Mr Brooks, Mr Rockman, Mr J. Stowman, Mr Seale.
(Mrs G. Valley)

Baptist Church, on the corner of Walmer Road and Bullen Street
(Bob Binnell Collection)

St Peter's Church in Rock Street
(Bob Binnell Collection)

Methodist Church in Pier Street
(Bob Binnell Collection)

14

Masjied Ul Abraar- Rudolph Street Mosque
(Bob Binnell Collection)

Masjied Ul Aziz (Pier Street Mosque)
(Bob Binnell Collection)

Mr Omar Cassim re-decorating inside of Masjied Ul Abraar
(Times Media Library)

Baptist Church Sunday School Staff and Pupils
(Baptist Church Brochure)

The Malays were among the first people to buy plots in South End when the original farm was divided. With a well-established community a mosque was required. In the early 1890's Imam Jalaludien Abrahams realized the necessity for a masjied to serve the community west of South Union Street. Together with his trustees, Mohammad Tape, Mossa Agherdien, Mohammad Idries Taybo, Malik Saban and Ayoob Sandan they set about the task of having a mosque built. On 29 August 1893 Lot 34, situated in Rudolph Street, was transferred in favour of the Imam and his trustees. The erf, measuring one hundred square feet, was purchased from William Earl at a price of one hundred pounds. The original masjied, Masjied Ul Abraar (Mosque of Righteousness) was completed in 1894. The masjied underwent a number of changes over the years and in 1950 it was extended to accommodate the growing Muslim community.

The fine artistry in the centre of the masjied is the original migrab[9]. In the early 1960s, before Omar Cassim was exiled, he redecorated the interior and reconstructed the new migrab of the masjied. The most recent construction was completed in 09 Thul Haj 1412 (30 May 1993).

Over the years seven Imams (priests) served the community, the first being Imam Jaludien, followed by Imam Tayboe, Imam Alawie, Imam Ayoob Sandan, Imam Abduraoaf Tayboo, Imam Omar Mallick and Imam Sadaka Abader.

MASJIED UL AZIZ (PIER STREET MOSQUE)

The origins of the Pier Street Mosque date back to when the Strand Street Mosque was sold in 1900. The Strand Street Mosque was registered and held in trust for the Malay community by Abdul Wahab Salie. The land on which the mosque stands was purchased by Abdul Salie. The mosque was designed by the architect JA Holland and was built by Messrs Trunick and Curtiss for the amount of 1345 pound sterling. The mosque was officially opened on the 27 July 1901.The congregation was served over the years by the following Imams: Imam Abdul Wahab, followed by Imam Salie, Imam Noorien, Imam Shieraaj, Imam Armien Connolly, Imam Abdulatief Kahaar, Imam Igsaan Nakerdien. The newly appointed Imam is Imam Isgaak Abrahams.

When South End was declared white there was an uproar from the Malay community because of the threatened destruction of the mosque. The matter went as far as the United Nations where the Moslem nations stated unequivocally that a mosque could never be demolished. The mosques survived the Group Areas bulldozers but in later years a further controversy erupted over the Pier Street Mosque when the Port Elizabeth Municipality wanted to build a freeway. Because the mosque could not be demolished, the Municipality decided to build the freeway over the mosque. However the dome was too high and the Municipality ordered the removal of the dome. The ensuing outcry landed the matter in the South African Parliament which decided not to built the freeway over the mosque but to change the routing. However by then, the mosque had already lost its dome. Today the Pier Street Mosque can be still seen without the original dome, stark testimony to the insensitivity and stubborness of the officials at the time.

Up to this day both South End mosques are still used by the community. The Rudolph Street Mosque stands in the present-day Walmer Boulevard, on the road leading to the Airport and the suburb of Walmer. The Pier Street Mosque is situated on the left of the freeway leading into Humewood.

PRESBYTERIAN CHURCH

On 10 November 1901 the opening services were held in St Andrew's Presbyterian Church in Upper Pier street, between Kenny and Bullen Streets. The foundation stone was laid on 24 November 1900. The Presbyterians later moved out of South End; the building was sold to the Dutch Reformed Church in 1928.

UPPER VALLEY ROAD TEMPLE

In the period prior to 1893 there were a few prominent families in the Tamil community, namely the R R Naidoo families, Appavoo families, the Namsoo family, the V D Pillay families. The S S Brothers

[9]A migrab is the place in the mosque from which the Imam leads the people in prayer.

were the Subramanies Subramanies Padayachee family, who were the leading members of the religious community. As their names were rather long, they were given much easier names. Due to the absence of any place of worship, they attended St Peters Church, but they felt unhappy, and decided to erect a temple. There were two schools of thought; one group felt that the Temple should be erected on the Old Quarry land in Fairie Street, while the other group were keen to have the Temple near the river. Finally concensus was reached and both groups joined forces. In May 1893, land was purchased for the sum of 125 pounds, and the temple was erected between 1893 and 1901 at Rufane Vale (Upper Valley Road) on erf 85. The Temple was consecrated in 1901 and is still in use today.

RUFANE VALE BAPTIST CHURCH (also called the `Mission of Queen Street Church')

The church was a wood-and-iron structure situated on the upper edge of the southern bank of the Baakens River. The funding of the church was initiated in 1903 by Rev A Hall of the Queen Street Baptist Church. Its building was made possible by funds made available by the parishioners of the Queen Street Baptist Church.
  The Rufane Vale Mission existed as a separate church from the Walmer Road Baptist Church until 1952. In that year the loose association between the two churches was tightened and it came under the direct jurisdiction of the Walmer Road Baptist Church. Many of the parishioners moved to Schauderville and other areas of the Northern Suburbs in the 1960s and 1970s when old South End was declared a white Group Area.

MARIAMMAM TEMPLE

The Mariammam Temple, which was situated on the corner of Gardner and Rudolph Streets in South End, was established in 1912. Under the Presidency of Mr .S R Naidoo and the guarantee of Mr Valayden of Veeplaas it was rebuilt and consecrated on 27 August 1940. The officiating priest was Mr B S Manian Pillay who performed the opening ceremony. On 14 April 1971 this Temple was sold by the administrators. The progressive members of the community opposed it. Protests were held and an appeal was made to the State president who agreed to re-transfer the temple back to the community on condition there was unanimity.obably around 1972. The administrators of the Temple refused and so the Temple was lost. This is a prime site in South End.

VICTORIA PARK BAPTIST CHURCH

Up to 1912 the entire South End-Walmer area was served by one church, namely the Walmer Road Baptist church. However, in 1913 the non-racial character of the church ended with the exodus of the larger European section of the congregation to form the Victoria Park Baptist Church in the predominantly European area of Walmer. This church still stands today and occupies a prominent position in the upper end of Walmer Road. It still serves as the place of worship of a predominantly white congregation.

SOUTH END UNION CONGREGATIONAL CHURCH (Robson Memorial).

This Church has its birth in the mission work started by Dr Van der Kemp at Bethelsdorp in 1804 under the aegis of London Missionary Society. The Bethelsdorp missionaries rode ten miles from Bethelsdorp to hold services in a small room with a clay floor and thatched roof, situated somewhere near the site of Union Church in Chapel Street in the city centre of Port Elizabeth.

17

Valley Road Temple
(Faizal Felix)

Mariaman Temple, corner of Farie and Gardner Street
(Bob Binnell Collection)

Dutch Reformed Church
(Bob Binnell Collection)

Rufane Vale Baptist Church
(Baptist Church Brochure)

18

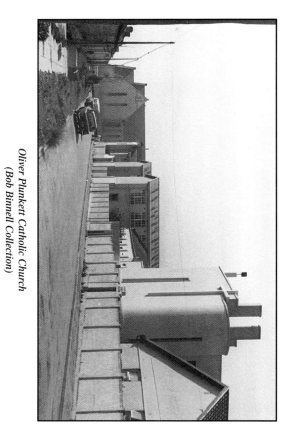

Oliver Plunkett Catholic Church
(Bob Binnell Collection)

Baptist Church, corner of
Walmer Road and First
Avenue, Walmer
(Faizal Felix)

Presbyterian Church
(Faizal Felix)

South End Union Church
(Bob Binnell Collection)

In these homely services were sown the seed from which Union Church grew. The first chapel building was completed with the assistance of Khoikhoi carpenters and Fingo labourers, and financially supported by local businessmen. The building, when completed and dedicated, was named `Union Church' in recognition of the non-racial and non-denominational nature of its congregants. In those days Port Elizabeth ended with Russell Road and the population was still small. Union Church was therefore used as a place of worship by Anglicans, Presbyterians, Baptists and Methodists, as well as Congregationalists.

The church building was consecrated in 1928 during the ministry of the Rev Weiss (1912-1932), who also initiated its planning and subsequent construction. Like other church schools it was a church- school unit in which the church building also served as classrooms. During the ministries of Rev CP Geldenhuys (1932-1946 and 1960-1965) and Rev Reneke (1947-1959), the church showed phenomenal growth.

Robson Memorial, through dynamic personalities, made a significant contribution to the spiritual and educational life of a vibrant South End. It was indeed a very sad occasion when it had to close its doors in 1968 because of the Group Areas Act.[10] The congregation was dispersed and most of the congregants worshipped in a classroom of the Papenkuil Primary School in Gelvandale for many years. It was only in 1976 that a new church building was erected in Parkside.

THE BLESSED OLIVER PLUNKETT CHURCH

In 1936 the Blessed Oliver Plunkett Church was opened. In 1938 an existing house next to the church was altered for the Maris Stella Convent. The congregation consisted of coloured as well as white members. Father John Little was the first parish priest and Mrs Felix was the organist and leader of the choir for a number of years.

The male church members organized themselves into a strong group, which was known the society of St Vincent de Paul. The female counterpart was known as the Ladies of Charity. These two groups did yeoman work among the poor. In the 1940s the church also started a youth group which consisted of young church members. The youth group was mainly formed to do work amongst the poor and needy. Oliver Plunkett Hall was a cultural centre where many games and indoor sports were played. The highlight of the Catholic calendar was the St Patrick's Day Celebration. On this day concerts were held; children did Irish reels and performed sketches of the funniness of the Irish. Many weddings, meetings, receptions, dances and cultural activities were held in the hall.

As a result of the implementation of the Group Areas Act the church finally closed its doors in 1970-71. This event cause great sadness amongst the congregation. At the ceremony of the deconsecration of the stone, many people wept openly. A remarkable feature of the church during its years in South End was that it kept its doors open day and night.

DUTCH REFORMED CHURCH

This Church, and the First Avenue Baptist Church, are the only two church buildings, besides the two mosques, which remain in present-day South End. The purchase of the Presbyterian Church building in Bullen Street in South End in 1928 led the way to the establishment of the southerly part of the Pienaar Congregation (Port Elizabeth Central) as an independent congregation. The church building had a seating capacity of 400. The church council of this congregation decided in principle on 3 June 1929 that the time was ripe to become an independent congregation. A motion was also accepted with a guarantee list, to make this proposal binding, to be circulated among the congregation in South End.[11]

On 7 September 1929 a meeting of the congregation in the South End church building was held. 65 members and 10 deacons were present. A proposal was unanimously accepted that the chairman, Dominee DL Steijl of the Pienaar congregation, would present the guarantee lists to the church authorities (Ring)

---

[10]Union Congregational Church, *150th Anniversary brochure, 1930-1980* (1980).

[11]H.O Terblanche, `Die Nederduitse Gereformeerde Kerk in Port Elizabeth: 'n Historiese oorsig van die eerste halfeeu, 1907-1957' (MA dissertation, University of Port Elizabeth, 1973), 124.

that the church become independent. The deacon, Van der Merwe proposed that the newly-independent church be called, Port Elizabeth South.[12]

On the instruction of the church authorities (Ring) of Graaf-Reinet the Ring Commission on Saturday 19 October 1929, meeting in the South End church building in front of a large audience, declared the Port Elizabeth -South Dutch Reformed Church independent.

This church also became a victim of the Group Areas Act and had to close in the 1970s. The building still stands on the hilly slope of South End and is used today by the Old Apostolic Church who purchased the building in 1983 from the Department of Community Development.

SEVENTH-DAY ADVENTIST CHURCH

The place of gathering was situated in Mackay Street in Port Elizabeth Central. Lawrence Meintjies and James Edwards were the first coloured people in South End to become members of the Church. About 1936 or 1937 Pastor BW Abney, an African-American missionary and pastor-evangelist from the United States of America, conducted meetings in Port Elizabeth where Meintjies and Edwards accepted the teachings of the Church. Seventh-day Adventists first met in a hall in central Port Elizabeth and later moved to the church in Mackay Street. The first Pastor, who originally came from Kimberley, was Jannie De Beer. He was succeeded by Pastors Kenneth Landers of Durban, and Daniel Gold Theunissen of Cape Town, whose father had converted the first Adventists in Port Elizabeth in the 1920s.[13]

Seventh-day Adventists did not have a large following in South End and the membership grew only as the families belonging to this Church grew. When the church in Mackay Street was expropriated under the Group Areas Act,[14] some of the members wanted to go to other Churches .

When members of the Church were moved out of South End, they hired a wood-and-iron building in Elkana Street, Korsten, from African members of the Seventh-day Adventist Church who were themselves, ironically, being removed from Korsten in terms of the Group Areas Act. As the membership of Adventists increased, due to an influx of other victims of Group Areas removals, proselytising, and the extension of the Northern Areas, more meeting places opened up. The Helenvale group met in the Toynbee Club in Kobus Road, Gelvandale; the Salt Lake group met in the De Heuwel Primary School in Hillside; the Springdale congregants met in the church at the corner of Geldenhuys and Stuart Streets and, lastly the Bethelsdorp group met in the church which is situated in Coombs Road, Bethelsdorp.[15]

NEW APOSTOLIC CHURCH[16]

The work of the New Apostolic Church started in South End on the instruction of the Apostle HF Schlaphoff. He commissioned Elder John Robert Bell, the son of Bishop Edward Bell who was in charge of the work in the Eastern Cape at the time, to 'throw in the net on the other side'. This meant - 'to make a start with the work in South End, as there were many souls who needed the help and the blessing of the Lord.' This took place about the years 1940-41. Early services were held in the home of a Mrs Wringquest and her son-in-law, a Mr Bagley. When this venue was no longer suitable, largely due to the growth in numbers, a new venue had to be found. The District Elder, JR Bell, then built a double garage

[12]*Ibid.*

[13]IF du Preez and R.H.du Pré, *A Century of Good Hope: A History of the Good Hope Conference, its Educational Institutions and Early Workers, 1893-1993* (East London: Western Research Group, 1995, Vol.2), 4. Vol 1 deals with the development of the Seventh-day Adventist Church among 'coloured' South Africans in the period 1893-1993.

[14]Abe Beaton, interview with authors, Port Elizabeth, 18 January 1996. Mr Beaton became a member of the Church in 1940. He passed away on 8 May 1997 before another interview could take place.

[15]Ibid.

[16]Information supplied by LH Bell of the New Apostolic Church, Port Elizabeth, 1997.

21

RIGHT: Seventh-Day Adventist Church, on the Hill (Faizal Felix)

LEFT: Union Congregational Church (Robson Memorial)

Masjied Ul Aziz - Pier Street Mosque (Port Elizabeth Municipality)

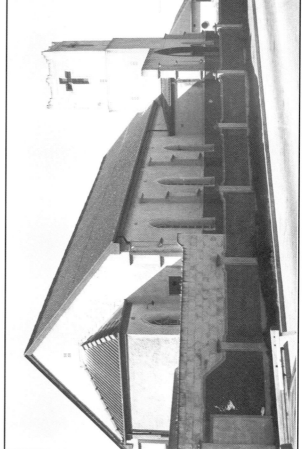

Apostolic Church, Corner of Rudolph Street and Forest Hill Road (Bob Binnell Collection)

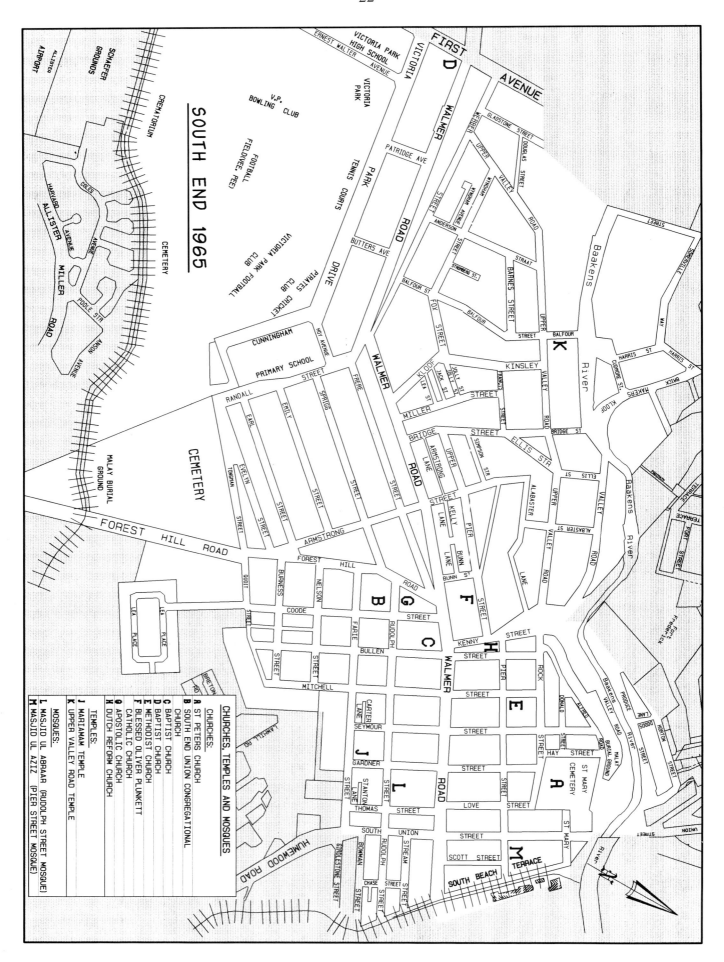

SOUTH END 1965

CHURCHES, TEMPLES AND MOSQUES

CHURCHES:
A ST PETERS CHURCH
B SOUTH END UNION CONGREGATIONAL
   CHURCH
C BAPTIST CHURCH
D BAPTIST CHURCH
E METHODIST CHURCH
F BLESSED OLIVER PLUNKETT
   CATHOLIC CHURCH
G APOSTOLIC CHURCH
H DUTCH REFORM CHURCH

TEMPLES:
J MARIAMAM TEMPLE
K UPPER VALLEY ROAD TEMPLE

MOSQUES:
L MASJID UL ABRAAR (RUDOLPH STREET MOSQUE)
M MASJID UL AZIZ (PIER STREET MOSQUE)

on his property. He told the authorities it would be used for his business vehicles, but he used it for the conducting of services on a regular basis.

The work then grew fairly rapidly and the congregation, then known as `Bunns Lane,' had to endure much discomfort because the `hall' was too small. A piece of ground was obtained in the area close to `Bunns Lane'. By 1945 the membership had grown to around 120 and Apostle Schlaphoff then consented, after a struggle in obtaining suitable ground on which to build a church, that the project go ahead. The church was built and the hall inaugurated on 11 November 1945 by Apostle Schlaphoff. This immediately after World War II, when materials were difficult to come by. Bishop Edward Bell made the windows in his factory. This building stood out in the area because of its tower and gothic-shaped windows. The work had grown even more by then and the congregation had swelled to around 300 members. A gallery had to be built later to house the growing congregation. New developments in the city, such as new housing developments, as well as the application of segregation laws, meant that many members left South End. Despite the continual exodus from the congregation, the membership remained constant as there were always new members being added.

During 1955 Apostle Abicht ordained Bishop JR Bell as Apostle of the Lord. By the 1960s the trickle of members out of South End became a torrent as the Group Areas Act began to force residents out of the area. The rest of the members left South End during the years 1972-75 and the church complex was taken over by members from the Southdene Congregation and used during the above period.

The South End congregation was a model congregation and `mothered' many congregations in Uitenhage, Fairview, Missionvale, Kleinskool, Raphael Crescent, Alexandria and Aberdeen (the first member of Aberdeen was adopted in South End). There were also many other aspects of the Lord's work where this congregation was a pioneer. There was the famous Brass Band which often performed in front of the church, and also in the residential areas of the suburb; the mixed choir which performed at other celebrations and activities of other organisations, and the Boys Brigade which at one stage which was synonymous with this congregation. The talent in this congregation was carefully nurtured by Apostle Bell who encouraged his family always to set the first example. Today these talents are enjoyed by many of the New Apostolic congregations, as the children and grandchildren of the original members are still performing in music and other activities of the work of the Church.

In this review of the various religious organisations existing in the old South End, one is struck by the great diversity of religions and worship. Yet, a remarkable feature was the ability of all these diverse religions to co-exist in harmony and without friction. Above all, the religious centres were not only places of worship but served a wider cultural role. They looked after the spiritual well-being of the community but also catered for the social, educational, welfare and sporting activities of their members. The religious centres held the community together. The coming of Group Areas legislation was therefore more devastating than historians and the media have ever indicated. The delicate fabric of the community began to unravel. By moving members and closing the churches, the Group Areas Act destroyed the strands that held people together. The rise of gangs and on-going gang activity and gang warfare in the Northern Areas today can largely be traced to the destruction of the social fabric by the Group Areas Act in the 1960s and 1970s. In this chapter one is also struck by the fact that none of the Church congregations survived the Group Areas onslaught and, except for two church buildings and the two mosques, none of the places of worship stand today. It becomes abundantly clear that the God-fearing members of the National Party were so obsessed with racial separation that they had no qualms about sending in the bulldozers to demolish places of worship and scatter `non-white' church members (many of whom were themselves members of the Afrikaners' Churches, like the Dutch Reformed Church) to the farthest corners of the globe. This fanatical obsesssion with colour showed scant respect for the worship of God and human dignity, where the worshippers happened to be a darker shade of white. Supporters of the National Party government, and proponents of the Group Areas Act might have rationalised that this law was merely about moving people of different colours into separate residential areas for their own welfare. This was furthest from the truth: it also resulted in the destruction of church buildings and the scattering of church congregations. The destruction of religious life in South End gave the lie to this lie. Religious worship suffered incalculable harm because of the single-minded determination of the National Party to pursue its obsession, the consequences of which are still with us today.

3

EDUCATION

The first school in Port Elizabeth was founded in 1824 under the aegis of the London Missionary Society by the missionaries from Bethelsdorp mission station. It was called the Union Chapel School since it was connected to the Union Church situated in Chapel Street.[1]

A missionary record dated 1829 stated that the school in Port Elizabeth had been better attended than formerly since the erection of the church, and `parents began to perceive the importance of education to their children.'[2] The record further states that colonial policy did not practice segregation neither did the small playground allow for social distinction. The little school went along happily with the only rule for the admission of pupils being that `they must be decently clothed.'

This school, which was part of the Union Church, was fathered by Captain Evatt and the Superintendent in 1841 was the Rev Robson of the Union Church. When Sir George Grey, the Governor of the Cape, visited Port Elizabeth he found the conditions of the Government Free School (Union Chapel), where white and black pupils of the town shared the same classrooms, totally unsatisfactory. As a result he was instrumental in having the Grey Institute established at a site not far from the Union Church. Unfortunately, this school was for white pupils only.[3] During his governorship Sir George Grey established the Grey Foundation which, in Port Elizabeth, saw to the establishment of exclusive English Schools for white pupils only. Nowhere in the London Missionary Society documents of the period is there any indication that Sir George Grey's government offered financial assistance to Union Chapel School which by this time only served `non-whites'.

From 1875 when it was taken over by the Congregational Union of South Africa (CUSA), the London Missionary Society was responsible for establishing eleven church schools for mixed-race pupils in Port Elizabeth, including two in South End. Other churches joined the London Missionary Society, and later the CUSA, in providing schools for `coloured' pupils in South End. The schools established were St. Peters (Anglican), 1865; South End Congregational School, Seymour Street, 1882; Dower, 1918; South End Union, 1924; St. Monica's (Roman Catholic), 1940; St. Thomas High School (Roman Catholic), 1942; and Hindu Primary,1942.

Education was important to the residents of South End. At the time of the passing of the Group Areas Act in 1950, the following primary schools existed in South End: Hindu, Dower, Forest Hill Road, Lea Place, South End Union, St. Monica's, Cunningham, St Peters, Victoria, Grey and the following high schools: South End High, St Thomas and Victoria Park.

The schools were attended by successive generations and strong bonds of tradition were built up. Most of the schools for `Coloureds and Indians' were also linked to certain Churches. There was a very close liaison between the Church and the school. The principal and teachers were invariably also members of the Church. The school principal would always consult with the Church before a major project was tackled. The buildings erected by the Church were hired by the State but the Church had to see to all the educational needs.

[1]AC George, `The London Missionary Society: A study of the Eastern Cape from 1852 to 1983', (M.Ed dissertation, Rhodes University, 1983)19, 70.
[2]Union Congregational Church, *150th Anniversary brochure*, 11.
[3]*Ibid.*

A. MISSION SCHOOLS IN SOUTH END

ST PETER'S CHURCH SCHOOL, 1871-1950

The school, like the church, was started in 1871 in temporary premises. Just like other Churches of the time, part of the school and church was housed in the same building. The church was also utilized for school purposes. The first minister, Rev George Smith ,was also the first principal. St Peter's school was also called `the mission' and was spread over a number of buildings in other parts of South End. A wood-and- iron building on the corner Mitchell and Farie Street housed the Sub As of St Peter's School. The school was the first church school in South End to produce pupils who reached the highest standard for coloureds at the time, namely Standard Six. On passing Standard Six they could then proceed to Dower College in Uitenhage where they could complete the post-Standard Six Teachers' Course. In the early years St Peter's, though an Anglican school, also served the Malay community, since they had no school of their own.[4] A memorandum to the Bishop of Grahamstown regarding the condition of the Anglican Church in Port Elizabeth reveals that in 1889 there were about 1500 Malays in the city. They had several priests and two mosques. Since they had no school of their own they had to rely on Church schools for their educational needs. Father Paddy decided to establish a High School. The foundation was laid at the lower end of St Peter's. The authorities stopped the erection opf the school. The foundation still exists. Except for some students who passed standard six and did teacher training at Dower Memorial College in Uitenhage, the rest were forced to go and work because no tertiary institutions existed in port Elizabeth at that time.

Due to the poor condition of part of the school building, it was regarded as unsuitable for educational purposes and St Peter's was forced to close its doors in 1950. All the pupils and teachers were moved to the newly-built Lea Place Primary School further up the hill in old South End. The Humewood Police Station was later built on the site of Lea Place Primary School. The enclave of Lea Place with its houses and white tenants is still in existence today. Among the teachers who were members of the staff before the school closed were Miss Isabel Rockman, Mr Clarence Peterson, Mr O George, Mr Quanson, Mr Aubret Langson, and the last principal, Mr Roberts, who later became principal of Forest Hill Road Primary School.

Teachers at the school in 1906 were: Manan Baartlett, Sarah Hughes, Dorothea (Dora?) Edwards, Violet Spearman, Elizabeth Blair; and in 1925 - Alfred Paddy, Effie Russel, Allie Cupido, Lena Adams, Janetta Ross, Gallie Bruwer, Werna de Klerk..

SOUTH END CONGREGATIONAL MISSION SCHOOL/SEYMOUR CHURCH SCHOOL/DOWER PRIMARY SCHOOL (1882-1968)

The London Missionary Society eventually relinquished its support of mission schools in 1875 and handed the reins to the Congregational Union Church of South Africa (CUSA).Although finance was in short supply it did not prevent the Church from expanding their educational work.

In 1880 the Superintendent General of Education received an application from Rev Macintosh for aid to a school which was opened in March 1882. This school was first called South End Congregational Mission School, then Seymour Street Church School, and finally Dower Primary School after Rev W Dower of the Union Church.

Edward Holbeck Burness, with 22 years of teaching experience, and his daughter Catherine Burness, 18 years of age, were the proposed teachers. The schoolroom was 28 feet by 20 feet and 10 feet high (8,5m x 6,1m x 3,1m). Temporary offices were provided and the furniture of the school consisted of writing desks and a blackboard. In 1883 the number of children on the roll of the school was given as:

---

[4] D Barth, Interview, 18 September 1996.

Boys: European - 3, coloured - 16; Girls: European - 32, coloured - 54.[5]

The school expanded rapidly during the 1900s and later moved to larger premises in Gardner Street and was renamed Dower Primary School. When the principal of Dower Primary School, Miss Griffin, retired at the end of 1949 her post became vacant. Out of the 11 applicants the School Committee unanimously nominated Mr O Salie[6] for the post.The secretary of the School Board pointed out that the candidate had English on Higher Grade, Afrikaans on the Standard Grade, but because most of the children were Afrikaans speaking, it was essential for the principal to have Afrikaans on the Higher Grade. Mr Salie's appointment as principal subsequently caused a difference of opinion between the School Committee and the School Board which led to a controversy which went on for more than three years. When the School Board refused to accept Mr Salie's nomination for the principalship, the School Committee nominated him as acting principal for the ensuing year. He was advised to complete his `A' bilingual certificate.[7] The Board expressed its disappointed in the decision of the School Committee to ignore their request to call for another nomination for the principalship.[8] They took a dim view of the stand taken by the Committee and only allowed Mr Salie to be appointed as acting principal for a period of three months, ending 31st March 1950. The Committee ignored the instruction of the Board and again nominated Mr Salie as acting principal after 1 April 1950. In response the Board informed the Committee that it regarded its actions in a very serious light and recommended that the Department make another appointment.

The Committee's stand was regarded as a `glaring example of wanton disregard of Departmental instructions and contempt of those in authority.' However, the Board acquiesced and allowed Mr Salie to continue as acting Principal for another term, on condition that one of the other applicants was appointed principal in the new term. The department subsequently nominated Mr Orrie as the new acting principal, this appointment to take effect from 1 January 1951. However, the School Committee refused to accept his nomination on the grounds that the new appointee had exactly the same language endorsement as Mr Salie.[9] As a result the Board was forced to back down and reappoint Mr Salie for the new year, up to 30th June 1951. At a subsequent School Board meeting, one of its members, Rev Windvogel, came out in support of Mr Salie, pointing out that `the reason why the Committee had nominated Mr Salie was that he was a Malay, and that the majority of pupils as well as the whole School Committee were Malays. He thought that Mr Salie was fairly good in Afrikaans, notwithstanding the fact that he did not possesses the necessary bilingual certficate.' Nevertheless, when the Superintendent General of Education later visited Port Elizabeth and addressed the Board on the matter of the principalship at Dower, he declared that he could not support Mr Salie's nomination and instructed the Board to inform the School Committee of his decision, insisting that they should make another nomination for the principal's post. If this was not done, the Department would have no option but to dissolve the School Committee, whose duties would then be carried out by the School Board.[10] In reply the School Committee pointed out that although Mr Salie at that moment did not have his Higher Bilingual Certificate, he had proved his capabilities as principal during his period as acting principal. Furthermore, he had mentioned in his application that he was in charge of Afrikaans for the higher classes and had entered for the Higher Bilingual, as well as the Hoer Taalbond examination. The School Committee also felt that it would not be in the interest of the school to change principals in the middle of the year. They included a petition signed by 123 parents in which they protested against the refusal of the Department to appoint Mr Salie as their principal. The Board was

---

[5]CC Abrahams, `A Pedagogical Evaluation of the role played by inter alia various Churches in the Education of the Coloured Child in Port Elizabeth area between 1803 and 1940.' (M.Ed dissertation, University of Port Elizabeth, 1989), 211.

[6]For a biographical note, see Appendix III below.

[7]Persons qualifying as teachers also had to complete a bilingual examination which certified that they were competent to teach either through the medium of English or Afrikaans, or both, depending on their proficiency. E/a indicated superior efficiency in English; A/a, Afrikaans and E/A , equal proficiency in both languages. No teacher was certified to teach without obtaining these symbols.

[8] *School Board Minute Books,* vols. 61-71 (1949-1957), 39.

[9] *Ibid*, 47.

[10] *Ibid*, 50.

not prepared to budge and, with the cooperation of the Department of Education, dissolved the School Committee, taking over all its functions, including that of appointing a principal of their choice.[11]

There is no doubt that Mr Salie was discriminated against by the Board because he was a high profile political figure fighting apartheid laws such as the Group Areas Act. He was the parents' and community's choice and was by far the best candidate. The unfavourable treatment he received thereafter from the Department of Education later led to his being forced to leave the teaching profession, primarily because of his political convictions.

The following were the School Committee members of Dower during the Salie debacle:[12] Messrs G. Fataar, N Baboo, A Adams, MB Savahl, A Agherdien, T Abrahams, S Samsodien.

Some teachers at Dower: 1906 - Bertha Ward, Amy Dent, Mathilda Ochse, Elizabeth Sydenham, Sarah McAdam, Ethel Todd, Miss Clark. 1907 - Miss Spearman, Miss Sydenham, Miss Clark, Miss Dent, Miss McAdam, Miss Ward. 1912 - Miss Sydenham, Miss Stacy, Mr J Diederichsen. 1922 - Miss Dickensen, Miss Ward, Miss Griffen, Miss Frazer, Miss Sydenham, Miss Nurick, Miss Murra, Mrs Flint, Miss Stacy. 1925 - Bertha Ward (Principal), Matha Rawnsley, Gladys Griffen, Jean Fraser, Anne Nurick, Emily Flint, Jessie Stacy, Winifred Adams. 1950 - Mr S Hendricks, Mr Agherdien, Mr Salie, Miss Baboo, M S Baderoen, G Lillah, K Hoffman, E Wicomb, B Wicomb, S Dennis, H Wilson.

SOUTH END UNION, 1928-1968

In 1912 when Rev Weiss started his ministry, a piece of ground was bought in Rudolph Street. Around 1926 he started a church school in a corrugated iron building in Seymour Street and this building served as a church as well. In 1928 a proper structure was erected. Initially, this school consisted of a church hall which was partitioned off into the two classrooms, a small room at the back and the church which was used as a classroom. During Rev CP Geldenhuys' ministry two extra classrooms were added and during Rev H Renecke's ministry, another two. These developments took place during the time that Mr George De Donker served as principal - a man who will always be remembered for his dynamic leadership. After Mr De Donker's retirement, Mr Davids, who served as his vice-principal, took over the reins. The school became well-known in Port Elizabeth for the many trophies it won at Eisteddfods.

This school was attended by children from different religious backgrounds. Today many of its products hold important positions in the community as well as society at large. One of its outstanding products is Prof Bhadra Ranchod who was the first Deputy-Speaker of Parliament in the Government of National Unity in 1994. In 1996 he was appointed South African Ambassador to Australia.

South End Union School finally closed its doors in 1968 after most of the families in South End had been forced to move as a result of the Group Areas Act, bringing a sad end to a momentous era. Today South End is a developing, upmarket, white suburb, but passing that hill, a remnant of the past will always remain a great memory in the minds of many.

Some South End Union School Teachers: 1925 - Winifred La Reservee, Kate Blignaut, Emmeline La Reservee. 1930 to1937 - Kate Meyer, Janet Ross, M.S. Eland, E.M. Crook, Sarah Prinsloo, Edward Van Vught, Mary Woodward, Robert Adams, Henry Williams. 1950 - Miss B Groener, EM Tobias, Miss Eland, Mr Davies, G De Doncker, Mr Vogel, Miss Jacobs, Mr Collins, Miss Marais.

ST. THOMAS HIGH SCHOOL, 1942 - 1970

Parishioners from Salisbury Park approached the Blessed Oliver Plunkett Church in South End to open up a high school for coloured children in South End as Paterson High School was too far for the pupils to travel. St Thomas subsequently opened its doors in 1942 in an adjoining building of the convent. The first principal of the school was Sister Mannes and she was assisted by Sisters Clara and Stephanie.

Since space was a problem at the school, only Catholic children were initially admitted. St Thomas

---

[11] *Ibid*, 60.
[12]*Ibid*, 67.

started off with Standard 7s and 8s and enrollment was low, numbering approximately 30 pupils. In 1944 the school presented its first matriculants. A number of teachers came from other institutions to assist the school. Some of the teachers at St Thomas were Dennis Brutus who taught English, Mr F Williams, Afrikaans, Sister Francis, typing, and Mother Louise Bertram.

Life at the school was characterized by a strong family spirit, enhanced by the fact that most of the teachers and pupils were Catholics. The school also had a manager who oversaw all aspects of the management of the school.[13] The school closed in 1970 as a result of the Group Areas Act but reopened in the Northern Areas where it became an important land mark on the corner of Beetlestone and Kobus Roads, in Gelvandale.

HINDU PRIMARY SCHOOL, 1942-1970

In the 1930s, Mr V A Pillay stood for councillorship for Ward 1 under the banner of the then Labour Party. There were five candidates, and Mr Pillay lost by thirty votes. The candidate who poled the lowest, Mr Maitland, referred to Mr V A Phillay as a 'coolie'. The next election, it appeared that Mr Maitland would be unopposed, and Mr Pillay decided to stand against him. Mr Maitland appealed to him to withdraw, and Mr Pillay conceded, on the basis that he sold a piece of land that he owned at the bottom of Rudolph Street to the Tamil Community. The building which was erected on this site was eventually called the Saraswathi Educational Institute. The first President was Mr Nagan Padayachee, and the second was Mr V A Pillay. Temple services were held here for many years. In 1939, the members realised that a more permanent structure should be built. Under the Presidency of Mr M S Nagan a fund-raising drive was initiated. The foundation stone of the new Saraswathi Educational Institute was laid on the 22 April 1941. The institute was the first of its kind in South Africa and its aim was to promote the educational, social and religious needs of the Indians in Port Elizabeth. It opened its doors as the Hindu Primary School, also known as a Sara-Swa Educational Institute, in 1942. The first principal was G Vasuthevan, followed by G K Nulliah. Yoga classes were held at the school. The building was used after hours by the community as a whole. In order to raise funds film shows were held on Sundays. Among the teachers who served the school were : Mrs G Fredericks, Mr O Fester, Mr B Benjamin, Mr E Yon, Mr L Redcliffe, Mr B Van Breda, Mr E Such, Mrs C Williams. The school finally closed its doors in 1970 with N V Coopoo as the last Principal.

ST. MONICA'S (Roman Catholic Primary School when it started).

St. Monica's and the Blessed Oliver Plunkett Church originated from the initiative of the St Augustine congregation in central Port Elizabeth in which Bishop Colby played an important role. Bishop MacSherry took it a step further by approaching the Dominican Sisters to take up teaching posts at the school. Initially the building was small and it was only later that the major buildings were completed. The school opened in 1940 with Mother Rose as the first principal, a post she held until 1960. At the start coloured and white children were admitted to the school. Later whites attended Sacred Heart School, which was situated on the corner of Pier and Armstrong street.

Some of the teachers who taught there over the years were Miss L Felix, Sister Emmanual, Monica Newton, Mr V Hagglund, Mr Hocketty, Helen Brutus, Julia Leyland, Mr K Barry, Mr Abraham Ganza, Mr F Williams and Mrs C Williams. The following principals served the school: Sister Alverez who took over from Mother Rose; Mr Ganza; and Mr Gerald Quontoi who remained principal until the school finally closed its doors in 1970, again as a result of the Group Areas Act..

---

[13]Mr and Mrs F. Williams, interview with authors, Port Elizabeth, 12 January 1996.

29

South End Union Church and School Building in Rudolph Street
(Bob Binnell Collection)

Dower Primary School Building
(Bob Binnell Collection)

Dower Primary School Buildings
(Bob Binnell Collection)

Teacher and Pupils of Dower Primary School
Back row L-R: S. September, I. Fontuin, R. Lalla, T. Blauw, Mr O. Salie (Teacher), R. Daniels, L. Rademeyer, S. Meyer, P. Parley
Middle row L-R: S. Sataar, H. Jappie, O. Salie, N. Boongard, L. Bassadien, G. Davids, M. Blauw, S. Peterson, M. Gentle, S. Hill,
F. September, ..., ..., J. Akeldien, R. Davids
Front row L-R: F. Williams, H. Bardien, I. Marriday, M. Raban, M. Akeldien, Y. Meyer
(S. Samuels)

Sports Day at the Oval - Dower Primary School Athletics Team
Back row R-L: K. Savahl (Teacher), Carol N. Boomgard, M. Baboo, G. Serfontein, D. Hendricks, L. Bassadien, ..., ..., ...,
F. Williams, J. Mooloow, B. Abrahams, ..., ...
Middle row R-L: A. Meyer, G. Hewson, S. Jappie, S. van Breda, H. Jappie, Y. Meyer, I. Fataar, F. September
Front row R-L: ....., ..., F. Raban, Van Breda, Simons, M. Abrahams, J. Rademeyer, Y. Peterson
(R. Petersen)

Hindu Primary School, at the bottom of Rudolph Street
(Bob Binnell Collection)

St Thomas High School
(Bob Binnell Collection)

St Monicas Primary School in Upper Pier Street
(Bob Binnell Collection)

*Teacher and Pupils of
Hindu Primary School
Back row R-L: J. Saul, R. Dolley,
F. Sandan, ..., A. Hendricks, E. Sataar,
B. Clark, A. Francis, J. Roberts, ..., ...,
G. Salie.
Middle row L-R: J. Baboo, ..., ...,
T. Connelly, Mr Coopoo, M. Nakerdien,
M. Roberts, ...
Front row L-R: F. Stellenboom, J. Roberts,
M. Lagardien, ..., ..., ..., Kulsum, ...,
L. Assumption.
(R. Peterson)*

*Teacher and Pupils of Hindu Primary School (Std 5 class 1956)
Standing R-L: J. Makan, O. Clark, G. Capri, M. Moodaley,
F. Kahaar, T. Padayachee, M. Lingham, L. Abrahams, B. Chetty,
O. Makan, B. Madhoo, D. Naidoo
Sitting L-R: S. Baboo, T. Naidoo, S. Dolley,
Mr Benjamin (Teacher), N. Fredericks, N. Meyer, K. Saunders
(W. Benjamin)*

*Teachers and Pupils of St Thomas High School
(Times Media Library)*

The school had as its main aim character-building. Bursaries existed for children to further their studies at Paterson High School. Some of the outstanding sportsmen and sportswomen at the school were Anna Hendricks, Alfonso Snyman, Rubin Kirsten, Celestine Hutton and Godfrey De Kock.

Two of the many pupils who later distinguished themselves were Louis Kathan, who obtained a Doctor of Education degree and Dennis Brutus who became Professor of English in the United States of America. Brutus also gained renown as a poet and a leading members of the Anti-Apartheid Movement abroad.[14]

The school was only partially subsidized by the state and the Church had to provide the rest of the finance. Pupils were exempt from paying school fees. St Monica's school also had a feeding scheme in which Mother Rose played an important role. Although there was no school committee, parents were always willing to come forward when their assistance was required.

Since 1871 when St Peter's Church School was opened, and up to 1950, schooling for coloured and Indian children was the responsibility of Churches. Mission schools exhibited some interesting features:

HIGHLIGHTS OF THE MISSIONARY SCHOOLS

Teachers
A shortage of `coloured' teachers was reported for the period 1900 to 1930. The following examples at St. Monica's (Roman Catholic) and St. Peter's (Anglican) served to demonstrate the shortage. The inspection report on St. Monica's stated that although the Education Department had sanctioned an extra teacher for the school six months earlier, up to that time the community had been unable to obtain the services of a qualified teacher, with result that the school work proceeded with great difficulty.
In a letter to the Superintendent-General of Education, the manager of St Peter's School pointed out that it had been very difficult for a number of years to obtain a suitably qualified teacher to teach Standard 4s.

Accommodation of Pupils
In 1911 the inspector of schools reported that due to a large increase of pupils in the infant class, an extra classroom had to be built at Seymour Primary School. When Seymour Primary moved from Seymour Street to Gardner Street, the enrollment increased from 180 to 290. This trend resulted in overcrowding because there were not enough classrooms available. The shortage of accommodation could also be attributed to the fact that coloureds at the time were denied the right to enrol at white schools.

In addition, no high school had been established for coloureds at the time. Thus, coloured pupils could not continue their education after having completed their primary school education.

Attendance of Pupils
One of the many factors which influenced the attendance of mission schools was that no compulsory education existed and no law prevented parents from keeping their children away from school. As a result many pupils stayed absent. The principal and staff worked hard to secure better attendance. Whereas education was not compulsory for coloured children, it was compulsory for European(white) children.

The Government and the Policy of Racial Discrimination
The government of the day adopted a policy of leaving the total provision for primary schools for coloured children in the hands of the Churches.[15] In 1922 Rev James C. Weiss (Manager of the Congregational Church schools in South End) wrote a letter to the *Eastern Province Herald* in which he expressed his disgust at the manner in which coloured schools were treated by the School Board. His strong feelings on educational policy were expressed in the following manner: `Free education loses all its benefits when children are packed like sardines and teachers are refused tables, etc. The churches which are over-burdened are constantly urged to supply accommodation, and keep premises clean and in repair. Our teachers cannot threaten the Department with a strike for it will not turn one hair grey. Hence, they must

---

[14]Ibid.
[15]Abrahams, `Pedagogical Evaluation', 228-256.

jog along, smile and keep their temper even, in spite of financial worries and domestic anxieties'.[16]

Father Paddy, Rector of St Peter's Church agreed with Rev Weiss and expressed his opinion in a letter: He doubted whether the general public realized how appallingly unequal the financial treatment meted out to the two classes of primary school (Board and Church) was. Church schools followed the same primary syllabus as European schools under the Board and were subjected to the same government inspection. The only difference was that Church schools were denominational while the Board schools were not. Furthermore, teachers in Church schools were paid less money than teachers under the Board.[17]

The above statements indicated that the government was happy to leave coloured education in the hands of the Churches as this involved minimal financial backing. This had a detrimental effect on coloured education. Differences in educational policy between the Churches and the State led to `non- white' parents leading the fight for the best education they could get for their children. It was therefore no surprise that a state non-white high school was eventually opened in Russell Road in 1925. Paterson High School was the first of its kind. Most, if not all standard 5 pupils of the primary schools in South End continued their high school careers at Paterson High School until South End High opened its doors in 1950.

B.   STATE SCHOOLS IN SOUTH END

As mentioned in the previous chapter, education for coloured and Indian children in Port Elizabeth as a whole and in South End in particular was provided by Churches from as early as 1824. The exception was Paterson High School which was built with state funds in 1925. In South End the Churches provided six mission schools from 1871 to 1950. In sharp contrast the state provided education for whites from as early as 1854 in Port Elizabeth and from 1875 in South End. The state schools for whites were Victoria Park Grey Primary School (1875), Cunningham Primary School (1916) and Victoria Park High School (1940). The state schools for coloureds and Indians were Lea Place Primary(1950), South End High (1950) and Forest Hill Road Primary(1952).

VICTORIA PARK GREY PRIMARY SCHOOL, 1875 to date.

This school was established in 1875 as the South End branch of the Grey Institute. The school started with 13 pupils and was housed in the Presbyterian Sunday School Hall in Bullen Street, South End. These were the same buildings in which Victoria Park High School started. The buildings were later taken over by the Dutch Reformed Church in 1928 when it was relinquished by the Presbyterian Church.[18]

In 1878 the South End Branch School was built in Walmer Road . In 1906 it ceased to be part of the Grey Foundation and was called the South End Public School. In 1916 enrolment stood at 225 pupils and the school had become overcrowded. During the principalship of Mr Bollen a new school was built in Mitchell Street and on 30 May 1916 Sir Frederick de Waal, Administrator of the Cape laid the Foundation stone.[19] In 1939 the school became South End Grey and choose as its motto `Honour and Service'.[20]

During the principalship of Mr SG Andrews some of the town councillors recommended that a new school be built next to Victoria Park High School. He recommended that the name should be changed, with the `South End' part being dropped, but in view of tradition, that the `Grey' part of the name be retained. Thus Victoria Park Grey Primary School officially came into being on 1 July 1949 and the foundation stone was laid on 12 September that year.[21] The new buildings could accommodate 600 pupils and were occupied in 1950. The school still functions as a well-known educational institution with a long

---

[16]*Eastern Province Herald (*16 May 1922).

[17]Abrahams, "Pedagogical Evaluation", 257.

[18] Victoria Park Grey Primary School, *School Magazine*, vol 7 (1995), 4

[19]*Ibid.*

[20]Harridene, *Port Elizabeth,* 67.

[21]Victoria Park, *School Magazine,* 4

and proud tradition.

When the school relinquished its buildings in Mitchell Street on 1 July 1949, it was taken over by South End High School, the first high school for coloured pupils in South End. This school eventually closed and the buildings were broken down in 1975 when South End was demolished under the Group Areas Act.

CUNNINGHAM PRIMARY SCHOOL, 1916-1994

On 22 February 1916 the School Board announced that the Provincial Education Department accepted in principle the establishment of a free school in South End. From 1 April 1916 the Masonic Hall in Pier Street was rented and used as premises for the Cunningham Primary School , named after a School Board stalwart, Thomas Henry Cunningham.[22]

As enrollment grew the school was spread over many halls in South End. In 1921 land in Randall Street was donated by the Council and on 24 March in the same year the foundation stone of the new school was laid. The school was designed by H Siemerink and was opened by Mr I Hoy, Chairman of the School Board's Building Committee, on 8 December 1922. As part of a rationalisation program, the school closed its door in 1994 and from 1995 amalgamated with the Walmer Laerskool (former Walmer Primary School). To date the school buildings still stand and are used for a variety of educational purposes; the University of Port Elizabeth for example uses them for music for all races.

PATERSON SECONDARY SCHOOL, 1925 TO DATE.

Formal education for `non-white' children in Port Elizabeth before 1900 was restricted to elementary education provided by the primary schools. After 1900 more `non -white' children reached the level of standard five and this led to a need for the establishment of a high school. In 1923 Miss Elton, Inspector of Education, requested the Superintendent of Education to have all the upper standards of the primary school in one school. The standard six pupils would come from Chapel Street School with five pupils, Dower Primary with six pupils, and other pupils would come from St. Marks School, St. Peters School and Mount Road Moravian School.[23]

The high school was slow in becoming a reality. A petition was drawn up by concerned coloured parents to the School Board showing support for a Standard 7 class to commence at any one of the schools under the jurisdiction of the Board. At the same time Chapel Street Primary School for coloureds was experiencing difficulty in accommodating all of its pupils. To overcome this problem, the Board decided to move both the pupils and staff of Chapel Street School into larger vacant buildings in Russell Road.

Before the opening of the long-awaited high school (to be named Paterson Secondary School after John Paterson who had opened the first senior government school at Chapel Street Union Church School) a number of parent meetings as well as School Board meetings were held during December 1924. The secondary school was to cater for non-white pupils and when the school board decided that the school would be situated in Russell Road objections came from the `non-white' deputation. Concern was expressed about the great distance pupils would have to travel from Korsten and New Brighton. Rev Newell and Rev Cowan suggested buildings which were closer to the residences of most of the pupils.[24]

The school board regarded the alternative buildings as unsuitable but pointed out that the Russell Road building would only be a temporary venue. Thus, the first secondary school for non-whites in Port Elizabeth was opened in Russell Road at the beginning of 1925.[25]

Teachers and Parents

[22] Harradine, *Port Elizabeth,* 139.
[23] SGE Report, 8 May1923, cited in Abrahams, `Pedagogic Evaluation', 261.
[24] *Ibid,* 263.
[25] *Ibid.*

The School Board appointed Mr Organ as acting-principal of the new school and the search was on for a permanent principal. Mr Organ was joined by Miss Gardner and both were given temporary posts. Since Africans (natives) also attended the school it necessitated the teaching of Xhosa, and the services of Rev James Gqamlana was acquired for this purpose. On 1 July 1925 Mr Arthur Howard Hemming was appointed as the first principal of Paterson Secondary School. The first staff appointed were:

TABLE 1 - First Staff Appointed at Paterson Secondary School[26]

POST	CLASSES TAUGHT	NAME	DEGREE	PROFESSIONAL CERTIFICATE	YEARS IN EDUC. DEPT
Principal	Std.7 Boys	AH Hemming	B.A.	P.C.	5
Sec Asst	Std 7 Girls	EM Magennis		P.H.	
Sec Asst	Std 7 Girls	DC Feather		P.H.	
Prim Asst	Std 6	SJ Redcliffe		T3J	
Prim Asst	Std 5	F January		T3J	
Part Time Asst	Xhosa Std 7	JR Gqamlana		T3	15

Despite the fact that many parents were poor they contributed financially and in other ways so that progress during those early years was rapid. Parents contributed the princely sum of 13 pounds (R26.OO) for the purchase of much-needed library books because many children from poverty-stricken homes could not afford to buy their own books. Interest was also shown by the parents in the selection of school colours and a school badge. By 1926 a healthy spirit had been fostered among parents, teachers and pupils. The involvement and interest of the parents was further demonstrated when 64 of them turned up for the first school committee election which was held on the 21 September 1927. The elected School Committee consisted of the following members: Rev ES Diedericks, Rev JC Weiss, Messrs WM Boggenpoel (Hon Secretary), W Kay (Chairman), A Koen, J Pietersen and H Triegaard.[27]

Enrolment, Instruction and Times

When Mr Organ and Miss Gardner started the school in January 1925 it had 113 pupils of which 48 were in Standard 7 (32 Native[African] and 16 coloured), 33 in Standard 6, and 32 in Standard 5.[28] On 1 March 1925 two extra classrooms were built in order to accommodate Woodwork and Domestic Science. Enrolment increased steadily over the years as the following tables reveals.

TABLE 2 -   Enrolment for the period from 1930 to 1937.[29]

---

[26]SGE 2/655, 7-9 December 1925, cited in Abrahams `Pedagogic Evaluation', 265.

[27] School Board's Minute Book (26 October1927), 204.

[28]SGE File (5 February 1926), cited in Abrahams,`Pedagogic Evaluation', 266.

[29]Cape Educational Department Survey, (1940), 185-186, cited in Abrahams, `Pedagogic Evaluation', 267.

1930	1931	1932	1933	1934	1935	1936
122	137	149	174	192	188	215

TABLE 3 - Enrolment, 1937

Standard	Coloured	Native	Total	Number of Classes	Room
7	59	55	144	5	Classrooms
8	54	16	70	3	Science Room
9	22	1	23	1	Woodwork Room
10	16	2	18	1	
Total	181	74	255	10	

Funds and New School

Parents were not exempted from paying for school fees and school books. The fee recommended by the School Board was one shilling and sixpence per quarter. Because many parents could not afford to purchase school books, the School Board decided to purchase the books out of trust funds.[30]

Since the School Board had decided that the Russell Road building was a temporary venue, alternative possible sites were considered on which to build a new school. The School Board's choice of site was on the Hill above Kent Road between the points where Gerard Street and Crawford Street joined that Road.[31] The building was soon completed at the cost of five thousand and forty five pounds sterling and it was taken over by the School Board on the 13 June 1929. However, the new school became a `non-white' island in a white area since it was surrounded by predominantly white families. It was therefore envisaged that the school should move again, but this time closer to the majority of non-whites. There were also plans afoot to establish another secondary school. However, before any of the options could be implemented, the school was burnt down in mysterious circumstances and a new school was built and opened in 1950 in Schauderville. Presently, Mr S Naidoo is at the helm.

VICTORIA PARK HIGH SCHOOL, 1940 TO DATE.

This school was established in January 1940 and used the hall of the Dutch Reformed Church, also called Petra Hall, between Kenny and Bullen Streets on the upper slope of Walmer Road in South End. Opposite the hall was St. Monica's Primary School and Sacred Heart Convent of the Roman Catholic Church.

The first headmaster of the school was Mr HW `Herby' Arnot. When he arrived on the first day of school he found an enrolment of 38 Standard 7 boys and girls and one assistant woman teacher.[32] There were no desks or other apparatus, not even a piece of chalk. These were the rudimentary beginnings of Victoria Park High School.

In 1941 a Standard 8 class was added and an additional assistant teacher was appointed. At the end of the 1942 school year Mr Arnot was allowed to go on active military service in the war and Mr de la Harpe was appointed acting-headmaster. In 1945 the school moved to new buildings on the present site at the junction of Victoria Park Drive and First Avenue, Walmer, and subsequently achieved high school

[30]Abrahams, `Pedagogic Evaluation', 269.
[31]School Board File (12 October 1925).
[32]Victoria Park High School, *A brief History (1940 - 1990)*, 2.

status.The subsequent principals were Mr TC Thorp 1947 - 1965, Mr Pearson 1965 - 1982 and Mr Blake 1982 - 1990. Today the school still functions as one of the leading educational institutions in South End.

SOUTH END HIGH SCHOOL, 1950-1972.

The `non-white' residents of South End agitated for a long time for a high school before they were granted the use of the school building of South End Grey Primary School in 1950. It was initially called South End Higher Primary School with Mr N.R. Myburgh as acting principal. The principal post was advertised in the school Gazette of 1950 and Mr N.R. Myburgh was the successful candidate from a list of 12 applicants.

The principal's first complaints included that the school grounds were being used as a public thoroughfare and the grounds were used by anyone. Due to the easy accessibility the building suffered much damage caused by irresponsible persons. The open stoeps were used by trespassers for a number of anti social activities such as gambling and the abuse of liquor. The grounds were used as a dumping ground and no sport grounds could be laid out while vandals had easy access to it.[33]

In 1950 the Standard 5s of the feeder schools were transferred to South End High. The main feeder schools were Forest Hill Road Primary, Lea Place Primary, Dower Primary and South End Union Primary. In 1954 the school had its first matriculants and in that same year the Standard 5s which the school had had since its inception were transferred back to the primary school.

As early as 1951 the school buildings were used for after-hours classes for Adult Education. In March 1957 the school needs were still catered for by only one laboratory which could accommodate only fifteen pupils. In a letter to the School Board dated 14 March 1957, the principal requested two additional classrooms to be used as science rooms.

Mr F Landman was appointed vice-principal on 1 January 1955. His nomination was unanimously endorsed by the School Committee and sanctioned by the School Board.[34] In 1957 the following persons were elected as members of the School Committee: Messrs JRH Bell, P Marks, J Potgieter, Rev H Renecke and Dr MAWarley.[35]

Of the first group of matriculants, a number became leaders in various fields such as medicine, education and law. South End High School developed rapidly and the number of matriculants presented for the matric exams increased over the years and additional classrooms were added to cater for the increasing number of pupils.

An ex-pupil, D Govindjee, stated that South End High taught him to achieve. He was motivated by his predecessors and his teachers who not only taught them about subject matter but also to face up to the demands of life. Pupils were guided through their subject matter and independent thought was regarded as a priority in the curriculum. He was impressed and influenced by Mr Howard Mackriel who joined the staff in 1965 after completing his studies at Natal University. Mr Mackriel introduced the Arts into the school and organised many theatrical productions at the school. Mr Y Johnson who joined the staff in 1965 brought new aspects pertaining to physical Education into the school program. He was fortunate to have worked under the guidance of Mr G Smith who had given yeoman service to the school over a period of many years. Soon gymnastic displays were conducted more frequently and Sport received more attention. Frequent use was made of the Victoria Park and Schaeffer grounds for inter-school and

---

[33]School Board Minute Book,vols. 61-71 (1949-1957), 40.
[34]Ibid, 49.
[35]Ibid.

*Victoria Park Grey in 1st Avenue Walmer
(Faizal Felix)*

*Cunningham Primary School in
Randall Street
(Bob Binnell Collection)*

*Paterson High School in Schauderville
(Faizal Felix)*

*Victoria Park High School, corner of 1st Avenue
and Victoria Park Drive
(Bob Binnell Collection)*

South End High School
(AC George)

South End High Matric Class of 1963 (Reunion)
L-R: Dr P. Gajjar, Dr J. Raga, Dr I. Tobias,
Mr D. Ranchod, Mrs H. Daya (nee Govinjee),
Mrs P. Ramjee (nee Bhagattjee), Dr R. Mitchell,
Dr L.Smith, S. Vaghmaria.
(Times Media Library)

South End High School Teacher and Students
L-R: 'Tumby', R. Peffer, E. Leslie, J. Donnelly,
W. Domingo, Mr A.C. George (Teacher),
T. Hitzeroth, F. Adams, D. Reddy,
-. Van Dayar, B. Moodaley, V. Simon.
(A.C. George)

Students of South End High
L-R: K. Ranchod, S. Potgieter, N. Bramdaw,
R. Williams, A. Mitha, E. Peffer,
S. Moodaley (Teacher), P. Uithaler, M. Adams,
M. Davids, M. Ahmed.
(A.C. George)

inter-house sports meetings. Inter-house sports meetings were contested between Trojans and Spartans.[36]

In 1963 Mr F Landman was banned by the Nationalist Government. He decided to leave the country with his family on an exit permit. In the same year the administration of coloured education was taken over by the Coloured Affairs Department. The new department send out their officials to meet with the teaching staff of South End High. The younger members of the staff took a strong stand against the Coloured Affairs Department (CAD). Most of the teachers were members of Teacher's League of South Africa (TLSA). This organization had as its main aim to fight against ethnic education in general and `Coloured Education', in particular. The teachers at South End High did everything in their power to circumvent the state's aim to undermine non-racial democratic education. They also did everything in their power to prevent education from becoming a tool of indoctrination.[37]

A particular incident occurred at the Westbourne Oval in 1965, when, after an inter-school Athletic Meeting between Paterson High, South End High, Gelvandale High and Spandau High, all the refuse drums were mysteriously emptied out in one big heap. A photograph of the pile of garbage appeared in the Afrikaans daily newspaper *Die Oosterlig*. The aim of the story and photograph was to demonstrate that the `non-white schools' could not keep the Westbourne Oval clean. As a result of the outcry which folllowed non-whites were banned from using the Oval. No-one made any attempt to ascertain whether the accused schools were in fact responsible for this incident. It was only in the 1990s that non-whites were again allowed to use the grounds. The non-white schools were forced to use the Schaeffer and later the Adcock grounds for inter-school and inter-house Athletic meetings.

After Forest Hill Primary and Lea Place Primary closed in 1969 and 1970 respectively, their buildings were used by South End High for the children of families who moved to the Northern Areas. This crazy situation developed when `non-white' families had to move from South End to the Northern Areas in terms of the Group Areas Act. However, the government had not made provision for sufficient school accommodation for pupils. Thus, pupils, who had previously lived and schooled in South End, now had to return to South End every day to attend school at South End High because of a lack of school accommodation in the Northern Areas. At one stage about 700 pupils traveled in 12 buses from the Northern Areas to South End every day. This ludicrous situation made a mockery of education and showed up the lunacy of the Group Areas Act. While the architects of this law saw only the need to forcibly remove `people of colour' to the Northern Areas, it was obvious that no-one had considered, nor appeared to be concerned that insufficient provision had been made for displaced pupils. Thus the haste in the implementation of the Group Areas Act superseded rational thought and logical planning.

A major shift of pupils and teachers from South End High School took place with the establishment of Bethelsdorp High on 1 July 1972 with Mr Ricks as the first principal and Mr R Uren as his deputy. Initially about 700 Standard 6s and 7s were transferred from South End High to Bethelsdorp High.

In 1975 Arcadia Senior Secondary School was opened in Arcadia in the Northern Areas with Mr R Doraswami as principal and Mr J Jardien as his deputy. The last of the pupils of South End High were then transferred to Arcadia Secondary. South End High with its rich traditions was no more.

Attempts were made to have the name transferred to any of the schools in the mushrooming Northern Areas. However the authorities refused to accede to this request, much to the disappointment of the former residents, and all past pupils and teachers of South End High.

Some of the teachers of South End High (1950-1965) were: Mrs O Landman, Mr F Landman, Mr O Fester, Mr R Meyer, Mr NR Myberg, Mr I Potgieter, Mr G Govindasammy, Miss Devi Govindasammy, Mr L Adrian, Mr Boet Simon, Mr R Simon, Mr RK Simon, Mr F Meyer, Mr G Smith, Mr C Peterson, Mr R Bath, Mrs Johns, Miss Balie, Miss Kleinbooi, Mr Pamplin, Mr B Van Vugt, Mr R Dolley, Miss E Williams, Mr AC George, Mr A Renze, Mr S Moodaley and Mr A Nortje (Mr Arthur Kenneth Nortje later became a world-renowned poet. After teaching at South End, he went off to Jesus College in Oxford University where he worked on his Doctorate in English. He passed away at a very young age in Oxford

[36]D. Govindjee, interview with authors, Port Elizabeth, 12 November 1995.
[37]R. Uren, interview with authors, Port Elizabeth, 24 November 1995.

in 1970).[38]

Teachers who left in June 1972 to open Bethelsdorp High School for Standards 6 and 7 were: Mrs F Jappie, Miss G Lillah, Miss Bramdaw, Mr Dollwy, Mr Hocketty, Mrs A du Plessis, Mrs Miller, Mrs O Naidoo, Mrs Adams, Mr A Bergins, Mrs Benjamin, Mrs A Smith, Mrs D de Donker, Miss Kannemeyers, Miss Blignaut.

Teachers at South End High when it closed in 1974: Mr L Maart, Mr S Moodaley, Mr R Uren , Sheikh J Jardien, Mr M Daya, Mr Doraswamy, Mrs J Udemans, Mr K Ah Goo, Mr Bowers , Mr C Accom, Mr Johnson, Mr D Jordaan, Mr Sampson, Mr N Attwell.

LEA PLACE PRIMARY, 1950-1969

The establishment of this school became necessary when the other primary schools in South End, namely St Monica's, St Peter's, South End Union and Dower Primary School became overcrowded. The school building was completed in 1949 and was ready for occupation on 1 January 1950. The first principal was Rev P Attwell who gave up his full time ministry at the Bethelsdorp Congregational Church to take up the post. At the same time St. Peter's Coloured Mission School was closed and all its pupils and teachers were accommodated on a double shift basis at Lea Place Primary.

As early as 1951 the parents agitated for a school committee. This can be attributed to the growing political awareness of the parents in the wake of the implementation of the policy of Apartheid in 1948; the Group Areas Act had been promulgated in 1950. The principal initiated the formation of a school committee by writing to the School Board, but the Board preferred direct management rather than supporting the formation of a school committee. The Board blamed the political involvement of the parents for their reluctance to agree to the formation of a school committee. However the pressure of the community in general and the parents in particular led to the election of the following committee, the first at Lea Place Primary:[39] Mr E Barth, Mrs M Dove, Mr OW Fester, Mr P St Clair Marks, Miss J Rensburg.

Lea Place was known for its effective kindergarten section which was responsible for laying a firm foundation for its pupils. They then continued their schooling at Forest Hill Primary and South End High. It was a sad day when it closed its doors the last time in 1969 because of the Group Areas Act. As in the case of Forest Hill Road Primary, its classrooms were also used by South End High when it had to accommodate high school pupils who were bused in from areas where little provision had been made for displaced South Enders.

Teachers at Lea Place Primary were: Mr P Attwell, Mr D Anthony, Mrs L Foster, Miss M Whitebooi, Mrs Williams, Mrs I Adams, Miss M Pilcher, Miss D Marks, Mrs E Marks, Mrs Lasker.

FOREST HILL ROAD PRIMARY, 1952-1971

The inability of Lea Primary to cope with the ever-increasing numbers of pupils, as well as the overcrowding at South End Union, St. Monica's and Dower, necessitated the building of Forest Hill Road Primary in 1952. In 1953 the principal requested additional classrooms because it had to accommodate 90 pupils from Lea Place Primary School and 131 from the South End Union Congregational School. The position would then be as follows:[40] The enrolment in 1953 of 304 would be added to by an additional 221 expected in 1954. This would produce a total of 525 with which the school was not able to cope.

The curriculum of the Lea Place and South End Union schools made provision for pupils up to Standard 1 and Standard 4 respectively. An additional factor was that whereas previously the Standard 5 pupils from South End Union would have proceeded to South End High, as from 1 January 1954 the latter would

[38]S Hendricks, *A Biography of Arthur Nortje: with the emphasis on the South African years 1942-1965* (BA [Hons] Extended Essay, Vista University, 1996).
[39]School Board Minute Book,vol. 61-71 (1949-1957), 27.
[40]Ibid, 25.

Teachers of Forest Hill Road Primary School
Standing L-R: M.M. Whiteboy, E.L. Marks,
M.J. Davids, M.H. Peters, E.C. Muller, A. Potgieter.
Sitting L-R: W.G. Quanson, M.L. Davidson,
C.H. de Harpe, C.B. Simon, D. Govindasamy,
M.L. Williams, W.N. George.
(E.L. Marks)

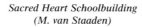

Sacred Heart Schoolbuilding
(M. van Staaden)

Forest Hill Road Primary School (Std 5 1961)
Standing L-R: Miss D. Govindasamy, L. Bruiners,
N. Jappie, -. Karsen, F. Abrahams, W. du Plesis,
D. Bowers, ..., E. White, ...
Sitting L-R: E. Prince, -. Mortimer, P. Chetty, ..., ...,
S. Dana, ..., ..., -. Nortje, Eileen, R. Cassim,
S. Pandie, ...
Front L-R: ....., H. Kafaar, ...

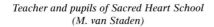

Teacher and pupils of Sacred Heart School
(M. van Staden)

Sheik Jamiel Jardien and pupils in Madressa - Movement Hall, Sprigg Street
(F. Hendricks)

Madressa Classes in Movement Hall, Sprigg Street
(F. Hendricks)

Madressa Classes in Movement Hall, Sprigg Street
(F. Hendricks)

Muslim Movement Hall in Sprigg Street
(F. Hendricks)

Moslem Public School in Burness Street
(A. Cassim)

Teacher and pupils of Madressa in Burness Street
(A. Cassim)

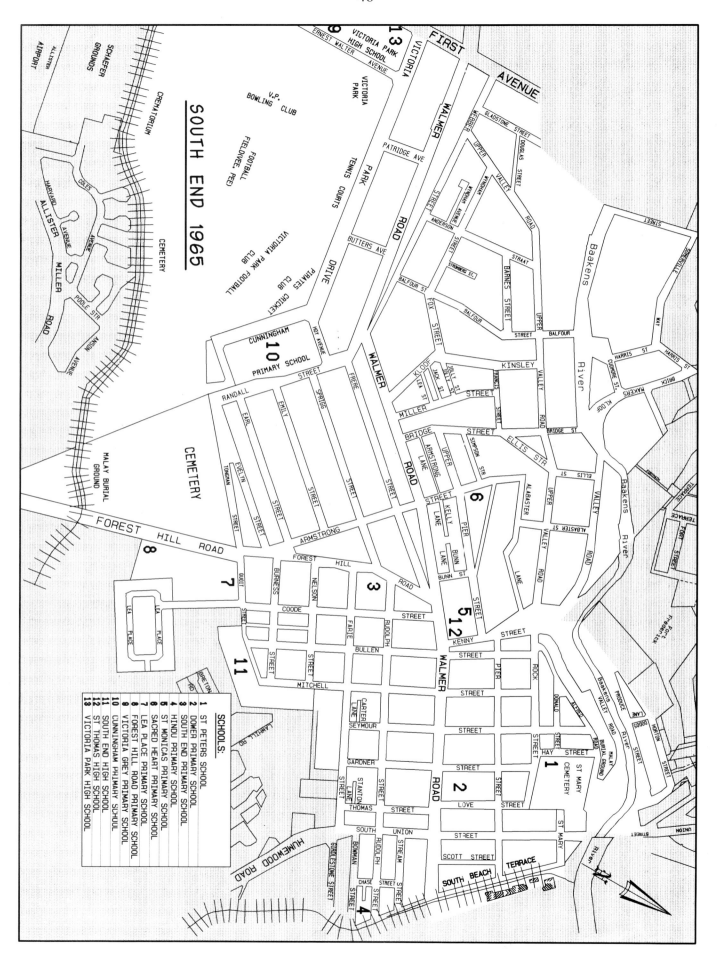

SOUTH END 1965

SCHOOLS:

1 ST PETERS SCHOOL
2 DOWER PRIMARY SCHOOL
3 SOUTH END PRIMARY SCHOOL
4 HINDU PRIMARY SCHOOL
5 ST MONICAS PRIMARY SCHOOL
6 SACRED HEART PRIMARY SCHOOL
7 LEA PLACE PRIMARY SCHOOL
8 FOREST HILL ROAD PRIMARY SCHOOL
9 VICTORIA GREY PRIMARY SCHOOL
10 CUNNINGHAM PRIMARY SCHOOL
11 SOUTH END HIGH SCHOOL
12 ST THOMAS HIGH SCHOOL
13 VICTORIA PARK HIGH SCHOOL

not be able to take these pupils as it had to provide for Standard 10 classes as from 1954. Thus, the Standard 5 classes at this school would be abolished with effect on 31st December 1953. The principal put his needs in a letter dated 3 March 1953: that adequate accommodation be provided for the expected 200 pupils in advance of January 1954; that three of the rooms to be built be fitted with partitions so that provision could be made for assembly purposes and a hall; that sanitary facilities be provided as soon as possible; that a storeroom, staffroom and principal's office be erected in the near future.[41] On 4 March 1955 the principal reported the completion of two new sections of additional classrooms. However, the school was short of adequate playground space.

Forest Hill finally closed its doors when most of the people had to move as a result of the Group Areas Act. The building was used to house excess pupils of South End High. The significance of Forest Hill Road Primary was that it was a major feeder school for South End High. Its products had played and are still playing a prominent role in various walks of life in different communities in distant places as far as Australia and Canada.

Some of the teachers who taught at Forest Hill Primary between 1954 -60 were: Miss RE Hector, Mr Roberts (Principal), Mr CF Snyman, Miss C de la Harpe, Miss SR Kleinbooi, Miss DE Markes, Mr CB Simon, Mr GE Muller, Mr M Peters, Miss M Davidson, Mrs Williams, Mrs Govindasamy, Miss B Groener, Miss M Davis, Mr Quanson, Mr George, Miss Baboo, Mr Baadjies, Mr H Effendi, Miss P Rhoda and Miss Whitbooi..

SACRED HEART CONVENT SCHOOL

In January 1898 the Dominican Sisters decided to open a girls' school in upper Pier Street, South End, called Sacred Heart. Teachers who taught at the school included Mother Patric; Sisters Bernadette, Christopher, Athanasium, Stephen, Aidan, Cleophas; Mrs Holfelder, Mrs Marshall, Mrs Pringle, Mrs Luck and Miss Audouim. As a result of the implementation of the Group Areas Act, the school closed its doors in 1970. [42]

From 1824 up to 1940 the Churches were solely responsible for providing all 23 schools for non-whites existing in Port Elizabeth and the surrounding Areas (except Paterson High School, 1924). These Churches, and the number of schools provided are: Union Congregational Church (11), Anglican (6), Roman Catholic (2), Moravian Church (4). As a result of the Group Areas Act all the schools were closed and most of them were demolished. Today only Victoria Park Grey Primary School and Victoria Park High are still functioning as schools in South End. St Thomas and Paterson High Schools are found in the Northern suburbs of Port Elizabeth.

---

[41]Ibid, 23.
[42]Mrs Van Staden, interview with authors, Port Elizabeth, 1996.

4

SPORT AND RECREATION

Education in South End was interlinked with sports and recreation. It was on the sports fields and in recreational centres where most of the socialising in South End took place. Although for a long time separate sports clubs existed for different racial groups, ample opportunities existed for interaction in sports and recreation in old South End.

Sport and recreation played a significant role in the lives of the people of South End. Formal and informal sports were played on a number of sports fields which were distributed over the whole of South End. Great rivalry existed between various clubs with a variety of exotic and exaggerated names, many of which were South African versions of British clubs. The progress and development of sport flourished due to the hard work of dedicated administrators. However, while former sportspersons from South End look back with great nostalgia at `the old days', it must be remembered that sport was played under trying conditions. Because `non-white' residents of South End were regarded as `second-class' citizens in South Africa, the government and local authorities made no attempt to provide adequate sport and recreational facilities for these communities. Rugby and soccer were often played on fields which were overgrown or lacking grass. Molehills and gravel patches were not unusual. Also, `non-white' sportsgrounds were used as public thoroughfares and the public used these grounds as a short cut home, or to work, or to school. Cricket fields were uneven, poorly-grassed and maintained, and lacking in proper pitches. Most cricket pitches were concrete or gravel and had to be covered with a cricket mat. Turf (grass) wickets were unheard of. The Paladins Hockey Field where ladies' hockey was played was not even level. It had a slope and was covered with a carpet of stinging nettles.

In almost all cases, even rudimentary dressing rooms were unheard of and participants had to use their cars, a big tree, or the back of a building as a changeroom. It made `non-whites' very bitter when they passed sportsfields set aside for whites and saw the top-class facilities provided for the `privileged' group; the well-kept and manicured cricket, rugby and soccer fields, looking like so many billiard tables; the pristine and well-provided dressing rooms; the neat and well-stocked clubhouses. In addition, because of their second-class status in South Africa, there were no coaching or training facilities, in fact, no facilities of any kind for most `non-white' sports. And despite the large variety of sports played, and the number of participants involved, no press coverage was available. Thus, `non-white' sport was played in a vacuum. It is almost as if in the eyes of white South Africans it never existed. Yet, despite these adversities, sport was played with great enthusiam, attracted huge followings, and produced quality sportspersons who would have excelled in the international arena, if given half a chance. Unfortunately, the apartheid policies of the South African government meant that no `non-white', no matter how good they were, would ever be able to represent their country because they had `the wrong skin colour'. `Persons of colour' had to go overseas to get recognition for their prowess, as in the case of Basil D'Oliviera and many others who followed him.

SPORT

Soccer - Soccer was by far the most popular code of sport in South End. A number of clubs were established over the years and most became household names. Among these were Bayonians, Fair Plays, Break of Days, Paladins, Swallows, Blackpool, Shamrocks, Primroses, Daffodils, Lads, Wolves, Swans, Evergreens, Rangers. In the early days soccer was played under the auspices of three associations, but as the game grew one unified soccer body was formed.[1]

---

[1]P Clarke and E de Kock, interview with authors, Port Elizabeth, 4 April 1996.

Bayonian A.F.C.
Winners of 1st League, S.M. Naidoo & Son Trophy - Season 1937
Standing L-R: A. Abdol, A. Agherdien, S. Pandie, O. Cassem,
A. Bruce, A. Jappie
Sitting: O. Salie (Secretary), H.M.I. Kahaar (Capt.),
S. Achmat (President),
A. Manan (Vice-Capt.), H.A.L. Kahaar (Treas.)
Front row: A. Salie, A. Lagardien (Mascot), M.Z. Nordien

ABOVE: Swallows A.F.C. First Team
Winners of League and Mala Moodaley Trophy 1964
Back row: D.J. Septoo, N.C. Stowman (Secr.), D.H.E. Cherval,
V.R. Henry, K. Moodaley, S.H.H. Lookwhy, M. Moodaley,
T.A.S. Hendricks (Ass. Secr.), R.N. Kisten
Centre row: C. Naidoo, F.A. Bailey (Captain),
W.S. Hendricks (Hon. Vice-Chairman),
G.W. Potgieter, (Vice-Chairman and Vice-Captain), G.G.S. Hendricks
Front row: C. Moodaley, R.L Pather, S. Prince, L.P. Hughes,
D. Dullabh (Treasurer)
Inset: Late L.R. Knipp (Chairman)
(A. Bailey)

LEFT: Blackpool A.F.C.
Back row: S. Moodaley, C. Rensburg, A. Bailey,
J. Pentolffe, J. Augustine
Second row: P. Williams (Treasurer), C. Burton, D. Jacobs,
L. Niekerk, A. Pathon, P. Jacobs
Middle row: I. Patterson (Vice-Chairman),
N. Bosch (Trainer and Coach), L. Bailey (Captain),
D. Williams (Chairman),
N. Burton (Vice-Captain), G. Groenewald (Secretary)
Front row: W. Muller, L. Moodaley, M. Abrahams, A. Williams
(H. Burton)

ABOVE: Paladins Football Club
Back L-R: T. Shovell, M. Johns, E. Weelson, G. Billing, J. Bramwell,
V. Pillay, C. Witfield.
Front L-R: R. Stowman, R. van Breda, T. Hendricks, 'Boy' Rockman.
(E. Tobias)

ABOVE: LADS A.F.C.
Winners of March Trophy, winners of
Knock-Out Trophy and Shield - Season 1966
Back row L-R: J. Kagaar, Y. Davids, I. Nakerdien, E. Manan,
A. Kahn, G. Loggenberg, S. Abrahams, J. Abrahams
Centre row: Y. Sandan, H.N. Agherdien (Pres.),
C. Mooloo (Capt.), G. Spiers (Coach), G. Connelly
Front row: R. Morley, O. Abrahams
(A. Connelly)

Eastern Province non-white soccer team on the Victoria Park Field

Back row L-R: S. hendricks, R. Barth, F. Frisler, 'Tortoise' Assam, 'Blackie' Ryan, ..., Carletti, 'Doolie' Hendrickz, C. March

Front row L-R: H. Barends, K. Knipp, G. Smith, A. ....., 'Troy' January, A. Prins (C. Simon)

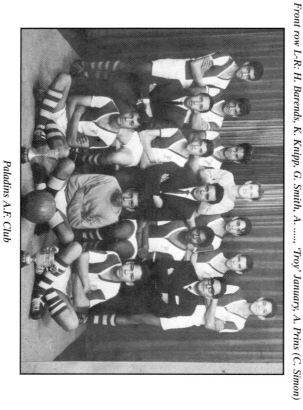

Paladins A.F. Club

Winners of the U-16 League Knockout Trophies

Back row: V. Naidoo, S. Smith, S. Naidoo, A. Johns, C. Parshotam, H. Pereira, A. Stowman

Middle row: D. Bowers (Sec.), K. Moodaley (Vice. Capt.), W. Dixon (Chairman), P. Moodaley (Capt.), L.A. Sajoe (Manager)

Front row: L. Scott, T. Davies, I. Schovell (S. Naidoo)

Eastern Province Coloured Soccer Team
(Taken on the 'Vee-Pee')
(C. Simon)

Swallows A.F.C. - Uner 14 A Team

Winners of the League and Knock-Out Trophies 1960

Front row L-R: D. Bowers, T. Felix, J. Dorothy (Captain), L.R. Knipp (Chairman), J. Adams, S. Rockman, B. Frieslaar

Middle row R-L: N.C. Stowman (Secretary), D. Holloway, D. de Vos, G. de Kock (Vice-Captain), L. Higgins, T. Sutch, R.J. Potgieter (Vice-Chairman)

Back row L-R: H. Felix, G.G.S. Hendricks (Treasurer), B. Adamson

Shamrocks Football Club
(Founded 1918)
Top row: S.S. Padayachee (Treasurer), D. Pillay,
Mr G. Naidoo (Hon. Life Vice-President),
D. Lala (Secretary),
P. Michael (Hon. Life Vice-President),
W. Padayachee, T. Hutton (Vice-President)
Second row: A.X. Hutton (Hon. Life Vice-President),
N.S. Padayachee (Vice-President),
V. Jeevan, W.J. Maggot, A. O'Brien,
B.N. Hutton, S.R. Padayachee (Vice-President),
A. Pillay
Third row: C. Nadasen (Hon. Life Vice-President),
V. Velloo (President), C. Moodaley (Capt.),
M. Frank (Hon. Life Vice-President), N. Samuels,
P.S. Vandayar (Hon. Life Vice-President),
T.N. Bandsa (Hon. Life Vice-President)
Bottom row: C. Naidoo, T. Padayachee
Absent: S. Moodaley (Vice-Capt.), R. Pather, William
Padayachee, B. Hutton, V. Naidoo,
S. Chetty

Daffodil Indian Football Club
Back row: O. Rafie, V. Augustine (Vice-Capt.) W.P. Nagan,
Mooloo,
H. Abrahams, Siva Moodaley (Secretary)
Middle row: S.R. Moodaley, I. Solomon, N. Moodaley (Capt.),
V.A. Moodaley,
Y. Davids, Isaacs, S. Mala Moodaley
Sitting: V.M. Moodaley, Dr S.V. Appavoo (M.O.H.),
T.F. Dullabh (Patron),T. Morgan (President),
S.R. Naidoo (Patron), P. Makan, I. Yakoob (Vice-President)
Front: T. Nayagar (Treasurer),
S.R. Moodaley

Primrose Indian Football Club
(Founded 1945)
Back row: S. Fredericks, H. Padayachee, J.P. Hendricks
(Hon. Treasurer), Mr A. John
Second row: S. Pillay, R. Saminathan, J. Franks,
M.A. Abrahams, S. Moodaley (Hon. Life Vice-President),
S.P. Naidoo, T. Moodaley
Middle row: E. Emmanuel (Patron), T. Naidoo,
S. Cooposammy, V. Padayachey, H. Dullabh, S. Appoo,
T.G. Naidoo, R. Daya (Hon. Life Vice-President)
Sitting: S.N. Moodaley, N.S. Vassen (Hon. Secretary),
T. devi Padayachey (Capt.),
J.A. Moodaley (President, Hon. Life Vice-President),
D. Dullabh (Vice-Capt.), S.R. Naidoo (Patron),
S.K. Moodaley (Hon. Life Vice-President)
Front row: J. Jattiem, R. Naidoo (Mascot),
S.M. Moodaley

Rangers Football Club
Top row: E. Bob, A. Laing, S. Pillay
Middle row: N. Pillay, A. Lagardien, S. Puckery,
R. Michael, R. Athie
Sitting: S. Appavoo (Treasurer), T. Vandayar (Capt.),
V. Moon (President), P. Athie (Secretary),
N. Pillay (Vice-Capt.) R. Vandayar (Mascot)
Absent: L. Pillay, N. Harri, B. Williams, M. Fredericks

Ramblers "A" Football Club
Top row: S. Padayachey, G. Cook (Secretary), P. Pillay
Standing: B. Nayagar, D. Doraswami, B. Francis,
D. Hendricks, G. Paddy
Sitting: D. Septoe, D. Chetty, S. Lalla (Capt.),
T. Chetty (President),
S. Pather (Vice-Capt.), G. Padayachey, O. Ahmed,
Y. Jamal (Mascot)

Ramblers "B" Football Club
Black row: D. Pather, R. Paddy, G. Cook
Standing: M. Davids, H. Williams, R. Dullabh,
A. Abrahams, L. Pather
Sitting: R. Paddy, H. Humphrey, D. Moodaly (Capt.),
C. Theunissen (Vice-Capt.), C. Naidoo

Cricket - Cricket in the earlier years was played with great spirit,and usually turned out to be a family occasion, with the ladies being great supporters at the fields. Earlier well-known clubs were Swipes, Lads, Star of East, South End United, Blackpool Cricket Club, Ottomans, Victorians, Hamadieahs and Cliftons. Pirates Cricket Club, later called Victoria Park Old Boys is still in existence. At the Schaefer Grounds cricket was played on a concrete pitch.[2]

Matches were accompanied by the serving of tea by the female supporters There was great loyalty to specific clubs. A player would start in the junior divisions and would rise through the divisions, and eventually retire, all the while remaining with the same club. Home ground advantage in cricket was treated with enthusiasm. The home club was responsible for rolling the pitch, and the carrying of the `carpet' to the grounds, where a mat had to be laid on a gravel pitch.

Rugby - The well-known rugby clubs of South End were PE Lads, Black Dominoes, Orange Blossoms, Wanderers, Swipes and Hamadieahs. Rugby was mainly played on the Schaefer Grounds.

Men's Hockey - Men's Hockey was played on the Schaeffer ground on Sundays. This became the main attraction on a Sunday in South End. The standard was high and the atmosphere electrifying. So great was the following that most players and supporters had their Sunday meal on the ground.

The Eastern Province Men's Hockey Union consisted of four teams, each having a second team, namely: St Peter's, Mobbs, Paladins and Olympia.

Women's Hockey - Women's Hockey was first played in the early 1930s in South End on the Paladins Hockey Ground at the back of the South End Crematorium, near the Airport. Two school teams, both from St Peter's in Rock Street under the late Father Paddy, were the beginners. Later three adult teams were formed, viz. Paladins and St Peter's from the Anglican Church, and Blackpool from the Walmer Road Baptist Church. Unfortunately records leading up to 1948 cannot be traced but from 1948 to approximately 1970 there appeared to be a good account of hockey played in South End on the famous Paladins Hockey Field.

The period under review was the dreaded apartheid era, and `Coloured Hockey', as South Enders were compelled to name their organization, was played on the one and only hockey venue in Port Elizabeth at the time - the Paladins Hockey Field. This field was not level and evenly grassed like today's sports fields. It had a slope almost as steep as the famous Bridge Street in South End and was covered with a carpet of stinging nettles. Yet, such poor facilities did not dampen enthusiasm for the game. Even though there were no coaching or training facilities, yet they were able to produce hockey of a high calibre.

The teams that made up the Eastern Province `Coloured Women's Hockey Union' of that period were: Paladins, St. Peter's, Blackpool, Protea, Albertons, Willow Grove, Stardrift, South End High School, Larkspurs, Dower Training College and Cavaliers. Hockey was played on Saturday afternoons.

During the early days Moslem women played hockey on the same field on Sundays under the leadership of Mrs Kayna Nakerdien. This did not last long and the Moslem women later joined the Eastern Province Women's Hockey Union.

There were two definite periods during the reign of hockey on the Paladins ground. There was the period just before 1948 to 1956, and then again from 1958 to the late 1960s when the Group Areas Act began to force people out of South End to the Northern Areas.

Table Tennis - Table Tennis was also one of the popular sports in South End, since every school or garage which had a table tennis board which could fit in, was utilized. South End formed one of the first non-racial clubs in Port Elizabeth. R Uren, D Govenjee, L Sammy and S Harry were included in the first Eastern Province team which competed against Western Province in Cape Town.[3]

The following Table Tennis clubs were formed in South End: PE Table Tennis, Gresham Table Tennis Club and Oliver Punkett Table Club . The venues for table tennis in South End were the Oliver Plunkett Hall, the Web and the Mariammam Temple Hall.[4]

Angling - The early inhabitants of South End, of which the majority were Malays, established themselves

[2] R Doroswami, interview with authors, Port Elizabeth, 15 November 1995.
[3] D Govindjee, Interview,12 November 1996.
[4] R Harry, interview with authors, Port Elizabeth, 17 May 1997.

along South Beach Terrace where fishing became the main source of their livelihood. This was the main motivation for the formation of Angling Clubs, the oldest one being the one at the Dom Pedro Jetty. Most of the fishing was done from the harbour breakwater. During the early years of its existence, the Dom Pedro Angling Club members held competitions among themselves. Later other clubs such as Birch's Angling Club (so named because the majority of the members were tailors who were employed by Birch's Clothing Shop in Main Street), Marine Rock and Surf, Bayonians, Marlins and Windsors were formed. The Eastern Province Angling Association was formed in 1951 and immediately introduced the Angling Week competition. Among the foundation members were Omar Cassim, Braima Kafoer and Ismail Nordien, who also donated the first trophies to the Association.

The venues for Angling competitions were Marine Drive, Blue Water Bay, St. George's Strand, Hougham Park, Gamtoos River Mouth, Jeffrey's Bay, Cape St Francis and Bushy Park. In 1965 the South African Angling Federation was formed with Eastern Province and Natal as the first members. The first tournament of the Association was held in Port Elizabeth in 1966. In 1967 Western Province joined the Federation and in that year the tournament was held in Natal.

Angling flourished as a sport in South End until the forced removals of its inhabitants in the late 1960s under the Group Areas Act.

Alpha Life Saving Club - The inaugural meeting of the Alpha Life Saving Club was held on 28 May 1958 at 36 Frere Street, South End. The foundation members of the club were FL Erasmus, M Agherdien, Y Solomon, C Jappie and A Jappie. It was the first `non-white' Life Saving Club in the Eastern Cape.

The first of its members who completed the Surf Proficiency Test with flying colours were, Anwar Abrahams, Cecil Domingo, Lionel Bruinders, Thomas Jordaan, Noorodien Adams and Jose de Silva. Most of the Club's Competitions were either held at the Schauderville swimming baths, Schoemakerskop (Malay Camp) or at St George's Strand , since all other beaches in Port Elizabeth were reserved for whites only in terms of the Separate Amenities Act of 1953. The club grew rapidly and still functions today. Its members perform regular life-saving duties along the coast at Joorst Park.

Tennis - Initially the only tennis court in South End was the Lea Place Tennis Courts where many interesting matches involving the well-known tennis twins of the time, namely M. Orsini and A. Bardien, took place. Later an additional tennis court was built in Stuart Township. As the years progressed many more players became actively involved. Tennis clubs of the time were: Lea Place Tennis Club, Sweet Pea Tennis Club and Universals.

It was impossible to give an account of the different cods of sport. It is the authors' desire that old South Enders may be motivated to research and publish each sport code in more detail.

RECREATION

Social events were very popular in South End and took place in halls of all kinds found throughout the area. The most well-known of these were the Lindstrom Hall in Coode Street, Oliver Plunkett in Bunn Street, Muslim Movement Hall in Sprigg Street, the Web in Walmer Road, the Boys' Club in Forest Hill Road and the Mariamam Hall on the corner of Farie and Gardner streets. Most of the churches also had halls built next to them. These halls were used for weddings, dances, birthday parties, stage shows, film shows and also for shooting competitions, kerm, snooker, bridge and indoor sports like table tennis. The church halls were used as venues for sports and social meetings. A popular social club was found on the corner of Walmer Road and Thomas Street where snooker was played. Other meeting places in South End where people of various ages could meet were the Palace Bioscope and the Roxy in South Union Street.

The very strong social interaction resulted in the formation of a number of well-known social groups

Break Of Day Cricket Club
Winners of 1st League Lion Cup Season 1935-36
Runners up Independent Social Cup
Standing: H.M. Agherdien (President),
K. Samsodien (Scorer), A. Hendricks,
A. Agherdien, A.B. Cassiem,
E. Bethanie (Hon. Secretary), S. Dolley,
I. Agherdien, A. Salie, T. Marcus (Vice-President)
Sitting: H.M. Kahaar, M. Boomgard,
H.M. Hendricks (Treasurer),
S. Hendricks (Captain), A. Kafaar (Chairman),
M.T. Jappie, H. Majiet
Front row: M. Morley, H. Davids, M.A. Hendricks,
I. Nordien
(F. Peterson)

P.E. Ottomans Cricket Club
(Est. 1950)
Winners of Searles and Kum Trophies
(1951-'52)
Standing L-R: A. Seale, A. Samuels,
I. Agherdien (Vice-Capt.), E.B. Savahl,
L. Matthews (Ass. Sec.), A.K. Ismail, H. Wilson
Sitting L-R: M.N. Moerat (Sec.),
J. Groener (Chairman), A.C. Abrahams (Capt.),
S. Dolley (Treas.), E. de Kock
Front row L-R: J. Prince, A. Abrahams,
I. Abrahams (Scorer), S. Agherdien
(E. de Kock)

Morning Star Cricket Club
(Established 1887)
Winners of 2nd League Trophy - Season 1952-'53
Back row: J. Gallant, D. Wilson, F. Francis,
C. Jackson, J. Wilson
Standing: J. Leander, D. Walters, A.J. Sutch,
G. Jassen, M. Goldman, W. MacKaiser, P. Wilson
Sitting: H. O'Rielly, H. Hollaway (President),
E. Conttell (Captain), M. Hendricks
(Vice-President), G. Soloman (Treasurer),
R. Hercules (Secretary), W. Williams,
Hendricks (Scorer)
(D. MacKaiser)

South End United Cricket Club
1st Team
Winners of League 1961/64
Standing L-R: G.J. Langson, M.C. Wilson
(Asst. Secretary), T.A.S. Hendricks,
A.M. Snyman, C.G. Simon
Sitting L-R: W.P. Nagan, C.E. Jeptha,
P.W. Snyman (Capt.-V/Chairman), W.S. Hendricks (Chairman),
G. Hendricks (V/Capt.-Sec.), P.A. de Klerk,
A.B. Snyman
(M. Wilson)

56

Moslem Sports Club
Back L-R: A. Jobson, A. Ally, A. Connelly, M. Agherdien, A. Ortell, A.L. Gardien, M. Demaine, C. Abdol
Middle L-R: K. Samsodien, G. Connelly, N. Baboo, M.N. Agherdien, K. Lillah
Front R-L: A. Morley, G. Fataar, G. Potgieter, F. Abrahams, S. Fataar (S. Hendricks)

Hamiediahs Cricket Club
Back L-R: Mr Willis, A. Shamar, A. Abrahams, Hadj. Y. Gamieldien, ..., 'Kallies', S. Fredericks, 'Dik Sand', 'Harry Oz', Mr E. Abrahams
Middle L-R: Mr S. Kam, Joel, N. Davids, 'Baatie', 'Boeta Tollie', A. Johns, ..., A. Ortell, Mr Dolley
Front R-L: M. Salie, W. Fredericks, A. Salie, S. Isaacs, A. Fredericks (A. Ortell)

57

Rugby on the Schafer Grounds. (Airport in left hand corner)
(S. Abrahams)

Windsor R.F.C.
Back L-R: 'Dan' ....., S. Turner, P. Swarts, ..., ... Middle L-R: L. Mattews, ..., G. Joel, A. Samie
Front L-R: A. Bruiners, ..., ...
(L. Mattews)

Orange Blossoms R.F.C.
Standing L-R: W. Ricketts, F. Francis, J. Rowan, S.C. Fick, M.A. Hendricks, E. Contell, A. Mortimer
Sitting L-R: G. Hendricks, A. Abrahams, A. Hendricks, Mr H. Abrahams, B. Abrahams, M. Boomgaard, I. Arkeldien
Front row R-L: G. Abrahams, Mascot T. Abrahams, H. Jaftha (A. Mortimer)

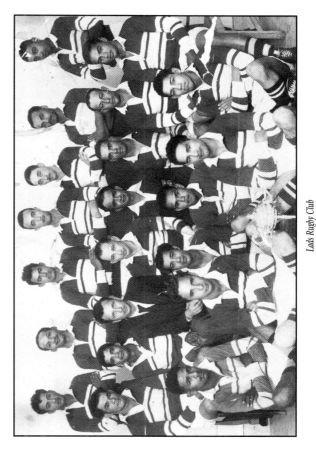

Lads Rugby Club
Back L-R: A.K. Ismail, ..., A. Ortell, E. Savahl, L. Mattews, -. Kamaldien, D. George
Middle L-R: F. Prinsloo, 'Seun' Claasen, M. Agherdien, I. Agherdien, 'Issie' Pandie, (Chairman/Treasurer), E. de Kock, S. Joel, J. Ricketts
Front L-R: A. George, Y. Agherdien, O. Raffie, M. Juluis, - Klein, B. Adams (Z. Astrie)

58

St. Peters Hockey Club
Back L-R: E. de Kock, R. Seale, J. Nelson, G. Hendricks,
L. Felix, D. Seale
Middle L-R: R. Stowman, N. Jenneker, Mr Rulser,
R. Potgieter, B. Johnson
Front L-R: A. Jenneker, A. Meyer, K. Naidoo,
R. Potgieter (L. Mattews)

1st. Team Baptist United Hockey Club
Winners of League and Five-A-Side Cups.
Season 1933
Top row: M. Bowers, O. Johns, E. Marks
1st row: R. Matthews, C. Rensburg, L. Benjamin (Hon. Sec.),
R. Johns (Treas.)
2nd row: J. Rensburg, W. Matthews (Trainer), E. Rensburg (Capt.),
B. Nicholas (Chairman), I. Watson (Vice-Capt.)
Front row: M. Potgieter, H. Burton
(Mrs Burton)

1st Team Blackpool Hockey Club
Winners of League and Five-A-Side Trophies, Season 1938
Top row: S. March (Treasurer), C. Rensburg, R. Matthews,
E. Matthews, S. Sutch, F. Murphy
Sitting: M. Miller, J. Rensburg (Secretary), M. Matthews,
J.C.H. Rockman (Chairman), H. Burton (Captain),
M. Bowers,
M. Potgieter (Goalie)
(Mrs Burton)

Paladins Hockey Club
Winners of League 1945-1946
Winners of Cassidy 1945-1946. Winners of Dorice 1946.
Winners of Knock-Out 1946.

Standing: M. Dixon, C. Fick, S. Jenneker, G. Snyman,
C. Fillis, V. Perry
Sitting: N. White, I. Knipp (Vice-Capt.),
I. Rockman (Capt. & Chairlady), P. Stowman (Sec. & Treas.),
P. Hendricks
Sitting: P. Dorothy, F. Prinsloo
(Mrs Burton)

Dom Pedro Angling Club
G. Agherdien, G. Pillay, T. Plaatjies
Front: E.B. Davids
(S. Abrahams)

ABOVE: Mr A. (Manie) Abrahams
Mr A . Abrahams standing on the break wall with the famous game fish,
Katonkel, also known as Baracuda, caught regularly off the break wall.
Many people earned a living by catching fish off the wall and by selling it
at the Fish Hooks at the corner of Walmer Road and South Union
Street. Even on thie break wall the non-whites were discrimanated
against. Three quarters of the wall towards the point was for whites only
and the rest, further back, was for non-whites.

Birch Rock and Surf Angling Club
Back L-R: G. Francis, S. Kajee, A. Bruce, A. Abrahams, H. Kader
Front L-R: R. Lagerdien, A. Astrie, A. Dolley, S. Dolley, G. Bruce
(A. Abrahams)

Windsor Angling Club - Season 1959-1960
Winners, Grand Challenge Trophy, Eastern Cape Anglers' Association
Back row: B. Losper, D.A. McDillan (Secretary),
G. Isaacs (Vice-Chairman), N. Hearne, S. Abrahams
Centre row: A. Langford (Vice-Captain), J. Moolow (Captain),
G. Joel (Chairman)
Front row: H. Kemp, M.T. Hendriks
(S. Abrahams)

Foundation members of lifesaving in South End
L-R: M. Agherdien, F.L. Erasmus, "King" Daniels, M.C. Jappie,
N. Adams, Y. Soloman, (S. Abrahams)

Alpha Surf Life Saving Club, 1965
(L. Briunders)

Friendly Game
A friendly game of friendship to remember - 1961,
on Schafer Tennis Courts - Port Elizabeth

Miss Audrey Morley, Mrs. Miller

Les Redcliffe

A. Bardien
(E.P. Open Champ - 1968)

A. Kuscus, Mrs M. Cupido
(E.P. Doubles - 1952)

such as the Black Shirts and the Bullet Gang, which, despite their fearsome names, were not criminal gangs. One could walk around in South End at any time of the day and the night without the fear of being molested.

Dancing - Dancing was very popular in South End. The main venues for dancing were the Oliver Plunkett, Lindstrom, and Eldorado Halls. The South End folk also attended dances in halls in other areas in Port Elizabeth. These included the Walmer Town Hall, as well as the Feather Market, Korsten and the Mac Sherry Halls. The most popular dance on the calendar of South End was the Dahlia Ball which was held annually in the Feather Market Hall.

Miscellaneous - The quarry ,which was situated where the Fire Station is today, was well-known to South Enders. It had a pool where many children in South End learnt to swim, and it was also the venue of many `fair fights' to decide the winner of a conflict.

A game of chance, called fah-fee was played on a daily basis in South End. The winnings from this popular game provided a plate of food in many a homes in South End. There were usually three `banks' and winners a day. Persons who took the bets and collected the moneys were found all over South End. The bankers in most cases were Chinese.

Victoria Park 'Coloured' Sports Field in 1997
This was one of the most important and popular sports fields for non-whites in South End. It was situated in the heart of Victoria Park, surrounded by the whites-only cemetery, Crematorium, Victoria Park Bowling Club, Victoria Park Tennis Club and Pirates sport fields. Soccer derbys were played on this field between its two most popular soccer teams namely Blackpool and Swallows.
With the removal of the people out of South End, the toilet block and ticket box was demolished and the playing field was left to become a waste piece of land, overgrown with scrubs and bushes in the middle of Victoria Park.
(Faizal Felix)

Sweet Pea Tennis Club
Standing L-R: W. Wallenstein, S. Dolley (Captain), W. September
Sitting: Miss M. Bush, A.A. Abrahams
(Y. Patel)

5

DOWN MEMORY LANE

South End had some unique features which made it a special place for all its inhabitants, irrespective of race, colour or creed. It was a community which showed mutual respect for the cultural diversity of its members. The community was strongly religious, as illustrated by the fact that there were numerous Churches of different denominations, as well as two temples and two mosques. It is remarkable that no incidents of religious or cultural animosity are known to have occurred in what was a harmonious and tolerant community. It would not be incorrect to regard it as a microcosm of today's rainbow-nation.[1] To demonstrate the cosmopolitan nature of South End, we will briefly look at some of the features which made it such a unique community.

By far the majority of the grocery stores were owned by Chinese and the shop names Date Chong, On Hing, Forlee, Jackie, Lee Ching, Horman, Low Ah Kee, Ah Why, Leeson and Loyson were household names. There were vegetable shops and grocery stores owned by VM Pillay, Naidoo's, Pillay Brothers, Lindstrom, Poole Groceries, Dunn Groceries,Ideal Fruiterers, Kader, Banana Wholesalers and Wellington Fruiters, Imperial Fruiterers and Reddy's Cafe. Many were situated in Walmer Road. The prices were very competitive and buying your weekly vegetables at the cheapest prices might have required you to traverse Walmer Road for the best bargains. The butchers of South End were Imperial, Narkar, Oxford, Wiblin, Saibu and Nelson Pearson. The chemists of note were Eastmead and Henman. Of the dairies, Chelsea Dairy in Walmer Road always had supplies of fresh milk and cream and their milk suckers which sold for a penny. United Dairies had as its specialty a `twistee' ice-cream which sold for a tickey each. Both dairies delivered milk to homes. One had only to ensure that your empty milk bottle was put out the night before outside the front door and the next morning your supply of fresh milk would be in its place. Other dairies were Modern, and prince Wiltshire.

Evans and Son's factory in Forest Hill Road manufactured tombstones and marble ornaments. Evans displayed its tombstones in Walmer Road next to Elite Cafe and on the corner of South Union and Rudolph Streets.[2]

South End was well-provided for in the line of clothing; it was known for its expert dressmakers like Mrs Uren who attracted clientele from all over Port Elizabeth. The Malay and Indian tailors were well-known throughout Port Elizabeth for the fine quality of clothing they made. Some of the names of the tailors that come to mind are Abrahams, Agherdien, Nakerdien, Davids, Bruce, Nordien, Peterson, Savahl, Meyer and Noor. Their tailor shops were frequented by all and many would sit on the counter to pass the day away in idle chatter. The tailors were sought after for the `zooting' of trousers.[3] Dresses were also very seldom bought in shops since dressmakers could be found all over South End, operating mainly from their homes. There were a number of well-known clothing shops in South End. The Makan Family owned one in South Union Street and two in Walmer Road. Others were Pamansky and Erics in South Union Street and Daya in Walmer Road.

One of the most familiar landmarks in Walmer Road was Dorasamy's hairdresser shop whose owner had continued what was a family business carried on by successive generations. In South Union Street Jamal's barber was a popular venue in which to catch up with the latest South End gossip. Ismail's barber which was situated in Mitchell Street next to Ismail's General Dealer on the corner of Walmer Road and Mitchell Street, was also well known.

Cars were a very scarce commodity because everything was in walking distance. From most parts of

---

[1]Mr S Pillay, interview with authors, Port Elizabeth, 23 April 1996.
[2]L. van Wyk, *Family Post,* 25 July 1987.
[3]A fashion fad in which the trouser leg would be altered to make it narrower.

South End, it would not take you more than 10 minutes down Walmer Road, through South Union Street to the center of the city of Port Elizabeth, or you could take the short cut down the `black steps' into Alfred Road, and then via South Union Street to town. Since a lot of walking was done there were ample opportunities to chat because everyone seemed to be everyone's friend.

At most schools children were served bread, milk, soup and fruit during the school breaks. In this way the poorer children of South End were provided for.

The postman was known by everyone and it was not unusual for him to enjoy a cup of tea at some of the homes where he delivered his mail. Birthdays, weddings, sickness of neighbours was also shared by all in the neighbourhood, no matter who you were.

The central recreational area in South End was called Quoit Green which was a large stretch of open veld bordered by Forest Hill Road, Sprigg Street and Armstrong Street. Here children of the neighbourhood would gather after school, and it was not unusual to see cricket, rugby and soccer being played at the same time on different parts of the field.

In the streets hop-scotch, rounders, jackstones, bok-bok or any ball game was enjoyed by the children of the neighbourhood. At the lower end of Quoit Green was the Boys' club which consisted of a community hall and a day-care centre. Everyone was allowed in the Boys' club where one could learn many disciplines, of which the most popular was boxing. One of the boxing instructors was Brian Elliot who later became the Empire Middleweight in the 1950s. Working parents could leave their children at the day-care centre. Presiding at the centre was Ma Fick, the matron, who for many years cared for children of all colours and creeds. Tree-climbing and soapbox rides down Kingsley Kloof were popular pastimes for young boys on a Sunday afternoon. The Baakens River Valley and the Krantz leading up to Fort Frederick were popular adventure trials.

The first canteens in Walmer Road and South Union Street in old South End were licenced around 1860. One of the first was called the `Woodman' situated in Walmer Road, and operated by TL Holdstock. In 1877 it became known as the `Walmer Castle', and finally the Queens Hotel in 1884. This was the name known to most of the residents of old South End.[4] William Buckley was the proprieter of the `Prince of Wales Hotel' in Strand Street and he opened his namesake in Walmer Road in November 1878. This hotel was rebuilt in 1929.

Round about 1880 there existed also the Royal Hotel in South Beach Terrace. The `Walmer Road Hotel' was a canteen opened around 1879 by T Jordaan. About 1898 it was taken over by WH Berry who bought it in 1903. After his death his widow ran it until Ohlsson's Breweries bought it about 1915 and renamed it the Collins Hotel. Directly opposite on the corner of South Union Street was the Tyrone Hotel which was started in 1883 by Johnson McWilliams.[5]

Thus, within walking distance, there were two hotels situated opposite each other, namely the Tyrone and the Collins Hotel. Not very far up Walmer Road were two more hotels, the Prince of Wales and the Queens Hotel.

Victoria Park was a popular recreational centre frequented by courting couples, families or young children, and was always bustling with activity. Today it is still a popular venue for married couples to have their wedding photographs taken. One of the famous 'coloured' sports fields was situated in Victoria Park, known as the 'Vee Pee', where many exciting soccer derby's were played between Blackpool and Swallows.

The Schaefer Grounds near the Airport were also very popular venues for rugby, soccer, cricket and tennis. In the same vicinity towards Walmer was the 'dorsie dam' where you would find many children enjoying a swim after heavy rains.

A common method of purchasing goods, especially groceries, was on `tick'. Purchases were recorded by the shopkeeper in a little notebook. The account only became payable when one had the money. Also widely practised was the phenomenon of 'basella', which was an additional item such as a sweet which you received from the shopkeeper when you made a large purchase. A well-known practice by the stores

[4]Harridene, *Port Elizabeth*, 47.
[5]*Ibid.*

was that of home deliveries. One could either phone in one's order of goods, or leave a list at the shop.

South End had a number of shops and restaurants that made excellent food: the Kasbah for its curries, the Chinese Lantern for its Chinese foods, Gee Dees for its hot curries and CR Pillay for the best fish and chips in town. Well-known cafes in Walmer Road were the London Cafe and the Elite Cafe. London Cafe was particularly popular because of its slot machines, viewer and toy crane in a glass case. Laurel and Hardy and Charlie Chaplin flick films could be watched on the viewer. When a light went on, you slowly turned a handle which would flick the pictures over one at a time giving the impression of a moving film. The machine which operated the toy crane had a watch as a prize, which nobody ever seemed to win.[6] At the bottom of Walmer Road were iron rails where the fishermen daily sold their fresh fish. Next to the Queens Hotel was Chetty's Fresh Fish supplies which had their own fishing trawlers supplying a wide variety of fresh fish. Ice vendors were very popular in the streets and were very much a part of the South End scene. The ringing of their bells attracted children.

Also popular was Lailee's home-made toffee bars covered with coconut, and costing only a tickey. Syrupy koeksisters were made and sold by Lee Ching in Walmer Road and also by many Muslim Families. No South End family would be without a fresh supply of koeksisters on a Sunday morning.

One of the cinemas in South End was the popular Palace Bioscope in South Union Street. Sunday matinee and night films were also shown in the Oliver Plunket hall. The Palace was a well-known meeting place of young people and held regular stage shows. Mr Lingham was the manager for many years and because it was owned by the Grand bioscope ,all first release films were screened.

Buses from town passed through South End via South Union Street. They would groan up the steep slopes of Walmer Road on their way to Fairview, Salisbury Park and other areas further north. When the bus conductor was busy upstairs on the double decker buses, the young boys would `fly' on to the open end of the bottom deck at the bottom of Walmer Road, and then jump off when the bus had reached the top of the Road.

The cane and wickerworks in Walmer Road ,where caneware and baskets were manufactured, was known to schoolchildren because this was where the teachers obtained their canes used to mete out punishment in the classrooms. There were also two electrical shops, Warwick's and Hodges. Mr Hodges was a genial old man who would repair any electrical appliance, very often without charge to poorer people in South End. Horman, General Dealer, on the corner of Walmer Road and Armstrong Street was known for its wide variety of goods offered for purchase. One could purchase anything, up to live fowls. In Walmer Road, there was a picture framer by the name of Anderhold who was of Scandinavian descent and `hop beer' was bottled by Robertson's who had a bottling plant in Frere Street. Joe Davis and Finro were the two hardware stores situated opposite each other in Walmer Road. Joe Davis had an advertisement in front of the shop which said `Keys cut while you wait'. This was precisely what he did, besides also specializing in paint and hardware equipment.

Nick's cafe which was situated in Webber Street was owned by a Cypriot . It was the point of distribution of the *Evening Post* for the boys who sold it in the streets of the upper part of South End. The boys who sold newspapers in the lower parts of South End and town received their supplies directly from the back of Newspaper House in Produce Street. Many high school pupils earned extra pocket money by delivering the morning newspaper to householders in South End and other parts of Port Elizabeth. `Uncle' Bill Matthews served as the agent for Newspaper house that printed the *Herald*. If you wanted to be a successful agent you were expected to start your round of *Herald* delivery at 4:30 a.m.and end in time to be at school.

One cannot talk about South End without mentioning the bridge which was located where South Union Street joined North Union Street. The bridge was the area where the bus terminus was situated. There you could get your bus to Schauderville, Cadles, Perl Road, Fairview and other areas of Port Elizabeth. The bridge was bounded by Baakens River on the one side and Nelson Pearson on the other side, where the best quality meat was sold. There were a number of well-known vendors who sold fresh fruit and other refreshments at the bridge. This was a strategic spot because it had to be passed by everyone coming from

---

[6]E Oliver,*Weekend Post*, 18 July 1987.

South End via South Union Street on the way to the centre of town.

In the 1930s non-whites were not allowed to trade in the Hill area. In defiance of this, Mr VA Pillay opened up five shops without a licence. He was taken to the Supreme Court on this matter, and he won. The Council appealed, and he won the appeal. The next year eighteen licences were issued to the non-white community.

South End had a number of shoe repairers, each one of whom was a character in his own right. Names that come to mind are Mr Mahdoo in South Union Street, Lingham in Mitchell Street (he was also an usher at the Palace Bioscope), Mr Karson in Bullen Street and then in Forest Hill Road, Mr I Cedrass in Rudolph Street and Daya in Walmer Road. Mr Parshotam was know as a cobbler to whom you could go and chat on any subject, besides shoes, especially herbal medicine. He often took the responsibility of looking after stray cats.

A landmark known to young and old in South End was the clinic situated in Upper Pier Street. Here all children irrespective of race, colour or creed received their inoculations after birth and in later years. There, mothers use to collect their supplies of Cod Liver Oil and other essential medicines. The building still stands today. However, it has been incorporated into a group of newly-built flats so that it cannot be seen from the street.

In 1973 the Council wanted to make South End white below the ground as well as above the ground. The excuse was the building of a road through the cemetary. With this in view, approximately 3000 bodies were to be exhumed. The council called for objections. The Young Peoples Hindu Cultural Association took up the matter. Mr Shun Pillay met Mr Shelton of the Parks Department, who offered that a cemetary and parlour would be erected in Malabar if the council was not opposed. Mr Pillay refused, and organised a series of meetings. 650 objections were lodged. This protest action stopped the council in their wild endeavours. Apart from the moral and religious reasons this exercise saved the tax payer over 3 million rands.

A walk down memory lane in old South End will not be complete if we do not visit three well-known `relics'. Firstly, the mosques in Rudolph Street and Pier Street which have been documented in another part of the book. Secondly, the ruins of St Peter's Church and School which still vividly remind old residents of South End and Port Elizabeth of the life-sized crucifix named the Fishermans's Cross by the locals. Thirdly, the old fig tree which stands prominently along the South Union Street freeway.

The Fisherman's Cross

The `Fisherman's Cross' stood in the grounds of St Peters Anglican Church. It was so called because it stood as a symbol of love and hope for the men in the trawlers and line boats in the bay. It could be clearly seen from all parts of Algoa Bay and far out to the sea, and faced across the mouth of the Baakens River. The Cross was unveiled and dedicated as a memorial to those who served in the Great War of 1914-18. The figure on the cross was a life-sized one and had been imported from Belgium. Kohler Bros supplied the 12 foot high teak cross and a parishioner John Hendricks, did the concrete work and stone masonry. A copper plaque read: `The glory of life lies in serving and not in being served'. Somewhere in the late 1950s the figure, for some unknown reason, fell and broke and it was replaced by a cement fondu sculpture by John Hooper, a member of the staff of the Port Elizabeth Technical College. Amazingly, the Cross survived the might of apartheid laws and the bulldozers of the Group Areas Act in the late 1960s and early 70s. It was taken to the church of St Mark and St John in Parkside in the Northern Suburbs, to which coloured people had been forcibly removed. Today it overlooks the noisy N2 motorway, still bearing witness.[7]

Restoration of St Peter's Church Buildings

In 1983 , the St Peter's building had reached such a state of ruin that the roofs of the building were gone;

[7]B.Durham, *A brief history of the Church of St. Mark and St. John the Evangelist*, Parkside, 1989.

part of the thick stone walls was all that survived among the ever-encroaching weeds. Mr George Holliday, Director of Port Elizabeth's St George VI Gallery, was so impressed with the ruins that he proposed a restoration to some `like-minded people' in that year.[8] The proposal was that `what was once the spiritual home of fishermen in Algoa Bay is to became the spiritual home of the residents of Port Elizabeth as a special museum depicting the history of the city'.[9] The art gallery's trustees supported the move and the trustees of the Anglican Diocese agreed to sell it for R30 000. Two anonymous donors offered to meet this cost and further donations were also pledged. Mr Holliday commented: 'This place is a history book in stone'. The ruins of St Peter's Church stand above St Mary's cemetery whose history which dates back to the 1820 settlers. Although the old buildings were skeletons, their concrete structures had weathered extremely well and the foundations were `as solid as rock'.[10] Unfortunately, the plans for a museum on the site of St Peter's Church and School never came to fruition for varying reasons, among others, insufficient finance.

Fig Tree

Along the freeway, near the South Union Street and Walmer Road intersection, stands an old fig tree, an immovable and living memorial to the people who used to stay in the old South End.

As far back as 1970 ,when most of the people who had not already moved, knew that their time had come, one of the residents, Mr S Isaacs, wondered if government officials would spare the old tree which then stood in Chase Street, South Beach Terrace. The old fig tree had stood there for as long as anyone in the neighbourhood could remember. The tree's heavy, wide, spreading branches, densely covered with foliage, formed a canopy over Mr Isaac's house and also covered the house next-door. Its roots were thick and uncoiled from the large bole of its trunk, to burrow under the surrounding houses, through solid concrete foundations and under the surface of the street, to come out and go down again on the other side, anchoring itself deep beneath the rock and sand of South End. No gale had been able to bend this old giant to its will. It had grown sturdily erect and stood the strain of what could possibly have been a century of buffeting by the wind.

A reporter who wrote an article on the fig tree in 1970, doubted if the authorities would leave the relic of old South End standing. He stated that what the wind was unable to do man and his bulldozers would most certainly do when the last remains of old South End were razed to make way for the smart new one.[11] Fortunately, a spark of sanity appeared to enter the minds of the single-minded officials of the ironically-named Department of Community Development, who had zealously carried out the task of evicting `non-white' residents of South End and demolishing their homes, schools and churches. The old fig tree miraculously won the battle against the bulldozers and, just like the two mosques, is a living reminder that about 30 years ago people of all population groups lived harmoniously together in a cosmopolitan suburb.

The residents of old South End regarded sports, recreation and socialization as important aspects of their way of life. This cemented the community into an integrated unit over a period of over 125 years. It also explains in very vivid terms the reasons for so much resentment, hatred and bitterness among its residents when old South End was declared a white group area under the Group Areas Act. This chapter has perhaps provided a clearer insight into why the Group Areas caused so much pain and suffering in South Africa as a whole, and old South End in particular. The aim of the following chapters is to foster a greater understanding among all South Africans of how `non-whites' in general, and coloured and Indian South Africans in particular suffered firstly as a result of British Colonial rule with its policy of `divide and rule', and then, after 1948, the Nationalist Party's policy of apartheid.

---

[8]B.Dennhy, *Eastern Province Herald*, 21 February 1983.
[9]*Ibid.*
[10]C du Plessis, *Weekend Argus*, 7 May 1983.
[11]J Michales, *Weekend Evening Post*, 7 September 1970.

68

Tyrone Hotel, corner of South Union Street and Walmer Road
(Times Media Library)

South Union Street
(Bob Binnell Collection)

Queen's Hotel, corner of Walmer Road and Mitchell Street
(Times Media Library)

Collins Hotel, corner of South Union Street and Walmer Road
(Bob Binnell Collection)

ABOVE: A. Horman's General Dealer
(V. Kwong)

RIGHT: Opening of Makans in
Walmer Road 1914
(J. Makan)

BELOW: Joe Davies The Hardware Store
in Walmer Road
(Bob Binnell Collection)

70

Blacks steps next to St Mary's Cemetery
(Faizal Felix)

The Fig Tree, 1997
(Faizal Felix)

Ruins of St Peter's Church
(Faizal Felix)

Imperial Fruiterers
(Samoo's Corner, as seen from the Fish Hooks)
(Bob Binnell Collection)

Scene at the Fish Hooks
(Times Media Library)

Fresh fish daily at the Fish Hooks
(Times Media Library)

A view of the harbour from Rock Street
(G. Astrie)

72

Imperial Fruiterers, corner of Walmer Road and South Union Street
(Times Media Library)

The Boy's Club, corner of Forest Hill Road and Armstrong Street
(Bob Binnell Collection)

Erics Stores in South Union Street
(Times Media Library)

Erics Stores in South Union Street
(Bob Binnell Collection)

Scene at the bottom of Walmer Road
Girl on left: Miss G. Wackie,
and her nephews on the right
(S. Wackie)

Children at the bottom of Walmer Road with student
(Times Media Library)

Walmer Road, between Seymour and Mitchell Street
(Bob Binnell Collection)

Oliver Plunkett Hall
(Bob Binnell Collection)

Lions Clothing factory in Farie Street
(Bob Binnell Collection)

Cassim"s" Building in Walmer Road
(A. Cassim)

Clinic in Upper Pier Street
(Bob Binnell Collection)

Floods on the first of September 1968 when the Baakens River overflowed its banks. It was also the weekend when a lot of residents had to move to the Northern areas
(Times Media Library)

Boys playing top games in Bullen Street
(Times Media Library)

The Black Shirts
Standing L-R: 'Milly'Tank, 'Milly', 'Manie', 'Brian', 'Doela', Dressie, 'Bobby'
Sitting L-R: 'Doela', 'Manie', 'Little Henry'
(S. Hendricks)

The Bullit Gang
Standing L-R: T. Mohamed, T. Hendricks, P. Muller, 'Gumpai',
D. Frost, D. Boomgard, A. Abdullah
Sitting L-R: S. Fataar, S. Fataar, A. Abrahams, J. Abrahams
(S. Fataar)

Group of youngsters on the corner of Gardner Street and
Walmer Road
(A. Abrahams)

6

THE GROUP AREAS ACT

The most devastating phenomenon to affect the residents of old South End in its illustrious history was undoubtedly the Group Areas Act. This Act was part of a clutch of apartheid laws passed soon after the National Party came to power in 1948. The Act was intended to give effect to the Population Registration Act of 1950 which labelled and racially classified all South Africans as part of a defined population group. To begin this process of racial separation, the Group Areas Act was passed in the same year.

The Group Areas Act had as its main purpose to restrict each population group to specific places as far as ownership, occupancy and trading was concerned. Up to this time Africans outside the homelands were already closely monitored in their movement and residence and employment by a policy of influx control. They were forced to carry a pass, failing which they were immediately arrested, and they had to obtain official permission if they wanted to change and accept jobs. Indians were subject to a number of restrictions in Johannesburg and Durban, and were prevented from living or earning their livelihood in the Orange Free State. However, the ultimate goal of the Group Areas Act was to extend the restrictions which already existed for `Coloureds, Asiatics(Indians) and Natives(Africans)' as well as to establish separate residential areas for different population groups by shifting people from one place to another. In this process coloureds and Indians (Asiatics) in long-established communities were uprooted and forced to move to areas far from the city and workplace. Africans were forced to give up their limited freehold areas, and a limited number of whites had to move. On the whole, the entire non-white population of South Africa was forced into a state of impermanence.

According to Du Pré `If one law could be singled out as the one which caused the most suffering, the most humiliation, and the most deprivation, and about which non-white people still talk today with hatred and bitterness, then it was the Group Areas Act. (No 14 of 1950)'. He further states that this law was `nothing more than legalized robbery. Under its guise, an immoral goverment and greedy whites stalked the non-white areas, buying up properties at pocket-money prices. This Act impoverished ... people... killed them economically... killed many of them physically.' He concluded that `this Act will go down in history as the most odious and devastating, as far as [its victims] are concerned.'[1]

The importance of this Act to the Nationalist Government was underlined by Dr TE Donges, Minister of Interior, who guided the Bill through parliament. According to him the Bill was introduced because `we do not believe that the future of South Africa will be that of a mixed population, and this is one of the major measures designed to preserve white South Africa.'[2] This fanatical desire to separate the entire population purely on the grounds of skin colour, and protect the supposedly `fragile' white people of South Africa, resulted in the forced removal of entire communities; the demolition of their homes, schools and churches; the destruction of suburbs; the fragmentation of religious, familial, educational and sporting bonds, and was to have repercussions which are still evident to this day. The Group Areas Act affected suburbs like South End and hundreds of other suburbs, towns and villages like it all over South Africa: places like District Six and Schotse Kloof in Cape Town, Sophiatown and Fordsburg in Johannesburg, Cato Manor and Phoenix in Durban and North End in East London and Oudtshoorn, to name but a few.

GROUP AREAS PROCLAMATION

The proclamation of the Group Areas in Port Elizabeth was a very emotional and contentious issue, since

---

[1]RH du Pré, *Separate but Unequal* (Johannesburg: Jonathan Ball , 1994), 82.
[2]AJ Christopher, `Formal segregation', 7-8.

the areas in and around the centre of the city were integrated communities dating back to the colonial period.[3] Proclaiming these areas `white' meant that all `non whites' living in the area had to move. Christopher states that the proclamation of the group areas had been anticipated by the municipality, since all land which was available for private sale after 1949 included `racially restrictive clauses for occupation and ownership which specified that it was intended for Europeans, Asiatics or Coloureds.'[4] These restrictions had not been previously included in the title deeds of sale.

TABLE 4 - DISTRIBUTION OF POPULATION IN PORT ELIZABETH 1951.

Popula-tion Group	Residents in Group Areas as eventually proclaimed				
	White Area	Coloured Area	Asian Area	Native Area	Total
White	78 622	733	-	153	79 508
Coloured	23 534	18 436	-	3 547	45 517
Asian	3 313	659	-	88	4 060
Black	14 938	15 525	-	40 235	70 698
TOTAL	120 407	35 353	-	44 023	199 783

The proclamation of the Group Areas Act evoked a storm of protest in Port Elizabeth, which took the form of letters written to the local newspapers (*Eastern Province Herald* and *Evening Post*), protest meetings by the Anti-Coloured Affairs Department (Anti-CAD) movement and the formation of an umbrella body, the Group Areas Action Committee. The Anti-CAD was established in opposition to the creation of the Coloured Affairs Department (CAD) by the Smuts' Government in 1943 to provide for separate administration of matters pertaining to coloured people. They saw this as the beginning of the application of segregation measures to coloured people, which had already begun to be applied to Africans. However, instead of the CAD succeeding in providing a platform for the improvement of the social life and political rights for coloured people, it led to a split and initiated the polarisation of coloured political life. Those who were in favour of the creation of the CAD were labelled as collaborators and sellouts and heralded the beginning of the Collaboration versus non-Collaboration issue which was to dog coloured politics for the next fifty years.[5] It is therefore not surprising that this organisation came out so strongly in opposition to the Group Areas Act.

The chairman of the Anti-CAD in Port Elizabeth was Frank A Landman and the vice-chairman was none other than Dennis Brutus[6]. The records consulted make no mention of any other executive member of the said organization. The Anti-CAD set out to oppose anyone who appeared to be in favour of collaboration with the Nationalist Government in the implementation of the Group Areas Act. The Group Areas Action Committee was an umbrella organization set up to represent all the community groupings in South End

---

[3] Ibid, (Figure 3 and Figure 4), 8.

[4] Ibid, 8.

[5] The Anti-CAD had strong support amongst coloured intellectuals and together with the Teachers League of South Africa (TLSA) and the New Era Fellowships (NEF), supported the Non-European Unity Movement (NEUM) which played a significant role in `non-white' politics in the 1940s and 1950s. For a more detailed discussion on this issue, see Du Pré, *Separate but Unequal*, 59-60.

[6] See Appendix III for a short biographical note on F A Landman.

who were prepared to fight against the Act. However, throughout this fight, there were many collaborators in their midst who believed the government propaganda that the implementation of the Act was not such a bad thing as it would bring benefits for those `non-whites' living in parlous conditions. Whites of course had their own hidden agenda for wanting to see the Act implemented. Both these groups were vigorously opposed and exposed.

Some whites put forward the most ludicrous arguments in favour of the implementation of the Act in South End. The arguments advanced were that there were many brothels, shebeens and gambling dens in South End; that the police could hardly cope with that; and that the area would become congested with non-whites if they remained there. They also stated that South End was a slum, that it was decaying because non-whites did not look after their homes; and that if the government planned to renew the area, the non-whites should be removed because they would be least affected by such a move. The real fear, which was readily expressed, was that there would be an influx of non-whites into the area, which would constitute a threat to the way of life of whites in adjacent areas.

Most of the reasons and arguments advanced were shallow and lacking in substance and were nothing more than an attempt to justify the enforcement of removals of non-white communities from South End. The accusation that South End was a slum was of course a gross generalisation. However, there were areas which had degenerated. Most often, this had occurred because after the promulgation of the Group Areas Act in 1951, owners and landlords had become mindful of the possibility that they might be moved. With this sword hanging over them, no-one wanted to commit hard-earned money to renovations and expensive maintenance with the possibility that it might never be recovered. It was thus the threat of government action which led to decay, and not the neglect of the communities and owners themselves. On the other hand, most tenants, owners and landlords had over a period of many years built, added-on and renovated on a regular basis. However, because the income of `non-whites' was less than whites, their homes were not as fashionable and smart as those of houses in upmarket white areas.To such whites, the humble dwellings of non-whites constituted a `slum.'

During one of the many protest meetings of the Group Areas Action Committee held in the Muslim Movement Hall in Sprigg Street in the 1950s, Dennis Brutus pointed out that `the Act would breed racial friction and once they were moved, there was no likelihood of any adequate compensation for homes or businesses. There was also the likelihood that non-whites would no longer be allowed to own property.' They could be reduced to`leaseholders'. Furthermore, he could not see any justification for the move and felt it was based on racial discrimination. It was a tool used by Nationalist Government to sow seeds of disunity among the non-white communities. Lastly, the Act was going to be exploited by the government: `In highly organized, patrolled locations, freedom of thought and speech would better be controlled.' Nationalist propaganda already insinuated that the non-white was an inferior being.[7]

FA Landman stated at a protest meeting in the Muslim Hall in Sprigg Street that `one of the most important tragedies of the Act would be the race hatred and friction it would stir up among non-Europeans. He declared that `it must be our chief consideration not to make it possible to let this race attitude develop'.[8] At another protest meeting of the Anti-CAD group, he advised the audience not to sell their property in panic and move to areas which were regarded as safe.

In the 1940s we were privileged to have a person of the calibre of Eric Erentzen, a teacher at Paterson High and a member of the Teachers League of South Africa (TLSA). He realised the need to develop progressive political thought among the people of Port Elizabeth, to oppose the establishment. He and a number of associates formed the Non European United Front (NEUF), whose emblem was the handshake of brotherhood. Among his associates were BS Pillay who became secretary, MM Desai who became councillor of Ward 7, Ofie Salie, Frank Landman, Cairncross of Uitenhage, Olive Landman, Harry Japtha, Dr Davids, Kolloi, DS Pillay and Fanie Pillay. They took up various matters; the election of Dr E Diedericht as coulcillor for ward 1, the rescinding of the ban of the use of the City Hall by non-whites, the removal of the segregation of station benchesa and the prevention of the removal of Dowerville. They

[7]Newspaper Resources, File 2/4, vols 1-4 (1951-1958).
[8] Ibid.

encouraged their members to join the school committee of Paterson High to advance the appointment of non-white principals and teachers. They made a vehement stand against the Coloured Affairs department (CAD) legislation and the Coloured Advisory Council (CAC) The council maintained that the new Schauder Township housing scheme was a sub economic scheme. The secreatary of the NEUF took up the matter and proved conclusively in a heated debate with the then mayor Adolph Schauder that the scheme was an economic one.

The trade union offices were at 92 Queen Street and leading members of those unions were MM Desai and DS Pillay who were also members of the Communist Party. In 1962 Mr Govan Mbeki, Alf Every, Eric Attwell and his wife, DS Pillay and many others were imprisoned for ninety days.

At St Andrews Street off Main Street the Foreign Club used to meet regularly where lectures and debates were held. Another political grouping was the Fourth International Group which took an active part in politics and were mainly Trotskyites.

Shun Pillay , Vice president of the Port Elizabeth educational forum, vividly recalls lectures conducted by Benny Kies on ' the law' and the Rev. Victor Wessels on ' The Role of the Non-White in Western Civilisation'. Both these gentlemen were prominent members of the Anti-CAD and TLSA of the day.

The 1952 Defiance Campaign was planned at a meeting between the ANC Cape Branch under the leadreship of Dr Njongwe and the Cape Indian Congress under the leadreship of SR Naidoo at the home of BS Pillay at3 Rock Street.

The attitude of many whites was reason for grave concern for the Action Committee and the non-white community at large. An example of this was the reaction to a proposal was made by the Government appointed Reference and Planning Committee of the Group Areas Board that Chinese, Indians and Malays be moved to an area on the Cape Road beyond Westering. George Hayward, United Party MP for Port Elizabeth, vigorously opposed this suggestion. Instead, he suggested that the Indian, Chinese and Malay communities be allocated Group Areas beyond Schauder Township in the direction of Bethelsdorp.[9] A leading member of the Indian Community, Mr BB Ramjee, retorted: 'Mr Hayward's proposal shows a complete disregard of the fate of the non-Europeans. He simply wants non-whites moved out and away from any area in which he may have interest, without considering for a moment how non-whites will live'. Ramjee indicated that the Indians objected to Group Areas moves which would cause hardship to one group at the expense of another. Mr HO Cassim[10], president of the Moslem Movement in Port Elizabeth concurred: `We do not accept the original proposals much less than this one made by Mr Hayward. The Act will strangle the Malay Community economically. Most of us are tailors. We cannot live in separate areas, making suits for one another.' Mr Wing King, chairman of the Chinese Association, also echoed similar sentiments when he declared that the Chinese objected in principle to group areas in which the people of a single group had to live and trade: `In a Community (South End) of 1300 Chinese, we have 248 shops. Obviously we cannot trade among ourselves.'[11]

On the other hand, Hayward's sentiments concerning the siting of a non-white area next to Westering, drew strong support from residents of Kabega Park, Westering and Linton Grange. Their major fear was the devaluation of their properties. Captain P Cumming, a resident in the Westering area, appealed `to the white group in the area to unite and oppose the proposals to protect the future generation.' Mr Naude, vice-chairman of the special action committee formed to address this issue, stated that a petition signed by Linton Grange residents objecting to the proposals had already been submitted to the Group Areas Board: `We would not like to see the Chinese or Indian community cutting into Linton Grange. It would be better to support proposals by the city council that these two communities be accommodated at Driftsands'. At the same time, many white (European) residents who were approached to sign the petition calling for South End to be zoned for a Group Area exclusively for whites, refused to do so. One resident explained: I told him that I did not want to sign it and gave him my reasons. He persisted to such an

---

[9] Ibid.

[10] See Appendix III for a short biographical note.

[11] Ibid.

extent that I was forced to throw him out'.[12]

In a letter to the *Evening Post* in 1955, a reader took his fellow-whites of Port Elizabeth to task over their attitude to the Group Areas Act, with all its ramifications. To him 'one of the most tragic and incontestable facts is that even in a predominantly non-Nationalist city like Port Elizabeth, no European voice' (except one honorable letter writer) was raised to criticize `baaskap Group Areas proposals', neither did any of them (European voters) suggest that those who desire to live in racial isolation should themselves make the inevitable sacrifice.[13] The letter also castigated members of local Christian congregations: 'Neither clerical nor lay voice has been heard locally vindicating the declared national standpoints of Anglicans, Roman Catholics, Methodists, Presbyterians, Baptists and Jews, in a city whose Archdeacon rebuked Canon Collins for distressing those who are doing the real spade work in South Africa.' He stated that it could be rightly said that all Europeans, `by our silence, our apathy, our indifference, the supine timidity which prevents us from sticking our necks out because the fear of officialdom, have at best passively condoned, and at worst, actively connived at a monstrous injustice perpetuated against those we are pleased to call our friends. (Our) primary aim is to perpetrate and preserve white civilization by jettisoning the morals ideals and values which alone make it worth preserving.' The letter writer launches into what he calls `a terrible and true indictment of one of our bishops. Injustice may stalk through South Africa, but God remains God. He is not mocked. No, nor is he white. He pleads with Europeans of goodwill to speak up: (to) refuse to acquiesce in this policy of pushing non-whites around to suit white comfort and convenience, pockets and prejudice[14] In conclusion he warns that whites must not allow their position as the friendly city to be tarnished and to be named in the same breath as Nylstroom, Nelspruit and Lydenburg.

Unfortunately, this letter writer was a lone white voice in an apathetic wilderness. The majority of white residents largely supported this Act. Those who did not, might as well have, as their silence allowed an injustice to be perpetrated. The philosopher, Karl Popper, put it succinctly: `For evil or tyranny to prevail, it is sufficient for good men to do nothing in the face if it.'[15] Yet, despite the absence of support from whites, the struggle continued. Protest meetings went on unabated as those affected by the Group Areas Act struggled to make their opposition known.

Since the Group Areas Act had as its main aim to separate the various communities in South End and dispatch them to separate designated areas, the government tried to play on group interests. However, the reaction of the communities was completely opposite to what the government expected. For example, at one of the protest meetings, the Malays included themselves in the coloured group rather than be seen as a separate group by the government.The meeting further decided that members of the Malay community would take part in a mass prayer meeting in the Feather Market Hall to pray for all these who would be affected by the implementation of the Group Areas Act. Members of all the non-white communities were invited to attend the meeting.[16]

Of particular concern to Malays was the position of their mosques under the Group Areas Act (in Port Elizabeth and Uitenhage there were 3000 Moslems at the time). The Chief Moslem Priest of the Cape Peninsula, Sheikh E Behardien, informed the Group Areas Board in Cape Town that when a mosque had been built and the ground dedicated to the service of God it could never be deconsecrated. The Sheikh warned the Group Areas Board of international complications that would eventuate, if any steps were taken to `alienate' a mosque. He further stated that a mosque could never be destroyed or the land on which it stood be used for any other purpose. He indicated that he was busy consulting Muslim leaders all over the world, and asked the Government to do the same. There were indications that the government was sensitive to this issue.[17] (This in itself is a shocking indictment of Christian Church denominations,

[12]Ibid.
[13]Ibid.
[14]Letter to the Editor, *Evening Post,* 1955.
[15]Du Pré, *Separate but Unequal,* 7.
[16]Ibid.
[17]Ibid.

82

that no such pressure was put on the government, itself a professedly christian government, to spare Christian churches. That the government showed no such sensitivity to the issue of Christian church buildings, suggests that it had no fear that it would face pressure by white Christians in South Africa, nor Christians in other countries).

In a memorandum dated 26 October 1956, a proposal on the Group Areas Act in Port Elizabeth was drawn up and presented to the full Port Elizabeth City Council.[18] In the preamble, various definitions in relation to the Group Areas were given: `A Group Area is regarded as an area established for any particular group, with the aim that it shall be owned or occupied by persons only of the group for which such an area is declared. It would be contrary to the law for a person of a non-conforming group to own property in such an area'. [19]

In the Memorandum it was decided that the City Council would participate in the enquiry into the application of Group Areas in Port Elizabeth which was to be conducted by the Group Areas Board between 12 and November 1956. It is worth noting that the Cape Town City Council, at the same time, refused to give evidence to the Group Areas Board when it held its hearing in Cape Town. The Port Elizabeth Council, however, argued that if they ignored the Group Areas Board `it will provide ammunition to those persons and bodies who maintain that City Councils are incapable of carrying out the proper functions of local government'.[20] This was a transparently weak, hackneyed excuse, and a spurious rationalisation, because the Council had already openly given evidence of if its wholehearted support of the concept of residential segregation. The following statement clearly shows that the City Council had freely applied a system of segregated group areas in the city before 1950, and that without any objection from any of the citizens of the city: `This council has recognized and put into practice over a long period an acceptable policy of what it called limited segregation'. According to the Council, `the continued development of separate residential areas is desirable' and they could not see that the persons involved would object to move into those areas voluntarily.[21] However, the Council conceded that because of its social and economic responsibilities, any application of the Group Areas Act which would cause existing businesses or trading areas for non-whites in `European Zones' being removed within a short space of time, would be undesirable.[22]

The non-white residents who would be forcefully removed from South End, reacted with shock and horror at the realisation that the Port Elizabeth Council and whites of Port Elizabeth were not going to defend their right to remain where they were, and that they were, in fact, going to conspire with the Group Areas Board to evict South Enders from their homes. The reaction of a 68-year old woman is one such example. She was born in Port Elizabeth of a Jamaican father and a St Helena mother and moved with her husband to South End in 1939. She recalled that `every spare penny we made went into the house. When our children grew up, they helped financially and the house would soon be ours.' If they were forced to move they would have to give up their home and start afresh in a place they did not know. She saw `nothing but bitterness and trouble if the Group Areas Act is enforced.' This was but one example of how non-whites in South End felt.[23] Under the Group Areas Act about 16 000 Port Elizabeth non-whites stood to lose their homes and give up properties with a valuation of 3 500 000 pounds. The Indian community stood to lose the most with 1 067 properties valued at 2 000 000 pounds.

The next phase of the struggle was to fight the Group Areas Board, because it represented the interests of the Nationalist government of the day. The Board's main purpose was to hear evidence which would help them map out Group Areas Zones which would form the basis of proclaimed group areas which

---

[18]`Memorandum for Consideration by the City Council" was a private and confidential document on Group Areas proposals to be submitted to the Group Areas Board which was to hear evidence at a public enquiry at the New Laws Courts between 12-26 November 1956. It was drawn up by Messrs McWilliams and Elliot and dated 26 October 1956.

[19]`Memorandum', 26 October 1956.

[20]Ibid, 6.

[21]Ibid.

[22]Ibid.

[23]Newspaper Resources, File No 2/4, vols 1-4 (1951-1958).

would follow.

GROUP AREAS BOARD

Before the implementation of the Group Areas Act in various parts of South Africa, the government appointed the Group Areas Board to conduct a public inquiry to hear evidence from local authorities for proposals for racial zoning; to make inspections *in loco,* and to call for objections[24].Their recommendations were to be submitted to the Minister of Interior who would make the final decision on Group Areas.

It must clearly be stated at the outset that the Board was in no way sympathetic to the objections of the people who were to be directly affected by the Act, but rather regarded as its priority the justification of the Group Areas Act. As it turned out, much of the evidence also submitted to the Board gave insight into why covetous whites wanted to drive non-whites off every piece of land which, to them, was too good for non-whites to own. Some of the evidence given by whites unfortunately displayed the intense streak of callousness and selfishness which had come to serve as the foundation of apartheid.[25]

However, it was the stand of the Port Elizabeth City Council on this matter and the opposition of the Group Areas Action Committee which represented all the non-whites affected by the Group Areas Act, which came to dominate the hearings of the Group Areas Board. In the months before the public inquiry the Port Elizabeth Council debated and finally decided to make proposals and submit evidence to the Group Areas Board on the implementation of racial zones[26]. The stand taken by the City Council was vehemently opposed by the Group Areas Action Committee. They made urgent representations to the Council to withdraw its Group Areas proposals for the city. They made this appeal on behalf of the 50,000 non-whites who were expected to be affected by these proposals.[27] Their appeal, in the form of a memorandum, was sent to the mayor, Mr IE Struan Robertson, and copies were sent to all the city councillors. It was supported by the entire coloured, Indian and Malay communities, with the exception of the Chinese who had been given a specific understanding by Councillor Dubb that they would not be affected by the Group Areas Act. After much criticism from all concerned, Councillor Dubb was forced to withdraw this assurance. As the Group Areas Action Committee put it: `We ask your council to extend a similar attitude towards group areas proposals for all other Non-European communities...The people for whom we speak are no less an important part of the economic life of the city.' [28]

Submissions were also made by a mainly Afrikaner group who gave evidence in support and justification of Group Areas Act. Rev JA Venter of the Dutch Reformed Church of Algoa Park was concerned about the proposals made regarding the non-white areas. These proposals, according to him, would make Algoa Park a `white bottle neck' and the `better off' members would leave the area. He felt Schauder Township and New Brighton should be pegged at their limits. The `surplus' Coloureds could go to Bethelsdorp and `surplus' Natives could go to Coega Kop.[29] Mr LH Jordaan, Chairman of the Ratepayers Association of Algoa Park and Cradock Place, requested that the sale of plots to the coloured community in Gelvandale be stopped because the Algoa Park residents feared being a white wedge between coloureds on the West and Natives on the East. Mr Jordaan argued that no acceptable reasons existed why a permit was granted to the council for the sale of plots in Gelvandale before the public inquiry of the Group Areas Board was held.[30] Rev Gutch, representing the Anglican Church of Port Elizabeth wanted to know: `Would it not be easier to remove the white people from Algoa Park, and put them elsewhere? Would they not be willing to go?' Furthermore, he felt that their attitude was not

---

[24]*Herald*, 11 November 1956.

[25]Du Pré, *Separate but Unequal*, 82-93.

[26]Full details found in `Memorandum' 26 October 1956.

[27]*Herald* , 28 October 1956.

[28]*Ibid.*

[29]*Evening Post,* 29 November 1956

[30]*Ibid,* 28 November 1956.

`Christian-like.' However, Algoa Park residents did not see why they should give up their land, which they had saved and struggled to buy, and start somewhere else all over again.'[31] (Yet, ironically, this was exactly what whites expected of non-whites in places like South End).

Mr Burmeister, principal of a school in Algoa Park made the following bold and expansive submission: (i) For Coloured people, he suggested setting aside the whole of Bethelsdorp on the west of the National Road to Uitenhage, starting from Missionvale, and developing northwards. He said that no Coloured development should take place west of Bethelsdorp, as this would be an ideal buffer between the Coloureds and Europeans; (ii) For the Natives: A large area above the Swartkops River Valley in the vicinity of the railway lines to the Swartkops Valley, Saltpan and Coega Kop quarry; (iii) For the Indians and Chinese: Driftsands as suggested by the Council for Indians. He further submitted that the above arrangement of Group Areas had as one of its advantages that the Native traffic could be removed from the National Road to Uitenhage and other streets in the city. In addition, a Native area at Coega Kop would have the attraction that New Brighton was for `strange natives' from the country. There would be more control over this influx and penetration into the European parts of the city. He then urged that South End and Schauder Township should not be proclaimed a Coloured group area, so that it could eventually become a European group area. [32]

Some submissions were presented in a convoluted way so as to give the impression that concern for non-whites was uppermost in the minds of the petitioners concerned. However, while purporting to have the welfare of the `non-white' community at heart, the racial prejudice and bigotry nestling below the surface of many whites in Port Elizabeth, were barely disguised. A certain Mr Marais, on behalf of (some of the white) voters in South End stated that it was `the duty of Europeans, if they are sincere about working to help the Coloured Community, to move them from South End.' He said that twenty years earlier South End was an `attractive European area', but it had become a `horrible mixture of Europeans and Coloureds' and in thirty years it would become a slum if the situation remained as it was. He advanced a number of additional reasons why `Coloureds' should be removed from South End: (i) Their congested living conditions led to friction and crime. They had to roam the street for recreation; (ii) Europeans from Walmer and Forest Hill had to pass through the lower part of South End which was unsafe late at night; (iii) South End was far from the industries where Coloureds worked; (iv) There was heavy bus traffic through South End because Coloured workers from Salisbury Park and Fairview had to pass through on their way to the North; (v) Sailors from visiting ships had to pass through South End to the Seaman's Institute. The present mixed nature of the area led to brothels, shebeens and other houses of vice.[33]

Rev RD Seagar (Anglican Church) contested Marais' argument. As a parish priest in South End, he was of the view that white and coloured people lived quite contentedly together in the same neighbourhood. He refuted Marais' assertion that South End had been a white area up to twenty years ago. The baptismal records of his church dating back to 1876 indicated that South End had always been a mixed area. Furthermore, there were only three businesses belonging to Europeans in the area. On the matter of the `unsafe' nature of South End, Seagar conceded that it would be utter folly to say no crime or hooliganism existed, but it could be controlled by `good and continual' police supervision. He objected to the notion that he as a European had the right to move anyone and he rejected the idea that he had any moral obligation to remove coloured people from their homes.[34]

The City Council also weighed in against views such as those expressed by Marais: `We were told the Coloured children were playing in the streets and that crime was prevalent. That is irrelevant to this inquiry. One fails to see how sending their families somewhere else will improve the position.' However, they made some firm Group Areas proposals. The Council suggested that, while non-whites remained in South End, the lower section, with Randall Street and Kinsley Kloof as the boundary, be set aside for coloureds (this included Malays). It was also considered that both sides of the lower section of Walmer

---

[31]Ibid.
[32]*Evening Post,* 29 November 1956.
[33]*Ibid.*
[34]*Ibid.*

Road should be a free trading area.[35] This highlighted the difference between the Council's Group Areas proposals and that of the Government's regarding the division of the coloured people. The City Council had not planned separate areas for `Coloured' people and Malays. It had also not separated the Indian and Chinese Communities from each other. On the Malay and `Coloured' issue they argued: `The Malays are so closely integrated with the Cape Coloured people that there is no need to make separate provision for them (in the Coloured housing areas) but if the Malays were to object to the Council's proposals it would be easy to do so within the Group Areas allocated to Coloureds.' However, they agreed to the implementation of Group Areas in South End.[36]

   Much of the evidence which was submitted up to now was in favour of the implementation of the Group Areas Act with all its tragic ramifications. Up to now the legal team of the Group Areas Action Committee, the major opposition to the Group Areas Act at the Board hearings, had played a minor role in the deliberations of the Group Areas Board. The Group Areas Action Committee officials were Mr Erasmus (chairman), Mr J Skidow (vice-chairman) Mr TF Dullabh (treasurer), Mr A Chetty (secretary), and Mr VT Pillay (assistant secretary). Mr V Vandayar, the Rev D Davids and the Rev A Taybo were committee members. The committee of the Group Areas Board which sat in Port Elizabeth consisted of Messrs WJ Gouws (chairman), VJ Nel and MP Prinsloo. Messrs C Isaacson IOC and M Selligson were the legal representatives of the Group Areas Action Committee which represented those who were going to be mainly affected by the application of the Act, viz. `Non-Europeans.'[37] Early evidence was led on behalf of the Chinese Community. After some initial confusion, the Chinese declared emphatically that 'they opposed a group area for Chinese in Cape Road because the establishment of a Chinese group area would mean the removal of Chinese traders from their clientele, with consequential effect of depriving the members of the Chinese group of plying their trade as general dealers.'[38]

   The hearings were marked by an incident which not only gave an indication of the pettiness of the officials of the Board, but left no-one in doubt of the unsympathetic nature of the inquiry as far as non-whites were concerned. The incident arose out of the fact that the audience at the hearings was segregated on racial lines and people were seated in cubicles. The previous day, Mr O Cassim, representing the Malay Community on the Action Committee, objected to the fact that the `Non-European section was over-crowded' while many seats were vacant in the European section. On 20 November 1956 there were vacant seats in the European and non-European public seats. On this matter the chairman Mr Gouws sarcastically asked Mr Cassim:`Are you satisfied now? By the second day you get half the people who were there at first and the next day only a third. Eventually you have only the representatives present.'[39]

   On 27 November 1956 the situation took a dramatic turn when the legal team of Group Areas Action Committee, Mr Dison (who replaced Mr Isaacson), Mr Selligson and Mr BB Ramjee walked out of the proceedings of the Group Areas Board. The point of contention was whether the Board had obtained prior information concerning proposed racial zones from the City Council, without making it available to the rest. If this was so, the feeling was that trust in the inquiry had been broken and the hearing had to be declared null and void. The chairman refused to accept the matter as reason enough to stop the hearing. He was then requested by Dison to recuse himself and co-members from the hearing. However, the chairman refused to accede to this request.[40]

   Dison also protested the action of the chairman of the Board `in asking the Port Elizabeth Divisional Council for particulars about ownership and occupation in Bethelsdorp before the hearing had started.'[41] Mr Ramjee wanted to know how the chairman could have an open mind on free areas since he was quoted at a public meeting on 10 March 1956 as saying: 'Free areas cannot be proclaimed because they would

[35]*Ibid,* 27 November 1956.
[36]*Ibid,* 29 November 1956.
[37]*Herald ,19* November 1956
[38]*Ibid.*See also K Harris, `Accepting the Group, but not the Area' for the Chinese attitude to Group Areas.
[39]*Evening Post,* 20 November 1956.
[40]*Ibid,* 27 November 1956.
[41]*Herald,* 27 November 1956.

defeat the object of the Act.' A Free Area was one in which the Act was not in force so that there was none of the control envisaged by the Act. The existing legal position would obtain in such an area[42]. In reply Mr Gouws stated: 'This Committee is bound by the Act. There is not provision for what you call "free areas". That is all I intended to convey at the public meeting. If the City council nevertheless insists they want "free areas" that is their affair.'[43] Mr Gouws elaborated that he had asked the Divisional and City Councils for information beforehand, so that the hearing was not unduly delayed. At this juncture, the Board adjourned to consider the issues before them. When the meeting reconvened, the chairman Mr Gouws, addressed the hearing. `Although there may be some substance in your request, from your point of view, the committee is of the opinion that it is not necessary to call anybody to counteract the argument that the Committee had obtained prior information from the City Council and the divisional Council'. In his reply Dison stated: `The responsibilities of this Committee (of the Board) are tremendous. I do not think in recent history there has been such responsibility on a few individuals, to recommend the determination of the fate of thousands of people.' He amplified his point by stating `One would have expected that there would have been a hearing of all proposals, as contemplated by the Minister, who said that the Act must be administered with justice.'[44] Selligson openly mocked the ruling: `The effect of your ruling is tantamount to a situation where a man is on trial for his life. The court has the evidence of any eye witness, which is not available to the defence, and which will be used by that court in making a decision.' To which Ramjee aded: `I am having to fight an enemy I cannot see. I am fighting against unseen odds.'[45]

Mr Ramjee did not leave the situation there . He took up the case up with a Supreme Court action, with Mr Justice G. Wynne presiding. Described as Mr BB Ramjee an Indian living at 28 Nelson Street, South End, he was refused an application for an interim order restraining the Committee of the Group Areas Board from making recommendations to the Minister of the Interior for Group Areas in the Port Elizabeth Municipality.[46] Ramjee then requested the court to rule the respondents (The Committee of the Group Areas Board's inquiry in Port Elizabeth in November) to have been constituted irregularly; to declare that the Chairman should have recused himself; and that the proceedings should have been declared null and void. Finally he felt that the Committee should have been restrained from submitting a report of the inquiry to the Minister of the Interior or the Group Areas Board. The judge ruled against Mr Ramjee's submissions and ordered him to pay the costs of his application.[47]

So determined was Mr Ramjee about his case that he appealed to the Appellate Division of the Supreme Court on the grounds that
(i) The Judgment was contrary to the evidence and the strength of the proposals of the Municipality and was not filed in time;
(ii) Furthermore the judgment was based on erroneous points of law because (a) Mr Ramjee and the other objectors did not have a proper opportunity to make representations of objections,and (b) All the material facts were not disclosed and/or the proposals of the Reference and Planning Committee were not explained;
(iii) The Court wrongly held that the public inquiry before the chairman of the Group Areas Committee was an administrative inquiry;
(iv) The Court erred in holding that the chairman had a discretion whether to call a representative of the Planning and Reference Committee to give evidence or make a statement;
(v) If the chairman had the discretion as a matter of law, the court should have held that he exercised his discretion improperly in refusing to call such a representative;
(vi) The Court should have held it essential that the proposals of Reference and Planning Committee

---

[42]`Memoradum' (26 October 1956), 2.
[43]*Herald*, 27 November 1956.
[44]*Ibid.*
[45]*Ibid.*
[46]*Evening Post*, 22 January 1957.
[47]*Ibid*

should have been explained at the public hearing, and that the facts on which the proposals were based should have been stated;

(vii) The court should have held that the applicant and other objectors were substantially prejudiced;

(viii) The Court should have held that the applicant and other objectors were not allowed to lodge proper proposals after the original closing date for proposal - other objectors were not allowed to do so;

(ix) The court should have held that the public hearing was irregularly held as the Board had not advertised for proposals;

(x) The Court should have held that the Chairman was bound to administer the oath to witnesses; and/or to permit cross-examination by, or on behalf of people who had made representations; and/or to subpoena people with information material to the purposes of the inquiry.[48]

This appeal to failed. No further information concerning this appeal could be obtained from the records of the Group Areas Action Committee. Presumably, this was because the Group Areas Action Committee did not take any further part in the inquiry of the Group Areas Board because it realised that the Board had no other role to play but make Group Areas a reality. The stand taken by Mr BB Ramjee must be lauded since he exposed the narrow-mindness of despotic officials of the government. For his brave stand, he was banned in 1964 for five years and placed under house arrest. He passed away on 7 October 1977.

It is recognised that other political groupings could also have played a role in the protests against the Group Areas Act in South End. However in the archival sources researched only those mentioned in this chapter were recorded.

The reality for South Enders of this valiant but futile attempt to halt the pending mass eviction of whole suburbs and entire communities, was that coloureds and Indians, who had been resident there for 125 years, were going to be uprooted, and forced to move from their homes close to town and places of work, to soulless, undesirable areas far from the city and work place. However in those early years of the Group Areas Act, South Enders were not fully aware that whatever protest and opposition they did mount, it was never going to have any effect on the single-minded Nationalist Afrikaner because the government had already made up its mind. The many hearings of the Group Areas Board, in Port Elizabeth and all around the country, were merely an expensive and puffed-up charade carefully designed to give the impression that the implementation of apartheid legislation would be carried out in an atmosphere of consultation, open-mindedness and fair play. Thus, the inhabitants of South End continued their heroic effort to prevent their being uprooted from their homes, little realising the utterly futility of the whole exercise.

At the end of the hearings, the condemned inhabitants of old South End sat down to await their fate - they had to wait for a number of agonizing years before the government gave the word. South Enders knew it was coming, but when it came, it was still a shock. Unfortunately, many of the older residents did not live to see that day. They died of a broken heart - before the bulldozers came and the trucks rumbled in.

---

[48]*Ibid,* 7 July 1957.

BB Ramjee
Banned in 1964 for five years. Passed away 7 October 1977
(R. Ramjee)

Dennis Brutus
(African Network)

House of BB Ramjee at Number 28 Nelson Street in South End
(Ranchod)

7

DESTRUCTION OF SOUTH END

The Announcement

The final blow in the battle for the right to retain South End as a non-racial suburb was heralded with a bold front page headline and article in the *Eastern Province Herald* of 1 May 1965: `Port Elizabeth's 125-year old South End will be rebuilt. A far reaching scheme announced by the Government last night will entail moving 8742 people of all races to other areas in the city, demolishing hundreds of slum dwellings, rebuilding streets and designing new developments.'[49] In his announcement the Minister of Community Development, PW Botha described South End as a depressed area in one of the major harbour cities. He further stated that the whole area would be given over to urban development which meant that most of it would be razed and rebuilt. As a consequence all the properties required for the new South End would be expropriated. Advance planning was already well under way for the few whites in the affected area to be accommodated in Walmer and in a flat scheme in Algoa Park. While the whites would be virtually unaffected, all coloured people were to be moved to Bethelsdorp and Gelvandale, Indians to Woolhope (later named Malabar) and Chinese to an area in the vicinity of Kabega Park . These areas were undeveloped and a great distance from South End. After the program of urban renewal was completed, only whites would be allowed back into the area.   This factor, of course, spelt out clearly that forced removals from South End had little to do with the need to `clear a slum'. If it was merely this, then all former residents would have been allowed to return after the renewal had taken place. However, the fact that the area would become a white group area and only whites would be allowed to return, clearly indicates that the `slum clearance' argument was merely a very transparent excuse for what was really the opportunity to carry out the deep desire of the Nationalists to enforce racial segregation.

TABLE 5: DISTRIBUTION OF POPULATION IN PORT ELIZABETH 1960

Popula-tion Group	Residents in Group Areas as eventually proclaimed				
	White Area	Coloured Area	Asian Area	Black Area	Total
White	94 253	344	-	290	94 887
Coloured	24 989	41 629	-	1 428	68 046
Asian	3 336	945	104	63	4 448
Black	10 776	4 545	1	105 792	121 114
TOTAL	133 354	47 463	105	107 573	288 495

[49] *Herald,* 1 May 1965.

In an editorial on 3 May 1965 the *Eastern Province Herald* commented as follows: `South End was proclaimed for whites against all the weight of evidence of two public inquiries, and against the wishes of the City Council... In spite of strong pleas on behalf of the six thousand non-whites living and doing business in the area, they were ordered to move - in time. Since then there has been a gradual exodus of Coloured families, out to Gelvandale Complex, Gelvan Park and Korsten'. The editorial further stated that `South End Indians have been, with timidity, living with the prospect that as soon as the Government had created a group area for them out on the edge of the city they too would have to move from their homes. The fate of their business has never been clarified'. And finally, according to Mr Botha's announcement `all Non-Whites who remain in South End and the Whites too, will have to go quickly, to suit his haste.'[50]

The area to be expropriated first was bordered by the sea, the Seamen's Institute, the Walmer - Port Elizabeth boundary, and South Union Street robots. Official figures which were released in March 1962 indicate that 539 properties in South End were owned by `non-whites', of which 398 were occupied by 'coloured people' and 141 by a mixture of races. Population figures which were released at the same time indicate that there were 4 950 Malays and coloureds, 1255 Indians, 155 Chinese giving a total of 6 350 non-whites.[51]

The threat of eviction from South End conjured up a variety of fears among all the communities of South End. According to an Indian property owner, `If the expropriation is on the basis of municipal valuation plus 25 per cent - as in Maritzburg - it will be very harsh. Assets built up over a lifetime would be lost.' He further believed that `the Indian community realized that eventually their residential area would be moved but that business would be left intact.' Disconcerting news to many was that a housing backlog already existed for coloured people in Gelvandale, when it was realized that most of the coloured people were to be moved to Gelvandale.

The sentiments of the close on 8000 inhabitants who would have to leave South End were echoed by a grey-haired man while sitting on his stoep in South End: `South End is not a place .... It's a way of life.' A 56 year-old man whose parents had come from St. Helena stated: `I was born in South End. I have lived in this very house since I was married 26 years ago. I know no other place.' Indian and Chinese business owners were also worried. They were not certain if they would be able to survive being self-employed when they are moved to whatever group area was decided for them. But it was mainly the ordinary folk who suffered the most. They all echoed the same question: `What is to become of us?'[52]

The first properties to be expropriated were bounded by Baakens Valley on the North, Farie- Mitchell-Quoit streets and Sandy Lane in the South and on the West Randall - Barnes - Anderson Streets. The area went through to the railway property on the foreshore.[53] The heartless and unsympathetic nature of the Nationalist Government soon became evident as they systematically set about destroying the heart of South End. To them time was of the essence as is clear from the statements of one of their officials: `The whole approach in South End as far as the department is concerned is to bring slum clearance and urban renewal at an early stage.' To reach this end result `the department will naturally have to spend a sum of money because urban renewal implies the rehabilitation or rejuvenation of a depressed area.'[54]

Notices of Expropriation

Within days of PW Botha's announcement the jackboots began to move in. On 10 May 1965 the first people in South End received their expropriation notices from the Group Areas Development Board. With it came a threat that the Board had the discretion that `after not less than three months' they would take possession of their properties if their hapless owners and occupants did not respond accordingly. Officials of the Board swarmed around South End with `stacks of notices of expropriation.' Notices were served

[50]*Herald*, 30 May 1965.
[51]*Ibid*, 1 May.1965.
[52]*Evening Post*, 7 May 1965.
[53]*Ibid*, 8 May 1965.
[54]*Ibid*.

on Mr S Chetty, an Indian General Dealer, for houses he owned at 94, 96, 97 Rudolph Street and 28 Bullen Street. He had lived in the Bullen Street house for 39 years with his wife and ten children. A notice was also served on Mr AO Lou Pen, a Chinese hawker who had lived at 32 Farie Street for the past 10 years. In that time they had brought about a number of alterations to the house. To the family the notice of expropriation came as a shock. Mr Omar Cassim, a Malay interior decorator received his notice for 29 Farie Street. He, his wife and family had lived there from 1938. His eleven children were born there, ten of whom still lived with him. Mr Cassim stated that most, if not all of his customers lived in suburbs like Mill Park, Walmer and Summerstrand. To him, his workshop, which was in his backyard ,was convenient. He doubted if his clients would be able to come to him if he lived elsewhere. He had spent a large sum of money improving his house in order that it could become a `civilized' place to stay in.[55]

An Indian hairdresser explained that `this business has been carried on by my family for generations in South End. We have been told that we will live in better condition in our areas, but what will happen to our business?' A Malay resident commented: ` I was born in this house 28 years ago. Now I do not know where we will go. We have no other area to go to.' Residents also expressed misgivings that they would not be adequately compensated for their homes.

While the Group Areas expropriation notices for South End overwhelmingly targeted non-whites, many white families and houses dotted in and around those of non-whites were also affected. A white resident of Bullen Street `was dumbfounded when I returned from work to find the notice... I was under the impression that only the slum areas would be cleared. I have spent a great deal on my home over the years.' Another white property owner stated: `I have been running my business in South Union Street for 17 years. Now the property no longer belongs to me. This has come as a bombshell to all of us.'[56]

Officials of the Department of Community Development tried to appease the residents of South End by mouthing assurances that owners would receive a fair price for their houses and they would be ensured of alternative accommodation, but, they pleaded, ` all this cannot be done in a day.' Furthermore residents were assured that `considerable time will elapse before anybody is required to move.' Meanwhile, economic as well as subeconomic houses were being built for coloured people in Bethelsdorp and facilities would also be created for those who wanted to build their own homes. The Department also planned to erect a building for shops, which would be made available for basic trades, on the corner of Stanford Road and Cottrell Street near Korsten.[57] However, many of these assurance would later turn out to be empty promises.

By 13 May 1965 some 450 properties had been expropriated. This included the area which was bounded by South Union Street, Donald Street and Forest Hill Drive. A Departmental spokesman described this area as `the worst part of South End, the most depressed and the most mixed.' However, this frenzy of notice-serving elicited a number of letters to the Editor in the local newspapers. One such letter appeared in the *Evening Post* by one who signed himself Boerseun, Algoa Park. Boerseun lashed out against `the Frankenstein monster of the Nationalist Party politics - Apartheid - (which) has suddenly reared its head in our midst... In truly draconian fashion it has turned the South End of our city into a plea of misery and frustation. As a Afrikaner I am very puzzled as to what has become of the Christian principles which our leaders prefer to adhere to... 'do unto others'. He asked the question: ` Is the influential N.G.Kerk going to remain silent in the face of the abhorrent negation of the ideals of human decency and compassion?... Must I forever bow my head in shame for the misdeeds of my people?' Boerseun ended his letter by appealing to his fellow-Afrikaners to stand still and wonder what the country was heading for.[58]

In a letter to the editor of the *Herald* on 14 May 1965 VA Pillay wrote that `this course of action by the authorities means the economic ruin of the Indians as far as their future aspirations are concerned.... The Indians and other non-Whites in South End have lived in peace and harmony with their neighbours there

---

[55]*Evening Post*, 10 May 1965.
[56]*Herald*, 11 May 1965.
[57]See table 5, Distribution of Population in Port Elizabeth 1960.
[58]*Evening Post*,13 May 1965.

for more than a century.'[59] In a further letter he pointed out that the `compulsory ejections must harm many.' Moreover, the areas to which Coloureds and Indians were to be moved were totally undeveloped areas, which offered only limited trading opportunities. The government's policy concerning this matter was not in the interests of the people that were affected by it. It was a divide-and-rule policy which intended to exploit and embarrass the businessman who had built up his trade over a period of more than half a century. Furthermore, the department who on one hand said that churches and temples would not be destroyed, had also said: `the department would be glad to buy buildings in the area which belonged to religious groups if they wish to sell them.' Pillay reminded readers that `according to the Eastern tradition, a Temple or a House of God can never be sold. God can never approve of monetary compensation for a place of Worship'.[60]

Most of the letters raised a number of questions common to most South Enders, such as what would become of the tenants; where would Indian businessmen go; and how would property-owners be compensated? According to the editorial of the *Herald* of 19 May 1965 there were also a number of teasing conundrums. For example, it stated that churches, temples and schools would not be expropriated. However, while this would not prevent the non-white communities being moved to Woolhope(Malabar), Gelvandale and Bethelsdorp, it meant that schoolchildren would have to travel many miles across the city to schools which would now be situated in the `all-white' South End. Above all, was it practical to expect that on Sundays and holy days, the displaced would be required to travel to South End in order to worship?[61] The newspaper however applauded the acceptance of the sacredness of the Mosques which would never have to face the prospect of being deconsecrated and destroyed.

In a letter to the *Evening Post*, a resident, Peggy Prosamy expresssed a feeling common to many facing the dreaded prospect of having to give up family homes: 'In all our Non-European groups, houses were purchased by our parents after decades of sacrifice. They wanted to ensure that after they had passed we would be able to live in our own house.' She explained that when the title deeds were received they were accompanied by the parental words. 'No one can take away this roof which I have provided .' However, now that expropriation was a reality, those who were still waiting for alternative accommodation could continue to remain in their old homes but pay a rental of 5% of the value they received for their houses. This might have seemed fair to the Department of Community Development but it was a financial blow to many families. Firstly, these people were not paying any rent for their houses in the present circimstances because they owned the houses. Now, after expropriation, the pittance they were to receive in compensation for the expropriation would begin to be eroded in rentals for their own houses. When they then moved to the Northern Areas, the balance had to be used to purchase another house (which was unlikely as the compensation in most cases never even began to come close to what was needed to purchase another dwelling) or a piece of gound on which to build a house. This meant that they would have to apply for a mortgage bond and start paying for a house all over again. They would then have to budget for items like rental, mortgage bonds, and face risks they had never had to consider before. For many, this was the beginning of a cycle of poverty and struggle which saw purchases being repossessed; insurance policies being surrendered; and the removal of children from university.[62] These are the consequences of the Group Areas Act which the Nationalists never bothered to consider in their calculations.

As the disquiet and dissatisfaction of non-white residents of South End began to grow, the rumbles of discontent reached the floor of Parliament. Helen Suzman of the Progressive Party vigorously attacked the National Party MP for Port Elizabeth North, JA Nel . She said that the people of South End were unhappy to leave their homes, the home of their ancestors. She could not understand why it was necessary to move whole communities for ideological reasons. They did not want to move, they had to move because the Afrikaner people wanted to have that part of Port Elizabeth in spite of the fact that it had been

[59]*Herald,* 14 May 1965.
[60]*Evening Post,* 8 June 1965.
[61]*Ibid,* 19 May 1965.
[62]*Ibid,* 27 May 1965.

occupied by the coloured and Malay communities for almost a century.[63]

Nel tried to justify the evictions and argued that the people of Port Elizabeth had asked for, and the Minister had agreed to remove 'this bad patch' in the city. Suzman retorted that the people were prepared to accept slum clearance but to them `there is a considerable difference between the clearance of slum Areas, removing the excess number of inhabitants, improving houses and condemning others, while on the other hand moving an entire community. The Minister of Community Development, PW Botha weighed in by pointing out that the Port Elizabeth City Council had welcomed the move, and disputed the stories circulating that he had been given assurances that businesses did not agree with the scheme.[64] As if in confirmation of Botha's statement, a meeting on 10 June 1965 between the City Council, State Committee, and Estates and Industries Committee to discuss the replanning and redevelopment of South End, reveals a statement by the chairman Councillor Isherwood, who felt that he could speak on behalf of the Council , and state that the decision made by the government to clear the South End area was a most welcome one.

When residents finally had an opportunity to view the official notices of the `provisional basic value', the feelings of residents ranged from `disappointed' to `shock' at the valuations. An Indian property owner complained that the 'provisional basic' value of the properties was only half of his own estimated value of his property. He foresaw that at the end `we are going to lose on this, and most of our remaining money is going to be absorbed by legal expenses in trying to save what we have.' Many residents realised with a sinking feeling that they might have to withold their objections and simply accept what was ofered. If no objection was made within 21 days then the basic value would become the official value of the property.

Eviction from South End

The first indication to the non-whites that they had to move from South End was when they were served with eviction orders which stipulated that they had to move from their homes by a specific day. These eviction notices wreaked havoc in the community and were the cause of great uncertainty and widespread anxiety. The uncertainty and worry went on for many months and even years as people waited for the dreaded day to arrive. Meanwhile many became sick with worry and countless questions gnawed away at the mind: What price would they get for their homes? Which whites would want to purchase it? Would they only be compensated for the land and not the house? If this was so, they would not be able to afford to buy property in the new group areas, and therefore not even have enough to build a house.[65] They would then have to rent houses of a much smaller size than their original houses. Having lived for generations in their own homes how would they cope in terms of rent money, space and environment; away from their churches, mosques, schools, sport fields and clubs. In addition, friendships of long years standing would be broken.[66]

As the people sat down to wait, for what was for many something akin to an execution day, the people became obsessed about the impending removals, and for many of the older people the eviction notice was a death notice. Many of the elderly people died of a broken heart before the bulldozers and trucks arrived. Those South Africans who did not go through this experience, would find difficulty in appreciating the physical and mental trauma that accompanied forced removals.

And when the day came, the people moved. After years of discussion, protest, letters and petitions, the government got its way and the people moved. When the last non-white family had moved out, when the laughter and cries of the children had slowly died ; when the excited gossip had trickled to a halt; when the calls of the fishermen and other hawkers were finally silent - the bulldozers moved in and levelled the area. 125 years of history bit the dust. Within a short time, houses, shops, schools, churches and various

[63]*Ibid*, 3 June 1965.
[64]*Herald*, 3 June 1965.
[65]Du Pre, *Separate but Unequal*, 85.
[66]*Ibid*, 87.

94

businesses lay in a pathetic heap - just so much rubble. The life went out of South End.

The Group Areas Act was not merely an administrative procedure which resulted in people moving from one place to another; in this case from South End to the Northern Suburbs. It was more than that - it was a human tragedy. It was a process of fragmenting and uprooting settled communities. The cosmopolitan South End community was fragmented and dispersed in the ingenious way which only the minds of Nationalist planners and their collaborating counterparts in the Port Elizabeth City Councillors could have imagined. The `lower-income' section of the coloured community was settled in Salt Lake and Helenvale; the `higher-income' group in areas like West End, Springdale, Gelvandale and Salsoneville; and the `middle-class' bought plots in Gelvan Park and built their own homes. Indians were moved to Woolhope (Malabar) where many of them built luxury mansions amongst the more modest the homes of the majority; the Chinese went to Kabega Park and the handful of Africans were relocated in Walmer Location. This Great Dispersal also meant that many South End residents were now far away from their places of work. This additional burden upon their meager finances resulted in unemployment and when bus apartheid was introduced the situation was made even worse.

TABLE 6: DISTRIBUTION OF POPULATION IN PORT ELIZABETH 1985

Popula-tion Group	Residents in group areas as eventually proclaimed				
	White Area	Coloured Area	Asian Area	Black Area	Total
White	130 932	101	1	13	131 051
Coloured	3 574	126 712	285	579	131 149
Asian	175	1 805	4 936	-	6 916
Black	7 640	2 095	131	223 466	233 332
TOTAL	142 321	130 713	5 356	224 058	502 448

The Group Areas removals were also not merely a matter of racial groupings being consolidated and then dispersed. Unfortunately, churches, schools and sports clubs were dispersed; congregants, students and members were scattered all over Port Elizabeth . Friendships of many years standing between families and friends were broken up. For many years after the first removals coloured people still trekked pitifully back to their formal residential areas to worship in the churches which still stood there or to use the sports facilities which still existed there. The government soon stopped this practice by breaking down their churches and giving their meagre sporting facilities to whites.[67]

While whites today sit with the spoils of apartheid, and while `non-whites' sit with crippling bonds, matchbox homes or a pitiful existence, there will always be resentment against the National Party, the Afrikaner and those who benefited from apartheid, in what was done under the guise of this horrific Act. A number of the older generation will say, `we can forgive, but we will never forget'. The younger generation are not so forgiving and they may find some way to ensure that the National Party never forgets.[68]

[67]Ibid, 87
[68]Ibid, 93.

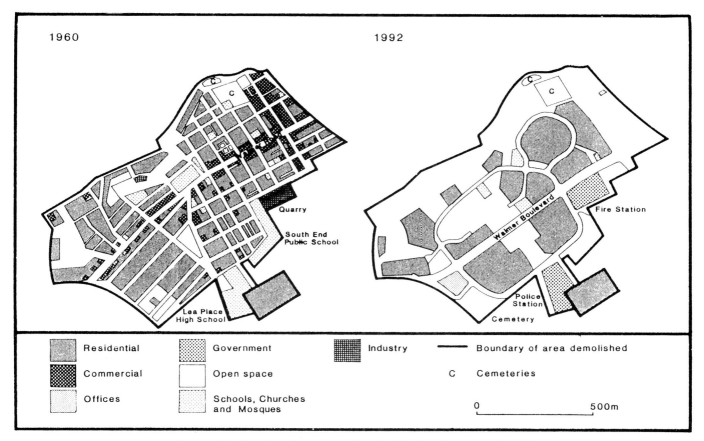

1960

1992

Quarry

South End
Public School

Lea Place
High School

Walmer Boulevard

Fire Station

Police
Station

Cemetery

	Residential		Government		Industry	——	Boundary of area demolished
	Commercial		Open space	C	Cemeteries
	Offices		Schools, Churches and Mosques	0	500m

Figure 4.28 The Transformation of South End, Port Elizabeth, 1960–92

Source Based on information from *Donaldson's Port Elizabeth Directory 1959/60*, 1959, Port Elizabeth
and air photographs for 1960, and fieldwork, 1992

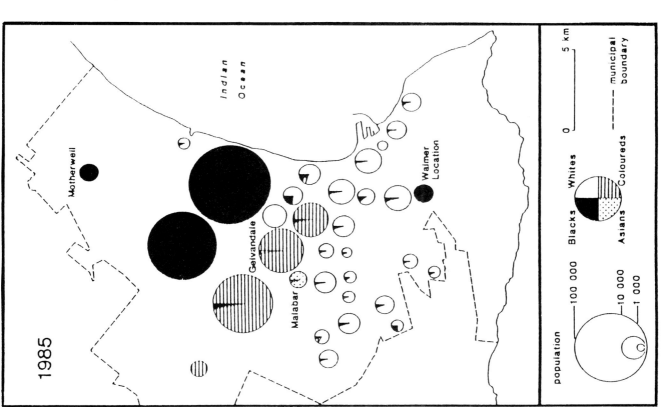

1985

Indian Ocean

Motherwell

Walmer Location

Gelvandale

Malabar

5 km

municipal boundary

Whites

Blacks

Asians

Coloureds

population

100 000

10 000

1 000

Distribution of population, 1985.

*The remains of
Apartheid
(Times Media Library)*

*What is now left of Bridge Street, 1997
(Faizal Felix)*

*All that remains of Walmer Road, 1997
(Faizal Felix)*

*Demolition at the
back of the
Methodist Church
in Pier Street
(Times Media Library)*

The bulldozers have come
(Bob Binnell Collection)

Demolition next to the Rudolph Street Mosque
(AC George)

Demolitions in Steam Street
(Bob Binnell Collection)

Fig Tree sheltering the last houses in Rudolph Street
(Bob Binnell Collection)

Demolitions in Walmer Road
(Bob Binnell)

A peep taken through the Apartheid window

8

EPILOGUE

THE RETURN OF THE DISPOSSESSED IN THE 1990s

Just before the 1994 electionsfor a new non-racial democratic government, new legislation was passed which made it possible for former residents to reclaim their property, or seek compensation for unfair prices paid at the time of expropriation. Reaction from the younger generation of the former inhabitants of South End and other affected areas, such as Fairview and Salisbury Park, was immediate. They formed the Port Elizabeth Land and Compensation Restoration Association (PELCRA) in 1993. A number of community organisations and NGOs have also been formed to facilitate the process of reclamation. PELCRA's main objective was to reclaim the land which was taken from their parents and grandparents by the Group Areas Act. Although no land could be reclaimed in South End, because original houses do not exist and vacant land is non-existent, the organization had succeeded in stopping a property developer from developing land which was on the site of the South End High School.

Under the Land Act the former tenants and property owners of South End and Fairview can claim back their original property. If the property is unoccupied, it can be returned to the original owners. If the property is occupied, the present owners will be approached to resell it to the government. If they are willing they will be paid the market value. If they are not willing, the original owners will be offered alternative land, monetary compensation or development aid. The claims of the former residents of South End could also be met by the utilization of land in Fairview and Salisbury Park.

PELCRA also decided to make group claims rather than individual claims because of the large number of individual cases in the country and the limited resources the government has available for compensation.

In the annals of history, the Group Areas Act and its effect on the non-white residents of South End will remain a shame and indictment on the perpetrators of the Act and those who benefited from it.

However, from the cosmopolitan nature of South End in the early years it is clear that all South Africans can live harmonious in a truly non-racial South Africa.

The older residents of South End may still feel embittered since they were deprived of a happy life and only now in the new South Africa can they experience some aspects life as it always should have been. They can see some of the aspects of the prospects of a free and equal life which they should have experienced. The younger generation have the future in their hands. They can only learn from the vicious experiences their parents had under the white man's rule and must ensure that they never again be allowed to lead a life of second class citizens in the land of their birth.

Although the Group Areas Act has achieved the physical movement of non-whites from South End it never succeeded in taking the spirit of South End, which has been enfolded in these pages. The legacy of South End remains in the hearts and minds of all those who inhabited its streets, churches, temples, mosques, schools, because truly its spirit was the spirit of a true rainbow nation.

APPENDICES

APPENDIX 1 -

SAMPLE OF INTERVIEWS WITH FORMER RESIDENTS OF SOUTH END

A. INTERVIEW WITH MR ARMIEN ABRAHAMS - 84 LIEBENBERG ROAD, GELVANDALE on 3 May 1997.

Q. How many members were there in your household when you moved from South End?
A. My whole family moved at interval stages to the Northern Areas. We were four members in the family and we moved to Liebenberg Road, which was situated in then-known Jarman Township. The area was undeveloped and bushy. Furthermore houses were not readily available. There was also a lot of underhand goings-on in the issuing of houses. Moreover we received a mere pittance for our property in South End.
Q. Where did you work at the time?
A. Opportunities for coloureds in those years were few. I was forced to leave school and work in a factory for One pound five shillings a week. Later I worked as a Taxi Driver, a Painter and from 1957 I was employed as a Customs Clerk at Good Year Tyres in Grahamstown Road, North End.
Q. How far was your place of employment from your home?
A. When we moved out of South End, I was working at Good Year Tyres, which was 6 kilometres away from my home.
Q. What is the approximate distance from your current home to the place of employment mentioned above? (if the latter still exists)
A. When we moved to Liebenberg Road the distance to work was more or less the same.
Q. What emotions did you experience at having to leave?
A. There was a feeling of mixed emotions. I was born there and after forty years we were uprooted. The family was a close-knit one and we lived in harmony with other races. We were moved to a different enviroment with people from different areas. Furthermore, we were not moved as a group, thus we did not have the same neighbours. It was difficult to explain apartheid to the children. Whites had all the opportunities and there was nothing for us. I curse the inventor of apartheid, because we were really a League of Nations in South End. It was an evil thing to move people, because the Group Areas Act broke up families. South End was a safe area. There were no gangsters, murders, rapes cases, etc.
Q. How did the relocation transform your life?
A. We carried on as before and we had to make the best of life. Life went on and we had to build a better future for the family and we had to educate our children. Religion-wise, we had to keep on track and we performed our duties to the best of our ability.
Q. How did the relocation affect your family's religious routine?
A. We saw to it that our children attend Madressa and we had to go all the way to South End to attend services at the South End Mosques. Fortunately my work place was near the Humphrey Street Mosque in North End where I could perform my daily prayers.
Q. How did it effect your children's education?
A. They had been at Dower Primary School and Hindu Primary in South End and then went to Gelvan Park Primary which already existed when we moved to Jarman Township. Later they proceeded to Gelvandale High School which was by then already in existence.
Q. Was there sufficient infrastructure in your area?
A. There were no shops in the area, only house shops. We also had to use the Schauderville Post Office as there was no Post Office in Gelvandale. Buses did not run on a regular basis, it had its times. Streets were also not tarred.
Q. Would you like to go back to South End?
A. No, never. One can relive the past, but can never go back to the past. You always go down memory lane with old friends. What is there in South End to go back to? Even our children, if they can buy there, they won't go back. Things will never be the same.

INTERVIEW WITH MR LES WILLIAMS- 27 CASSIA GARDENS, SUNRIDGE PARK - 20 MARCH 1997.

Q. How many of your friends or your household were moved as a result of the Group Areas Act?

A. Ten or twelve houses in Gladstone Street were broken down - I cannot state the reason why only some houses in Webber Street were broken down and the houses near Victoria Park in the upper reaches of Walmer Road up to 1st Avenue remained. I stayed in South End from 1916 - 1948, then up to 1958 in Grahamstown.

Q. Describe your emotions when South End was declared a Group Area for whites.

A. I did not see the demolishing of South End because we had already left the area by that time. However since I was a resident of South End from 1916 to 1948 I would empathize with the residents who had to leave their homes. The years from 1955 to 1971 - Having grown up in the area and having known as many people in area - regardless of colour, it shatters us .... we could see the iniquity of it ... there were people like the Marks family who lived in Anderson street .... and I particularly remembered Mr St Clair Marks who played a prominent role in the community - these people were all friends of ours and we realized what was happening but being out of town ... we were distant spectators... had we been here I think the impact would have been much greater ... The tones of many of our conversations were: how did the government of the day think? They were going to have a section of the community in a state of subjugation for ever and ever. How did their minds think? This is something nobody has ever been able to answer me ... A lot of people say Oh Yes do you remember what Adolph Hitler did in Germany... Adolph Hitler had 88 million people behind him ... we know he did go into Sudetenland - we know that he went into Czechoslavkia .. he ultimately lost out on everthing .. he did not succeed in subjugating these people for ever and ever ... how did the Afrikaner Government think that they were going to succeed?

Do not forget it was Verwoerd who said that the "Non-White man is going to be a servant for the rest of his destiny... Why educate him' ... these were his own words. I think quite frankly it had a devastating effect on these people particulary from the family point of view because you must remember ... the people who lived in South End worked fairly near to South End ... they   worked in the centre of town, they worked on the harbour... they were lorry drivers and of course the Railway absorbed a big number of them - They were suddenly removed miles away from their places of employment and this must have devastated these families.

INTERVIEW WITH MR AND MRS BENJAMIN - 49 FREEMAN STREET, SALT LAKE -26 MARCH 1997

Q.How many members were there in your household when you were moved out of South End?

A. My husband, myself and four children.

Q. Where did you live in South End?.

A. Hollywood Flats, on the corner of Gardner and Rudolph Street.

Q. Where did you work?

A. Both of us worked at Edworks Shoe Factory. We retired from Edworks.

Q. How far was your place of employment from your home?

A. We had to take a bus. We can't say what the distance is. (Mr) The distance from South End to Edworks was near, it is further now from Salt Lake.

Q. What was your emotions on moving?

A. We were shocked and very heartsore (Mr Benjamin). We didn't want to move. Especially me. (Mrs Benjamin). Salt Lake is a farm and it is still a farm today (Mr). When I came home from work one evening there was this gentleman sitting in the kitchen. He explained that we had to move. He took our particulars. We asked where we were going to and he said to Bethelsdorp. The gentleman said it was instructions from the government and there was nothing he could do about it. I told my wife we should move to Cape Town, but she did not want to go. I gave my wife the option but I was not keen to stay here in Salt Lake. And still I am not keen to stay here. I keep on telling my wife that I want to sell the house. We were very disappointed that we had to move. We were very happy in South End. We moved to Salt Lake on 22 June 1968. (Mrs Benjamin) It poured for a whole week. It wasn't nice. South End was so nice, in South End you were in heaven. The school for the children was just a stone's throw away. If you go to town you don't need busfare or taxifare, you take a nice stroll, it's just around the corner. Everything was convenient. The other thing is that we had to get rid of some of our furniture items, because the house was too small. We felt that we were put into a stable.

Q. How did the relocation affect your life?

A. Well we had to adapt ourselves to the situation (Mrs). There were no lights, shopping centres etc. we did our shopping in town. We were thrown together with bad elements. Now we are used to conditions here. We started a `missionary' at Machiu Primary School. We raised funds to build St Mary Magdelene Church. We in Salt Lake are the foundation members of that church. Father Bartlett was the first minister of the Church. He was also the last minister of St Peters Church (in South End).

Q. How did the relocation affect your children's education?

A. My eldest daughter had to travel to South End High. My other children went to Machiu Primary which is existant in Salt Lake. The high school (Bethelsdorp Senior Secondary School) was only built afterwards.

Q. Was there sufficient infrustracture, for eg. shops, post office, transport etc.
A. Nothing. We had nothing (Mrs Benjamin). We had to make use of the Post Office in Gelvandale and there were only a few house shops and nothing else. Everything we had to buy in town. If you run out of something then you're lost. You had to see that you buy everthing you need in grocery line. Because if you run out of that you have to wait untill the next day when you go to work to buy it. There were no butchers, no shops, nothing.
Q. Would you like to move back to South End?
A. Not at the present moment, not the way it is built up now. They gave us peanuts for the property when we moved out of South End. It must have been the people living in Walmer who complained about South End, because they had to pass South End. They regarded the area as a eyesore. South End was not a slum area. Everyone lived in harmony. South End was a clean place although some of the houses were wood-and-iron structures. South End will never come back again. It will never be the South End as it used to be. The government made the biggest mistake when   they instructed the Group Areas Act.

INTERVIEW WITH SHUN PILLAY, 2 ROCHLEASTREET MALABAR - 26 MARCH 1997.

Q. How many members were there in your household when you moved?
A. Mother, 5 brothers and two sisters.
Q. Where did you work previously?
A. We had a shop on the corner of Gardner Street and when they evicted us we eventually moved to 3 Rock Street in Malabar. We had to commute to Korsten because my father opened a shop in Durban Road.
Q. How far was your place of employment from your home?
A. Initially it was next door, but when we moved it then moved 5 kilometers away.
Q. What is the approximate distance from your current home to the place of employment mentioned above (if the latter still exists).
A. 2 - 3 kilometers.
Q. What emotions did you experience at having to leave?
A. My dad came to South End and opened his shop there round about 1901 and he died in 1948. When I locked our home for the last time it was like locking the door of a jail, in this case you were not locked in, you were locked out. You thought of all the moments of joy and suffering, the friends you made before the guillotine dropped, whether its going to be worse or good was to be seen. The pain the people had to go through, with all the sacrifices people had to make under difficult circumstances. I remember the depression of the 1930s, the fact that most of the people were not well-educated, however our parents had worked hard to provide those things which we could enjoy. The moving from South End had a devastating effect on the older folk because they had reached the end of their lives, they died virtually broken-hearted because they would not see their children enjoy those things which they had worked so hard for.
    It was a feeling of a tremendous amount of pain and no amount of words can describe it. Whether you were an ordinary worker - who had their meager possessions bulldozed and broken down and to move to areas they did not know, and also the family life that changed, moved to desolate and undeveloped areas where you had to re-establish yourself. You lost those friends you were so near to, you had to make new friends - and it was not easy.
Q. How did the relocation transform your life?
A. Firstly, we were very settled in South End. We lived very contentedly, the people were not very wealthy, the house might not have been brilliantly painted but they were homes - either owned or rented for a modest sum. Although land had been frozen in 1952 - in terms of most of our Community, land was not available in other areas so you had 10 - 15 years elapse before land was made available and costs had escalated. In the meantime we were paying rentals. The amount the government had paid owners for their homes, was completely dissipated in rents which they had to pay for the homes they had up to recently owned. This they had to do while they waited for plots or home to be made available in the new areas they had to move to.
    Land was much more expensive, we had to build homes at much higher prices which now brought a tremendous change in the family pattern. Previously most females stayed at home to look after their families, but were now forced to go out and work to augment the family income to meet the increased expenditure, this resulted in a lack of discipline at home - collapse of close family pattern which had existed in South End.
Q. How did it effect your children's education?
A. I went to the Dower Primary School, a mixed school in terms of teachers, we had quite a number of whites, among them was a Jewish teacher. We had coloured teachers, a Muslim teacher Mr O Salie, who was my Standard 3 teacher, ---- tremendous amount of discipline in the school-- you had to salute your teacher whether at school or out in the street. We grew up with a broader respect for one another, we also had Africans at school ---- we played together. Then I went to Weiss Primary School under principalship of Willem Kriel, coloured

teachers mainly; we learnt to respect each other --- we also had African and White teachers again. This kind of education gave me a firm grounding for later life.

When my children had to go to school, there was a school called Malabar Indian School, I could not allow my children to go there --- I did not want them to become more Indian than they were. I wanted them to be educated in a similar environment that existed in South End --- in a milieu where they could learn to respect people from various communities --- learning their weaknesses and their strengths. With that view in mind I sent all my children to Alfa Primary School - to Gelvandale High and finally to Theodore Herzl. My primary aim was that my children mix with children who were not as fortunate as they were --- a sense of humanity --- a sense of respect that others are as good as you are and in some cases even better.

I remember Mrs Peterson, the Maths teacher at Paterson High School in 1971, when Indian children had to leave the school telling me. "You know Shun I feel sorry that the Indian children are leaving now because the cosmopolitan composition of the school, the sense of rivalry among the different groups bought out the best in the pupils -- was going to be absent. That was one of the sad comments to be made besides other pressing the so called compartmentalization of education --- we lost that rivalry and respect which we could learn from one another.

Q. How did the relocation affect your family's religious routine?
A. Due to the selling of the temple in South End by certain Indian religious leaders without the support of the whole community --- we tended to become more private in our religious endeavors --- more time was spent in our prayer room --- we tended to become more private --- there was no temple built initially in Malabar --- we were deep rooted in our religious persuasion --- no amount of legislation could break us away from our religion --- we did more at home --- we taught our children the basic moral values at home.

Q. Was there sufficient infrastructure in your area? Shops, Post offices, transport, etc.?
A. Originally the roads were made in Malabar with no pavements--- there were no post offices, there were no shops, ---school came later --- transport services were absent --- you either had to buy a vehicle or share transport with people who owned motor vehicles. Basically the infrastructure was not in place.

Q. Would you like to go back to South End?
A. There has always been a yearning for the area you grew up in-- there was a value you attach to old Rudolph Street ---where this one lived --- where that one lived --- today it resembles something totally different --- today it is not the buoyant area that we grew up in. The location was so good --- you were two minutes from the airport and the CBD area --- the station is nearby the beautiful view of the sea and the harbour --- we never complained about the ore dust -- you could walk down the black steps and in a few minutes you were in town --- you had the easy means of transport, the trams were easily available. South End has become a mass of stereo-type match boxes --- there is a lack of community liveliness --- you could see a child playing with a ball, a bicycle or a cricket bat. All this is absent now --- virtually we have an extension of tombstones---there is no more this buoyancy about the whole area. I would love to have returned to the old South End --- it might have been a group of shabby houses but more especially they were homes to us, they housed so many memories. When the bulldozers pull down those houses they were now eradicating an entire epoch, it is a sad commentary to make. I love to go there to get a feel of old South End but I feel strange to go there alone. If we all went back and we could get our positions again. They said it was urban renewal. They could have allowed us to improve our homes and make funds available to improve it but that was just an excuse.

The big farce of urban renewal - what they wanted was our land. It was prime sites and legalized theft by a government who professed to be Christian in their approach and yet so non-Christian in its actions. They forgot the Ten Commandments that was used only for observance on a Sunday.

You always felt that South End was your home, and relocation is another reason for not wanting to return to South End. It would be far to expensive. We all have built bigger homes in the new areas and made major sacrifices to do so would not afford to relocate to South End. I do not think many people have the means to go and relocate that to the present day South End.

INTERVIEW WITH MR S H(SINKY) AH WHY- 14 OPAL RD. KABEGA PARK, PORT ELIZABETH- 18 MAY 1997.

Q. Where did you live in South End.
A. In Gardner Street.
Q. How many members in your household were moved?
A. My family, my mother and sister.
Q. Where did you work?
A. I had my own business. I moved out of South End in 1974 due to the Group Areas Act. They said it was a

slum area and we had to move. There were no facilities for Chinese. They only had this (Kabega Park) residential area up here. We had to close up. We laid idle for a year with no work. I struggled here for a whole year. Then thereafter I manage to strike a job at United Dairies.

Q. How far was your business from your home?

A. I did not have to travel anywhere. My shop was a walking distance from my home.

Q. What emotions did you experience at having to leave?

A. Well you had a heartsore feeling because I grew up there, I was born there. Then the government what they done, they used a slow poison tactic. They moved all the coloureds and the Indians gradually, and they left the Chinese in the desert island. So even if you don't want to move you had to move.

Q. How did the relocation transform your life?

A. Well we were all put up here (Kabega Park) and the government built a school here. That meant, for my kids it was easier for them to go to school. For myself employment was a problem. There was no work for us. So we had to hang on until we could find a job. Any type of job just to keep yourself moving.

Q. Would you like to move back to South End?

A. I would like to but now after they have built all the town-houses, how will I get back in there.

NOTES OF MEETING HELD ON THE 10TH JUNE, 1965, IN NO. 2
COMMITTEE ROOM, BETWEEN THE STATE COMMITTEE AND THE
ESTATES AND INDUSTRIES COMMITTEE TO DISCUSS THE REPLANNING
AND REDEVELOPMENT OF SOUTH END.

PRESENT:

REPRESENTING THE CITY COUNCIL
(Estates and Industries Committee
appointed as Council's representative):-

    Councillors H. Isherwood (In the Chair)
           R.K.Hancock
           I.Racki
           H.J.D.Toerien
           His Worship the Mayor
           (Councillor J.Graham Young)

ALSO PRESENT:

    Town Clerk
    Deputy Town Clerk
    City Treasurer
    City Engineer
    Medical Officer of Health
    Chief Town Planning Officer
    Housing Manager
    Chief Health and Licensing Inspector
    Mr.T.Barret (Resident member of
    Messrs. Mallows & Beinart, Town
    Planning Consultants)

STATE COMMITTEE:

    Mr.G.Nel (Deputy Secretary of
    Community Development Board) (Chairman)

    Dr.Loubscher (Deputy Chairman of the
    National Housing Commission)

    Mr. Strydom (Chairman of the Community
    Development Board)

    Mr.A.B.Nichol (Departmental Town Planner)
    Mr.D.P.Coetzee (Regional Representative,
    Department of Community Development)

    Mr.A.H.Nelmapius (Principal Administrative
    Officer, Department of Community Development)

REPLANNING AND DEVELOPMENT OF SOUTH END.

    Councillor Isherwood welcomed the Government
Departmental Committee representative to the meeting and
said that he was glad that the City Council and the
State were collaborating on the vital matter of redeveloping
South End, and that the meeting would be an exploratory one,
which would enable all those present to sort out the difficulties
involved in such an ambitious project.

    He said that the Council was aware of the action
taken by the Government Department in expropriating certain
properties in South End and that the Council had employed
Town Planning Consultants to undertake the replanning of

the Southern area of the City, which included the South
End area. He said that he felt that he could speak
on behalf of the Council and state that the move made
by the Government Department would treat the South End area was a most
welcome one.

    He continued that the Council was fully aware
that certain hardships would be experienced by moving
the non-conforming groups in the South End area, and
that he trusted that the Government Department would
treat the groups involved with compassion.

    He informed the Government representatives
that the Council was at the present time experiencing
a physical difficulty which was holding up its Town
Planning to some extent, in that, there was a shortage
of staff in the City Engineer's Department to copy with
Town Planning problems. He then requested the
representative to express their views on the South End
removal scheme and emphasized that these proceedings
would be regarded as highly confidential.

    The Town Clerk said that he wished to confirm
that the proceedings of any meetings held between the
State Committee and the Estates Committee would be
treated as confidential. He also requested all members
present to come to the decision in regard to the giving
of a statement to the press.

    Mr. Nel said that it would be possible for a
joint statement to be made to the press.

    Committee to the Council members. He said that the entire
project was new to the Government Department as well,
and that he was pleased to hear that the Council would
be co-operating with the Department in the matter.

    He then introduced the members of the State
Committee to the Council members. He said that the entire
have a preliminary discussion on the matter and that
he had heard that the Council had appointed Town Planning
Consultants to undertake the replanning of the Southern
area of the City. He continued that he would like to
know what the Council had in mind insofar as the replanning
or the area was concerned and said that he would also
like to know when the Council expected the technical
proposals for the replanning, in order that a further
meeting could be arranged. He said that the actual
acquisition of the properties would take some time but
planning could naturally proceed in the meantime.

    The Chairman said that the Town Planning
Consultants had been appointed just prior to the
Government's declaration and that a report would be
available in approximately 12 month's time.

    He continued that certain data was already available
as a result of the Consultant's investigations into a possible
civic centre site. Further information would however,
still be required before the full report could be submitted.

    The City Engineer said that the final report was
expected in June, 1966, but that three interim reports were
to be given at the end of September, December 1965, and
March, 1966 and the final report in June, 1966. He said
that the Consultants had been instructed to collaborate

with the Department of Community Development in the planning of the whole area and also to collaborate with other Government Departments.

Mr. Nel asked whether it was intended that an overall report was to be submitted by the Town Planning Consultants, and then the detailed report on the South End area.

The City Engineer in reply said that this was so.

The Chairman said that the Government's expropriation programme only applied to the land above South Union Street but the Council had road widening and freeway planning for the area and had foreseen the necessity for acquiring all the land between the sea and South Union Street. He suggested that the acquisition of that land could be facilitated if it was brought within the Government's expropriation scheme in the South End area.

Mr. Nel in reply said that his Committee had restricted its activities to the area above South Union Street, and that he had been informed that, in view of the Council's street widening and freeway programme, that the Council itself was proposing to deal with the area between the sea and South Union Street. However, if the Council wished the Government Department to undertake expropriation in that area, an application could be submitted by the Council for the Minister's consideration.

The Chairman said that this action would have to be sanctioned by full Council.

He added that most of the land was connected with the freeway scheme, and that while the Council had considerable experience in expropriation for street widening purposes, he felt that one body could deal with the whole matter more expeditiously and satisfactorily.

He said that after the expropriation had been effected by the Government Department, the Council could come to an agreement with the Department for the area it wished to retain.

Mr. Nel, in reply, said that he would consult the Minister on this proposal, but that he regarded the Chairman's statement as a personal view only at this stage.

The Chairman then referred to the future developments in the area which had prompted the City Engineer to put forward his proposal for the entire Southern area of the City to be replanned.

Mr. Nel said that he felt that any possible expropriation of the land between the sea and South Union Street should be left in abeyance until such time as the final details of the freeway had been settled.

Mr. Strydom said that South End needed redeveloping as a matter of urgency, and that it was possible that intensive development of flats in certain areas would be undertaken. He said that they tried to assist development in the right direction but were primarily concerned with necessity.

These were now empowered by virtue of recent legislation, to go into Urban Renewal generally, but the redevelopment of areas would still mean that local authorities should plan their own areas as they deemed fit.

He continued by saying that it was impossible for the Department to expropriate all land in need of development, as funds were limited. He felt that details of the proposed development in the area should be left over until such time as the Town Planning Consultants' proposals had been received.

The City Engineer said that the Consulting Engineers dealing with the freeway project were currently employed in planning the section leading into South End, and that they had recently been requested to extend their investigations with a view to the whole system being extended beyond the Seaman's Institute. The freeway scheme in that area was scheduled for completion in 1972.

Mr. Strydom asked when the first report would be available as he was a little disappointed in the time factor.

The City Engineer, in reply, said that the report would be available within three to four months and that the major part of the work had already been done. Details, however, were still being discussed with the South African Railway Authorities with regard to the intersection at the Baakens River Bridge.

Mr. Strydom said that why he was disappointed to hear of the time factor involved with the Town Planning report, was because the Government Department was anxious to proceed with the development of the South End area.

The Mayor said that the future of South End did not cover the whole of Port Elizabeth and that the overall Town Planning of the Southern area of the City must be given consideration.

Councillor Hanock said that he agreed with the Mayor's remark and that he felt that the opportunity presented to Port Elizabeth should be "grasped" in the broad sense. He said that the clock should be put back 150 years and that South End should now be envisaged as a hill with nothing on it, and that consideration must be given to transforming the hill into something worthwhile.

He said that he would not like to see haphazard development in the form of blocks of flats scattered here and there in the area.

Mr. Nel said it was not possible to anticipate the nature of the development which would take place in South End, and he did not think the time was opportune to go into particulars about the area. He said that the Department had perhaps acted too soon in regard to enforcing an actual re-development programme and that he felt that the question of development should be dealt with when the Consultants had submitted their final report on the replanning of the area, and after the City Council had considered and approved of it.

He said that the Department wished to help in the removal of schemes from the area and did not intend making money out of the project.

Councillor Hancock said that the members present should decide on whether to tackle the problem piecemeal or as a whole, and that the only people who could guide the members were those who held the finances.

He continued that it appeared as though the Department wanted to undertake the project in a piecemeal manner. He requested that a decision in principle be given on the whole matter.

Mr. Nel said that it was never the Government's intention to necessarily confine itself to South End alone, and that the Government was interested in the removal of all the slum areas of the City.

That the elimination of slum conditions was dependant upon overall planning, and it was decided that as the South End area was the worst one in the City, that it should be tackled in the first instance.

He said that it would be a mistake to tackle, at once all the "blighted" areas in the City.

Councillor Rackl asked whether it would be possible, physically, to provide, within a reasonable period, enough housing to to match the removal en bloc.

Mr. Nel said that he was not prepared to discuss. this aspect of the matter at this stage, as other areas were still to be proclaimed, and that he felt that it was a subject which would be one for subsequent discussion. His Department, however, would be prepared to speed up housing in Bethelsdorp.

He continued that he and other members of the Committee would be visiting Port Elizabeth regularly in regard to the South End problem.

The Mayor said that he was glad that Mr. Nel would be visiting Port Elizabeth regularly, as it was vital that the City Council discuss the question of housing with the Department.

He asked whether the Department intended rebuilding, all areas which had been expropriated, or whether such building would be left to the City Council and private enterprise.

Mr. Nel said that this aspect of the matter was not clear to him at this stage.

He continued that he did not know whether the Consultants would be retaining the streets in their present form, whether services would remain or be removed, and whether it was intended to plan the area on a contour basis. He said that it was not his Department's usual practice to develop schemes for flats and that this could be found to be impracticable in the future. It would possibly be the lot of private enterprise to redevelop the area as it was not his Department's intention to keep the whole area for itself.

Councillor Hancock again asked whether the whole area was to be developed at once or in sections, and what the procedure would be in this regard.

The Chairman said that all these aspects would be covered by the Town Planners.

The Chairman then read the Town Planners' basic proposals for the area.

between now and the submission of the final report by the Town Planners, and in the event of people being displaced, the properties formerly occupied by such persons would be re-occupied by Europeans.

Mr. Nel in reply said that a similar position had arisen in Johannesburg. After expropriation notices had been served, the Department could take occupation of the premises within three months. If the person living in the expropriated property wished to re-establish himself, he would be compensated. It was not the Government's intention to force people to leave the expropriated premises before the replanning of the area had been finalised.

Councillor Hancock said that the statement made by Mr. Nel was a very welcome one, and that, consequently it was even more vital that a time schedule be drawn up in order that persons who would be displaced could make their plans accordingly.

Mr. Nel said that he was "still in the dark" as regard to the time factor involved and that it would be in everyone's interest to await the Town Planners final report.

The Chairman said that as the Town Planners report was only expected in 12 months time, that a statement should be made to the press on the point raised by Mr. Nel in regard to persons remaining in their homes.

Mr. Nel said that after the preliminary report had been received from the Town Planners, he felt that the City Council and his Department could collaborate and proceed with the development of the area.

The City Engineer said that the bulk of the land in South End was of a sloping nature and was near the centre of town. When the area was developed, it would be more densely populated than at present. Topographically the area was not well situated for schools.

He said that he hoped that the position would not arise when the Council would be left with only certain areas of land, possibly unsuitable for school purposes, after the Department had utilised the land it required for housing development. He felt that some joint arrangement with a view to providing suitable areas for schools should be made.

Mr. Nel said that after the Town Planning report had been received, consideration would be given to the City Engineer's request.

The City Engineer said that those areas which the Department was not actively interested in, could possibly be used for a speculative purpose to the disadvantage of the public and to the redevelopment project.

Mr. Nel said that his Department was very aware of this aspect, and that in terms of the recent Act, his Department could define a limited area. It was vital that the City Council and the Department collaborate in the development of this area.

The City Engineer said that new buildings could possibly be put up in the wrong places, and that it was essential that development of the area was in conformity with the forthcoming Town Planning proposals.

Councillor Hancock said that the whole area should be "frozen" to avoid speculation.

The Chairman said that if a plan was submitted to the City Council and it conformed with the building regulations, the Council could not refuse it, and that possible unsuitable development could take place in the area.

Mr. Strydom said that the Department had limited itself to the nucleus of the area and that he felt that the less people knew about the expropriation of properties in the area, the better. It was not the Government's idea that private enterprise be permitted to develop in the area.

He asked to what limit it would be possible and it was suggested that the "freezing" of the area should be taken, as certain operations could be "frozen" and certain operations not.

Mr. Nel asked whether the Council would be willing to have a formal application for the area it suggested be defined in terms of the Act, to include full details of the size of the area required for definition, together with relevant plans connected therewith.

The Chief Town Planning Officer asked whether it was possible for the Government representative to let the Council know the standard of development envisaged in the South End area by the Department, and whether it would be on a sub-economic or economic basis.

Mr. Nel in reply said that he could not possibly foresee any sub-economic development.

Mr. Nichol said that the Government Department must be guided by the Consultants in this matter as to what development should take place.

Councillor Toerien said that he was satisfied that two very important aspects had been covered in regard to the area, namely that people would not have to be moved for some time, and that an area could possibly be defined in terms of the Act.

Mr. Nel said that there were 841 families affected in the area, and that he did not think that it would take very long to provide alternate accommodation for them, possibly a two to three year period.

(At this stage of the proceedings, the Mayor left the meeting.)

Councillor Hancock said that he had hoped that Mr. Barret would report on the matter as representative of the Town Planning Consultants.

Mr. Barret said that he had very little to add to the discussion except that there was a possibility that the Consultants' staff would be increased in order to expedite the submission of the project to the City Council.

He did, however, feel that in order not to provide undesireable development in the area, that the entire area be defined including the area that the Town Planners were to cover.

Mr. Smith said that the entire area mentioned by Mr. Barret was area (b) on the plan.

The Chairman said that in regard to the Council expropriating the area between the sea and South Union Street, that it was possible that no subsidy would be forthcoming from the Provincial Administration.

Mr. Nichol said that the Government Department would need guidance in the redevelopment scheme, and asked whether it would be possible, for the preliminary report from Messrs. Mallows and Beinart, which would be available in three months time, to be discussed when it was received.

Mr. Barret said that the staging of the first report would be the undertaking of necessary surveys. The basic guidance required would be available in the second report.

The Chairman asked whether it would be possible for a loan to be obtained from the Government in regard to services in the area and Mr. Nel in reply said that this would be possible.

Mr. Strydom said that he saw no reason why loan money should not be made available for any area as long as the necessity therefor was motivated. The granting of loans, however, was subject to a higher authority, namely the State Treasury, which controlled the whole loan market. The Treasury could refuse the loan and instruct that Port Elizabeth should go to the open market.

He said that as long as the application for the loan was properly motivated, he saw no reason for it being refused.

The City Treasurer said that he was glad to see a way made open to the Council.

Mr. Coetzee said that he would like to explain to the members present that the cause of the panic when expropriation notices were served, was activated by reason of certain landlords giving their tenants notice.

Mr. Barret asked whether the Department was going to hold matters in abeyance until such time as the plans were received, or whether the Planners were to collaborate with the Department during the preparation of such plans.

Mr. Nel said that the Town Planners had been appointed by the City Council and that he could not demand any information from them.

The Town Clerk said that the Consultants had been specifically instructed to collaborate with the Department of Community Development, and that the Town Planners should go ahead during the drawing up of their proposals and collaborate with the Department as they deemed fit.

The Chairman then thanked the representatives for attending the meeting and assured them that the City Council would collaborate with the Department of Community Development in expediting the redevelopment of the South End Area.

The meeting terminated at 10.30 o'clock p.m.

C H A I R M A N.

REPUBLIC OF SOUTH AFRICA.

G. 26 (E).

DEPARTMENT OF COMMUNITY DEVELOPMENT.

NOTICE IN TERMS OF SECTION 20 (1) *bis* (*b*) OF THE GROUP AREAS ACT, 1957 (ACT No. 77 OF 1957).

To _____ Mr. Ernest Ting King, _____

Address _____ 145 Villiers Road, _____

_____ Walmer _____

WHEREAS by Proclamation No. ___144___ dated ___30:5:1961___ the area defined in

paragraph ___8___ of the Annexure thereto was declared an area for occupation by members

of the ___White___ group; and

WHEREAS you are occupying the land or premises described as ___The dwelling house on___

___erf 1380, Walmer situated in the Municipality of Walmer Division___

___of Port Elizabeth known as 145 Villiers Road.___

that the ___Secretary for Community Development___

YOU ARE hereby notified, in terms of section 20 (1) *bis* (*b*) of the Group Areas Act, 1957 (Act No. 77 of 1957)

in respect of the said area;

WHEREAS you are not a member of the ___White___ group and are therefore a disqualified person

which land or premises are situated in the said area; and

by virtue of a delegation of the Minister of Community Development, has determined that the provisions of

section 23 of the said Act shall apply in respect of the said land or premises with effect from the ___30th April 1967___

and that you, together with all disqualified persons occupying with your permission are required to vacate the said

land or premises prior to the said date.

Signed at ___PORT ELIZABETH___ this ___28th___

day of ___April___ 19 66

_____ [signature]

_____ [signature]
Officer Designated by the Minister in terms of section 20 (1) ter.

SEE NOTES OVERLEAF.

NOTES.

1. Section 23 (1) of the Act reads as follows:—

" As from the appropriate date determined in terms of sub-section (1) *bis* of section *twenty*, and notwithstanding anything contained in any special or other statutory provision relating to the occupation of land or premises, no disqualified person shall occupy and no person shall allow a disqualified person to occupy the land or premises, or (as the case may be) any land or premises in the area or portion of the area to which the determination relates, except under the authority of a permit issued for the purposes of this sub-section ".

2. Section 20 (1) *bis* (*b*) reads as follows:—

" The provisions of section *twenty-three* shall—

(*b*) with effect from a date determined by the Minister, which shall be a date not less than one year after the date of publication of any such proclamation, and of which not less than three, or in the case of business premises, twelve months, prior notice in writing has been given by the Minister to the occupier of any land or premises situated in the area to which the proclamation relates, not being an area which is the subject of a notice under paragraph (*d*), apply with reference to such land or premises ".

3. Section 42 *inter alia* reads as follows:—

"(1) Any person who contravenes the provisions of sub-section (1) of section *twenty-three* shall be guilty of an offence, and liable on conviction to a fine not exceeding four hundred rand or to imprisonment for a period not exceeding two years.

(2) The court which convicts any person of occupying land or premises in contravention of sub-section (1) of section *twenty-three* may in its discretion order the person convicted to vacate the land or premises to which the conviction relates on or before a date to be specified in such order: Provided that any such order shall lapse in the event of the issue of a permit under section *eighteen* authorising the occupation of such land or premises concerned by the person convicted ".

RETURN OF SERVICE—SECTION 20 (1) TER.

I certify that I served this notice on (¹) ___28/4/1966___ by delivery to (²) the occupier personally/to

~~an adult inmate of the premises~~

___Ernest Ting King___

Place ___Port Elizabeth.___

Date ___28/4/1966.___

_____ [signature]
Signature of Person Serving Notice.

(¹) Insert date.

(²) Delete whichever is not applicable.

G.P.-S.2197154—1961-62—2,000.

APPENDIX III - BIOGRAPHICAL NOTES

Omar Cassim played a leading role in the 1960s in the fight against the Nationalist Government in genereal, and the Group Areas Act in particular. He was a representative of the Moslem community on the Group Areas Action Committee. Due to his political activity he was forced to leave South Africa on an exit permit. He is resident in London and recently revisited South Africa with his family.

Frank A Landman was a member of the Teachers League of South Africa and the Anti-CAD. Both these organisations were affiliated to the Non European Unity Movement (NEUM). During the 60s, in the fight against the group Areas Act, Frank A Landman served as the chairman of the Anti-CAD and the Group Areas Action Committee. After he and his family were forced to leave South Africa on an exit permit in 1963, he taught in Zambia, and later England. After thirty four years in exile, he returned with his family to South Africa in 1993. During this visit, he passed away peacefully in Port Elizabeth.

O Salie was born into a humble Muslim family in South End. He was a respected educationalist, and was known as 'Sir'. He drew up programs for Islamic studies and also taught in the madressa. He was committed to the political struggle, and played a leading role in the Anti-CAD, and the Teachers League of South Africa. He was dismissed from the teaching profession in 1965 because of his political activity in the early 60s. In 1967 he re-entered the teaching profession and taught at Gelvandale High School until his death in 1985.

> This section is confined to only three individuals because the authors felt that additional material was too exhaustive to be included in this publication; the politics of non-whites in Port Elizabeth could fill another book. It is the wish of the authors that this coverage will serve to motivate others to write a separate book on the topic..

STREET DIRECTORY OF SOUTH END IN 1964/5

ALABASTER LANE
RIGHT
---	Valley Road
1	Associated Hemmers.
	Teal Record Co.
---	Upper Valley Road
17	Diedericks,J.J J.
19	Omore,R.P.
---	Alabaster Lane

LEFT
---	Valley Road
	Polliacks Wholesale
---	Upper Valley Road
10	Pillay,S.
14	Humphries,H.
30	Mackay's Bakery
---	Armstrong Street

AH TONG LANE
2	Baboo,R.

ALFRED ROAD
RIGHT
---	Valley Road
1	Van Greunen,K.
5	Barnard,J.
7	Welgemoed,A.G.
9	Van Meyeren,_.B.
11	Matheus,J.
15	Hercules,R.
17	Sharrock,W.T.
19	Michael,E.
21	Boshoff,J.J.
---	Rock Street

LEFT
---	Hay Street
2	Strydom,C.J.
4	Herselman,P.A.
6	Hansen,L.D.
8	Van der Mescht,J.W.
10	Schroeder,V.
12	Botha,P.J.
14	Varrall,A.E.
16	Thompson,T.E.
18	Boucher,H.W.
---	Mitchell Stree:

ANDERSON STREET
RIGHT.
1	Such, A.
3	Assoim, J.
5	Van Breda, J. A
7	Botha, T. W.
9	Solomon, G. D.
11	Kopps, Miss S.

LEFT.
2	Johns, N.
4	Hendricks, C. T.
6	Leo, V. G.
8	Clair Marks, P St.
---	Walter Rad.

ARMSTRONG LANE
RIGHT
---	Armstrong Street
1	Van Vuuren,P.K.
5	Redlinghuis,F
7	Gerber,D.J.
---	Bridge Street

LEFT
---	Armstrong Street
2	Umley,M.P.
---	Bridge Street.

ARMSTRONG STREET
RIGHT
---	Alabaster Lare
1	Kaines,J.
3	Roberts,G.W.

3a	Davids,H.A.
5	Van Eyk,M.H.
---	Simpson Street
7	Stanford,R.
---	Upper Pier Street
9	Barnard,C.J.P.
11	Barnard,C.J.P.
---	Kelly Lane
13	Roberts,A.O.
---	Walmer Road
15	Ryan,L.
---	Frere Street
17	Howe,C.
19	Dolley,A.
19a	Gerber,M.J.
23	Kolesky,J.
25	Nel,B.
27	Martin,F.E.
---	Sprigg Street
29	Paul,I.B.
31	Coopoosamy,S.
35	Hornigold,T.W.
37	Watson, Mrs. V.M.
39	Ashworth,H.F.
41	Noli,A.
---	Emily Street
43	Ludwig,C.E.
45	Abbott,R.
47	Scheckle,E.H.
49	Burrough,L.V.
53	Pillay,D.S.
55	Dana,M.
57	Dana,H.

---	Earl Street
51	Dana,H.
53	Pillay,D.S.
57	Dana,H.
59	Beck,A.
61	Snyman,J.
63	Duff,A,C,
65	Scheepers,S.
---	Evelyn Street

LEFT
---	Alabaster Lane
2	Kebble, Mrs.J.
2a	Henwick,E.A.
4	Fick.D.
---	Upper Pier Street
---	Kelly Lane
10	Agherdien,A.
12	Gouws,B.
---	Walmer Raod
	Quoits Cash Store
---	Frere Street
14	Momberg,C.J.
---	Sprigg Street
	S.E. Boys Club
---	Earl Street

BALFOUR STREET
RIGHT
---	Webber Street
1	Duthie,J.
11	Moore,Mrs. M.
---	Wyndham Street
	Portview Flats
31	Maree,L.A.
33	Smith,G.
	Steps to Upper Valley Road

LEFT
2	Nelson.R.J.
---	Wyndham Street
4	Ungerer,D.
6	Jenkerson,L.D.A.
12	Scullard,L.M.
10	Ferreira,H.
10a	Ferreira,H.

12	Jonker,P.J.J.
12a	Emslie,V.R.
	Steps to Upper Valley Road.

BARNES STREET
1	Wesley,H.J.
3	Thomas,I.
5	Jeuneker,I.
7	Waasen,J.
9	Kleinbooi,A.

BOWMAN STREET
RIGHT
	South Union street
	Hindu Primary School
	South Beach Terrace

LEFT
---	Chase Street
12	Arnolds,A.A.
14	Madatt,A.
16	Moodley,S.
18	Abrahams,A.
---	South Beach Terrace.

BRIDGE STREET
RIGHT
---	Valley Road
1	Andersons Hardware.
	Abel Court.
---	Francis Street
3	De Bruin,M.J.
5	Plaatjes,I.
7	De Lange,D.
9	Sivinger,G.H.
11	Knoetze,J.
13	Randall,T.W.
15	Williams,W.
17	Breytenbach,R.H.
19	Manley,R.C.
21	Jansen,C.J.
21a	Vosloo,N.C.
23	Naidoo,L.L.
25	Wilson,V.P.G.
27	Moodaley,P.
29	Frosler,M.
33	Poole,J.L.
	Poly Flor Products Africa.
---	Walmer Road.

LEFT
---	Ellis Street
2	Sandan,J.
8	Strydom,H.
10	Swanepoel,H.
12	Human,M.J.
18	Kuscus,F.H.
20	Meyer,S.L.
22	Naidoo,G.S.
24	Ruiters,W.
---	Simpson Street.

BULLEN STREET
Right
---	Rock Street
1	Bopp,B.
3	Jones.B.
5	De Abreu,J.A.
5a	Kapp,H.
---	Pier street
7	Adams,A.
7	Cooper,R.
7	De Maine,J.R.
7	Von Hagen,L.P.
7a	Geyer,J.E.
9	Dutch Reformed Church
	Petra Hall
---	Walmer Road
	Buchanan Hall
17	P.V.A. Investments (Pty) Ltd

19	Padayachey, C.S.
21	Smuts, E.E.
21a	Minnie, C.J.
23	Frier, C.
23a	Warricker, G.S.
----	Rudolph Street
25	Tyler, R.H.
27	Rosslee, Ek.
27a	Van Staden, A.H.
29	Padaychy, M.
29a	Lagerdien, R.
----	Farie Street
31	Davids, H.M.
33	Davids, T.
35	Lalla, S.N.
37	Meintjes, F.
39	Steyn, H.J.
41	Chandler, C.
43	Assam, H.
47	Kow, Mrs M.C.
49	Abader, H.B.
53	Nayagar, C.
55	Miller, Mrs M.
57	Bailey, A.F.
59	Rensberg, I.
59a	Davids, S.
61	Noorshib, A.K.
----	Nelson Street
	LEFT
----	Rock Street
2	Knoetze, J.A.
----	Pier Street
4	Alfonso, P.L.
6	Bramford, V.
----	Walmer Road
8	Dickson, J.H.
8	Swanepoel, J.C.
8a	Kilian, G.
10	Wardle, V.G.
12	Naiken, Mrs G.
14	Narotham, T.
16	Gilbert, C.
18	Dorasamy, R.A.
20	Brown, S.
20	Hattas, A.
22	Ismail, E.
22a	Economy Cleaners Depot
22a	Adams, I.
----	Rudolph Street
----	Farie Street
24	Jeptha, C.E.
26	Solomon, J.
28	Chetty's
34	Kees, L.J.
34	Low Kee, D.
36	MacKay's, H.
38	Roux, W.A.
38a	Van Niekerk, J.A.
40	Quantoi, G.
42	George, E.H.
46	George, L.S.
48	Human, J.J.
48a	Lookwhy, S.H.H.
----	Nelson Street

BUNN LANE

2	Hart, B.
4	Fataar, G.
8	Jessem, M.G.
3	Thomson, Miss E.
7	Fataar, K.
9	Drake, M.R.

BUNN STREET

	RIGHT
----	Walmer Road
1	Mallinson, M.H.
3	Joel, J.
	Blessed Oliver
	Plunket Parish Hall
----	Bunn Lane
	LEFT
----	Walmer Road

| | London Cafe |
| --- | Upper Pier Street |

BURNESS LANE

4	Denson, B.
5	Nethling, S.M.
7	Hendriks, G.

BURNESS STREET

	RIGHT
---	Burness Lane
3	Jobson, R.
5	Safedien, G.
7	Schovell, J.
---	Lane
9	Uren, E.
9a	Contell, F.
15	MacKay, K.
17	Burton, A.
21	Langford's
	Upholsterers
---	Bullen Street
---	Nelson Lane
---	Coode Street
	Moslem Public School
25	Moodeley, N.
27	Moodaley, V.A.
29	Niekerk, W.A.
31	Danoo, M.
---	Forest Hill Road
	LEFT
---	Nelson Lane
2	Fellows, H.
2a	Adam, I.W.
4	Fond, A.A.
6	Jacobs, C.P.
8	Knitt, W.
12	Petterson, M.A.
14	Welcome Cash Store
14-16	Kahaar, H.M.
18	Bowers, T.
---	Coode Street
----	Forest Hill Road
20	Norton, M.
22	Greaves, M.
24	Prince, D.C.
26	Bhana, S.
28	Bhana, R.
30	Ferreira, P.E.
32	Mink, R.

CHASE STREET

1	Jappie, A.
8	Govindasamy, M.P.
12	Jappie, J.
18	Prinsloo, J.
20	Harris, H.A.

COODE STREET

	RIGHT
----	Walmer Road
3	Frieslaar, N.
5	Roberts, H.A.
7	Roos, Mrs E.A.
----	Rudolph Street
	Union Church School
9	De Vos, E.D.
11	Schovel, M.
23	Jim Carr
25	Perils, J.
27	Naidoo, N.
29	Armstrong, R.
33	George, E.L.
35	Cobb, E.F.
7	George, L.
39	George, J. W.M.
41	Oosthuizen, H.
----	Farie Street
----	Nelson Street
49	Linstroom, W.
51	Martimer, A.
53	Mortimer, W.M.
55	Louther, a.S.

----	Burness Street
	LEFT
----	Walmer Road
4	South End Laundry
4	Morar Kara Laundry
6	Williams, K.H.
6a	Shaw, W.W.R.L.
----	Rudolph Street
	Lindstrom Hall
12	Van Schaik, N.
12a	De Maine, J.
14	Sutch, A.J.
16	Domingo, W.
18	Hendriks, H.
20	Olivier, G.
22	Burton, Miss P.
----	Farie Street
----	Nelson Street
----	Burness Street
40	Knee-Chong, A.
	Fook Chong & Co.
----	Quoit Street

DONALD STREET

	RIGHT
----	Hay Street
3	Van der Merwe, D.J.
----	Seymour Street
5	Hamilton, D.G.
5	Wolfaardt, G.S.
5a	Thompson, K.I.
----	Mitchell Street
	LEFT
----	Hay Street
2	Radue, R.
4	Van Wyk, J.J.M.
6	Bosch, C.A.
----	Seymour Street
8	Erasmus, I.M.
10	Niemand, E.H.
12	Esterhuizen, J.
14	Kwong See, P.
14a	Li Green, S.
---	Mitchell Street

DOUGLAS STREET

	LEFT
---	Upper Valley Road
2	Poole, R.
4	Doyle, R.N.
6	Ingram, --.
8	Osborne, D.
10	Dyer, D.
12	Bosch, O.P.
14	Dyer, P.A.
---	Gladstone Street

EARL STREET

	RIGHT
---	Armstrong Street
3	Stockington, W.F.
5	Dana, D.
7	Prinsloo, P.
7a	Leslie, E.N.
7b	Du Plessis, B.
9	Heidsinger, E.M.
11	Nadasen, C.
13	Tobias, M.S.
15	Benjamin, Mrs H.
15b	Niekerk, W.
17	Alexander, C.
19	Prinsloo, F.
21	Abrahams, A.
23	Snyman, P.
25	Perreira, D.R.
27	Becker, W.P.
29	Jozaffe, L.A.
31	Herdian, A.
33	Printoos, J.
35	Udemans, H. & Sons
45	Meintjies, G.
47	Prince, P.L.
---	Randall Street

	LEFT
---	Armstrong Street
6	George, J.H.
14	George, J.
16	Turner, D.W.
16a	Bareira, D.C.
18	Clemence, D.
20	Domiggo, --.
22	Areington, L.
30	Paul, P.
32	Meiring, A.M.
----	Randall Street

ELLIS STREET
RIGHT

----	Off Valley Road
1	Van As, N.D.
3	Fisher, D.
5	Claassen, J.H.
7	Van Zyl, K.
9	Potgieter, P.C.
----	Upper Valley Road
----	Bridge Street
----	Lower Valley Road
2	Olivier, J.H.W.
4	Scholtz, J.F.
----	Bridge Street
6	Benjamin, Miss E.
8	Van Rooyen, J.C.
10	Carter, a.M.
----	Upper Valley road

EMILY STREET
RIGHT

----	Armstrong Street
5	Warner, E.P.
5a	Potgieter, J.
7	Prinsloo, H.
9	Prinsloo, N.
11	Coopoo, N.V.
15	Lagardien,
17	Lagerdien,S.
19	Neil,P.R.
21	Koekemoer,P.K.
25	Johansson,V.E.
27	Sa Joe,L.A.
29	Wong,D.
31	Spinks,C.W.
33	Mallick,H.A.
35	Mallick,M.A.
37	Van Rensburg,W.J.
39	Adlam,F.H.
41	Barnard,T.W.
43	Gardner,C.D.A.
45	Skolifa,M.
47	Van As,L.M.
49	Sutton,J.J.
51	Coupe,H.G.
53	Pretorius,J.N.
55	De Jager,A.J.
57	Corney,V.W.
59	Marais,J.B.B.
61	Morton,W.T.
---	Randall Street.
	LEFT
---	Armstrong Street
2	Coetzee,E.
8	Miller,J.
10	Bezuidenhout,D.S.
12	Rudman,D.L.
14	Lagerdien,J.
16	Lagardien,H.
18	Joorst,A.
20	Wagner,W.F.R.
22	Allison,J.
22	Soloman,M.
24	Martin,V.
26	Humphreys,M.
28	Smith,G.W.
30	Ah Tow,G.
32	Meyer,C.P.
32	New Apostolic Church(Africa).

32a	Bell,E.E.
34	Kliengeld,W.F.
34a	Comley,R.H.
---	Randall Street

EVELYN STREET
RIGHT

---	Armstrong Street
1	Van der Watt,A.r.
3	Potts,E.
13	Turner,L.
15	Grauman,H.
21	Williams,M.
---	Randall Street.
	LEFT
---	Armstrong Street.
2	Loyson.
4	Kitching,J.
6	Bell,L.H.
8	Gush,H.R.
10	Barnard,O.
12	Jappie,H.F.
12	Kohen,H.W.
14	Hendricks,A.
16	Forbes,A.A.
16a	Forbes,A.
18	Schultz, Mrs. M.A.
18	Friskin Transport Service.
---	Sandy Lane.

FARIE STREET.
RIGHT

---	Thomas Street
1	Lagerdien,F.
3	Serfontein,F.
---	Gardner Street
5	Poonoosamy
7	Theunissen,A.
9	Kafaar,S.
---	Farie Lane
---	Seymour Street
---	Mitchell Street
11	Talaludien,A.
13	Jooste,Mrs. A.
17	Carlson,J.C.
19	Randall,W.
19	Nel,B.
19a	Mon Yan,D.
21	Bibby,J.S.
25	Reid,W.
27	Padayachee,G.
29	Bezuidenhout,C.J.A.
---	Bullen Street
---	Coode Street
31	Gamiet, G.
33	Waite, A.G.
35	Knipp, K.
37	Jozaffe, R.
39	Ramasamy, C.
39a	Welgemoed, A.
39b	Van Rensburg, G.D.
41	Dorothy, J.
	Cover Girl Dresses.
----	Forest Hill Road
	LEFT
----	South Union Street Lyclo Building Lion Clothing Manu= facturers
----	Mitchell Street
26	Hendricks, A.
28	Abrahams, G.
28a	Govender, I.M.
30	Bardien, I.
30a	De Villiers, A.G.P.
----	Bullen Street
----	Nelson Lane
32	Lai Pan, A.O.
34	Rademeyer, P.J.
36	van der Mescht, N.J.
38	Manan, H.A.

40	Joshua, J.H.
42	Davids, A.N.
44	U.N. Cash Store
44	Kayser, D.
46	Joshua, J.
48	Pillay, I.
48	Frost, F.
50	Wallenstein, W.P.
50b	Wallenstein, R.
----	Coode Street

FOREST HILL ROAD.
RIGHT

---	Frere Street
1	Kason,N.
3	Agnew,M.J.
5	Sharp, William,A.H.
15	Koffinas,G.J.
---	Sprigg Street South End Boy's Club.
---	Evelyn Street.
35	Loyson,Mrs.L.L.
39	Loy Son,L.L.
39b	Nepgen,F.J.
45	Diedericks,R.P.
---	Tongman Lane
	LEFT
---	Walmer Road Coode Buildings
2	Jack Kee,E.
6	Wolfaardt,G.S.
8	Jacobs,A.J.
10	Barboo New Apostolic Church.
---	Rudolph Street
12	Liberty,V.D.
14	Key,J.S.
16	Sunrise Cash Store.
16	Key,J.S.
---	Farie Street
20	Strydom,K.J.
24	City Mission Full Gospel Church.
28	Chinese Restaurant.
30	Run,G.H.
32	Son Kee,W.
---	Nelson street
36	You Lee,L.
38	Ting Chong,D.
40	Begg,L.
42	Mitha,R.C.
---	Burness Street.
44	Dickenson,Mrs.N.
48	Ross,C.
50	Broadway Supply Stores.
----	Quoit Street.

FRANCIS STREET
RIGHT

---	Bridge Street
1	Nordien,C.
3	Kapp,M.H.
----	Kinsley Kloof.
	LEFT
2	Preston,J.
4	Berbie,H.
6	Johns,H.E.
6a	Moore,A.Q.
10	Mungur,B.
----	Miller Street

FRERE LANE
(Off Frere Street)

1	Chowles, Mrs C.J.
3	Pettit, M.S.
2	Van der Merwe, D.G.C
4	Gerber, P.F.

FRERE ROAD
(South End)

28	Du Randt, A.E.
72	Lillah, A.K.,
	Fruits & Veg.

FRERE STREET
RIGHT

----	Walmer Road
	Thelmyr Flats
1	Chowles, F.
3	Van Vuuren, K.E.
9	Hercules, A.
11	Serfontein, A.
13	Jappie, A.G.
15	Abdool, I.
17	Williams, D.
21	Bonthuys, F.S.
----	Armstrong Stret
23	Wilson, T.
27	Deacon, G.H.
33	Johnson, H.
35	Coopoo, D.
37	Du Preez, J.E.
39	Dalton, D.L.
41	Wilson, M.
43	Nel, Mrs V.
----	Randall Street

LEFT

----	Forest Hill Road
2	Cassim, V.
4	Cassim, N.
6	Fourie, T.J.
8	Forbes, D.
10	Kay, W.
12	Ganey, G.
12a	Ganey, S.A.
14	Davids, H.A.
14a	Kahn, S.
16	Dickenson, M.
18	Estrehuizen, J.
---	Frere Lane
20	Reneson, W.
22	Francis, L.
26	Du Plsis, C.J.
28	Du Randt, F.
30	Koen, n.
32	Domingo, C.
34	Johnson, T.
36	Jappie, A.
38a	Samuels, N.
38	Moodaley, V.
40	Labercensie, J.
42	Bruindres, A.
44	Daya, A.
46	Daya, A.
48	Abrahams, S.
50	Britz, J.A.
52	Neff, W.
54	Michaels.
56	Van der Spuy, B.
58	Wilson, I.
60	Goulding, G.
62	Henry, W.R.
64	Thomas, W.
----	Armstrong street
66	Gross, E.
68	Kendall, W.C.
70	McDillon, A.
72	Acherdien, G.
74	Abrahams, A.
74a	Abdulla, G.H.
74a	Midway Taxis
76	Davids, E.J.
78	Mullany, L.C.
---	Randall Street.

GARDNER STREET
RIGHT

---	Rock Street
1	Padayche, R.
3	Mathieson, H.
---	Pier Street
5	Dutton, L.D.
9	Jonker, N.B.

11	Miles, Alfred.
13	Vergadagenum, P.E.
15	Ragavall, A.
17	Muller, J.B.
19	Padayachee, T.
---	Walmer Road
	Prince of Wales
	Hotel
31	Moodaley, V.R.
33	Abrahams, J.
37	Rockman, D.
39	Pillay, D.
---	Rudolph street
	Tamil School.
	Shri Mariaman
	Temple.
41	Plaatjies, L.
41b	Padayachee, A.G.
45	Imperial Fruiters.
47	Fakir, G.
49	Rangesammy.
---	Farie Street.

LEFT

---	Rock Street
2	Ross, A.W.
---	Pier Street
	Dower Primary School
10	Coronation
	Hairdressing Saloon.
12	Essop, H.M.
12a	Makan, T.V.P.
14	Gutstien, F.
14a	Meyer, Mrs. K.
16	Makan Bhana.
	Standard Bank.
---	Walmer Road
20	Fattar, C.
20a	Baker, A.
22	Tukarom, T.
22a	Ah Why.
---	Rudolph Street
28	Adamson, J.

GARDNER STREET

30	Simon, S.H.
	Edward Searle & Co.
	(Pty.) Ltd.
---	Farie Street.

GARDNER LANE.

1	Kopps, D.A.
13	Mcbean, H.

GLADSTONE STREET.
RIGHT

---	Webber Street.
1	Mudford, K.H.
3	Mclachlan, D.
---	Lane
7	Styles, R.J.
---	Douglas Street

LEFT

---	Webber Street
6	Marx, L.J.
8	Mckay, J.R.
10	Burger, G.
12	Ranger, G.E.
14	Rudman, C.A.
16	Van Rooyen, D.
18	Van Heerden, F.
20	Botha, P.R.
22	Stear, J.F.
24	Will, A.
26	Cuff, C.N.
28	Renshaw, G.
30	Stanley , J.T.A.
32	Du Preez, Q.P.
34	Rosling, E.H.
34	Rosling, M.I.
36	Johns, M.

HARRIS STREET.
RIGHT

---	Brickmakers Kloof.
1	Davidson, E.J.
3	Kock, R.
3	Strydom, R.
5	Nel, W.J.
7	Pretorius, M.E.
7	Lutzke, C.S.A.
9	Kent, A.N.
11	Stevens, J.
13	Muller, M.
13	Mills, -
13	Sheenan, W.C.
15	Modern Steam Laundry
---	Cudmore Street

LEFT

---	Brickmakers Kloof
2	Teema Flats
---	Cudmore Street

HAY STREET
RIGHT

---	Alfred Road.
1	Long, R.C.
1a	Van Eyk, T.L.
3	Dart, L.
5	Clark, T.R.
7	Miller, P.
---	Donald street
9	Hughes, P.T.D.
---	Rock Street

LEFT

---	Alfred Road
2	St. Peter's Rectory.
---	Rock Street.

HOY AVENUE.
RIGHT

---	Randall Street
	Du Preez, A.D.
---	Victoria Park Drive

LEFT

---	Randall Street
	Cunningham Primary
	School
---	Victoria Park Drive.

JACK STREET
LEFT

---	Miller Street
8	Torrentee, J.

RIGHT

1	Prange, W.P.
5	Zimmerman, H.C.
7	Rockman, H.A.
---	Miller Street

JOLLY STREET

---	Miller Street
8	Torrentee, M.
---	Kinsley Kloof.

KELLY LANE

3	Stowman, S.R.
5	Hearne, c.
7	Pluke, V.
8	Grimsel, K.

KENNY STREET
RIGHT

----	Upper Pier Street
1	Maris Stella Convent
3	St Thomas School
----	Walmer Road

LEFT

----	Upper Pier Street
	Dutch Reformed Church
----	Walmer Road.

LEA PLACE
RIGHT

---	Quoit Street

1	Daniel, J.
3	Brooks, E. A.
5	Braamwoult, W.
7	Samsodien, B.
9	Abrahams, T.
11	Assam, J.
13	Prince, S.
15	Sammels, S.
17	Hughes, G.
19	De Vos, G. H. A.
21	Muller, P.
23	Barry, W.
25	Leo, H.
25	Minnie, M. J.
27	Mesmith, F.
29	Volkwyn, J. C.
31	Charles, --.
33	Devega, A.
35	Marsh, G.
37	Tim, D.
39	Kannemeyer, V.
41	Hendricks, S. P.
43	Samsolen, K.
45	Oliver, T.
47	Abader, A.
49	Harrison, J.
51	Hendricks, Mrs. W.
53	Felix, L. H.
55	De Kock, R.
57	Kemp, T. A.
59	Pereira, h.
61	Gallant, V.
63	Orsini, V.
67	Walters, S.
69	Scott, C.
71	Mallick, G. O.
75	Morley, H. A.
	LEFT
---	Quoit Street,
2	Bardien, A.
4	Thomas, T.
6	francis, J.
8	Johns, H. S.
10	Boltman, F.
12	Paterson, J.
14	Beckett, J. C.
18	Muller, W.
20	Bannesse, J.
22	Barth, E.
24	Bartt, R.
24	Potgieter, I.
26	BcBean, E.
28	Abrahams, F.
30	Julius, H.
32	Rockman, T.
34	Barry, H.
36	Holloway, H.
38	Connelly, S.
40	Beck, A. J.
42	Edinberry, J. W.
44	Hearne, D. G. C.
46	Samuels, L.
48	Rockman, D. W.

LEE STREET

2	Gedult,L.
4	Dixon,E.H.
6	Goliath,J.
8	Posthiusus,M.M.
10	Rockman,A.J.

LOVE STREET
RIGHT

---	Rock street
1	Peo,E.
3	Dalton,D.L.
5	Walters,D.L.
7	Le Villiers,N.
11	Francis,H.W.
5	Red Star service Station
17	Abrahams,G.

---	Pier Street
	LEFT
2	Rock Court
4	Barnard,A.J.
6	Anderhold,L.
8	Dezzel,G.R.
---	Pier Street
10	Dysel,M.
10a	Brophy,p.
16	Ranchod,G.
16	Ryan,A.
18	Dolley,a.S.
---	Walmer Road

LOWER VALLEY ROAD

9	Seahorse Pool (Pty.) Ltd.
9	Sapphire pools.
9	E.P. Anti Corrosives (Pty) Ltd.
9-13	Van Pitswick Joinery Works (Pty) Ltd.
21	Van Vuuren,P.J.J.
23	Van Gend,B.C.
25	Rupersburg,A.
27	Bosman,I.J.
29	Nell,W.A.
31	Lawrence,R.A.
33	Republic Motor Exchange.
33	Algoa Glassworks
39	Continuous Towel Cabinet Service. Valley Road Service Station.
39	Electrical Wholesalers (Pty)Ltd.
41	Brown,C.J.E.
43	Van Huysteen,J.L.
47	Nell,J.M.
49	Esterhuizen,S.
51	Tait,D.
55	Stander,H.J. Disca (Pty) Ltd Algoa Glassworks.
16	S.A. Druggist Ltd.
16	Winthrop Laboratories S.A.
22	Stokes,D.J.J.
24	Van as,N.D.
26	Posthumus,N.P.
28	Wait,J.W.
30	De Jager,H.
32	Paton,T.K.J.
32	Greef,D.
32	Liemecke,W.D.
34	Van Rensburg,I.
36	Van Loggenberg,N.E.

MILLER STREET
RIGHT

---	Francis Street
3	Nielsen,J.
7	Kock,C.P.
9	Jacobs,A.J.
9	Long,A.V.
9	Van eyk, Mej.H.
11	adams,Mrs. N.
11a	Holman,G.W.
11a	Adams,R.
11a	Sanders,R.A.
13	Sammy,P.
13a	Naidoo,C.M.
---	Jolly Street
15	Jackson,W.C.
17	Jubber,W.F.
19	Murran,A.E.
21	Payne,I.D.
---	Jack Street
21	Brown,A.C.
---	Lee Street
23	Johannie,L.

25	Wilson,C.R.
27	Pretorius,Mrs. B.
29	Van eyk,T.L.
31	Viviers,R.O.
33	Ranchod,E.
---	Walmer Road.
	LEFT
---	Francis street
4	Jackson,O.T.R.
6	Hassen,B.
10	Smuts,S.J.
12	Petzer,D.J.
14	Conway,T.
16	Smuts,A.N.
18	Van Heerden,P.
20	Johannie,N.F.
22	Van staden,J.
24	Johns,J.
26	Wasserman,H.J.
---	Walmer Road.

MITCHELL STREET
RIGHT

7	Moodley,M.
9	Young,M.M.
11	Frier,P.S.
---	Pier Street
13	Castro,F.
15	Nel,A,P.
17	Burrough,C.
19	Campbell,J.
21	Salie,A.
---	Walmer Road
23	Nipiagodien,B.
27	Ebraham,I.
29	Ismail,W.
33	Solomans, Dr.A.&S.
33	Kleinbooi Motors
35	Dorasammy,R.A.
37	Dorasamy,R.A.
---	Rudolph Street
41	Abdul Sain.
43	Chetty,K.
47	Williams,J.
49	Acherdien,I.
51	Kader,H.
53	Kader,G.
55	Domingo,L.
55a	Dolley,A.
57	Burion,W.F.
59	Rockman,J.R.
61	Pillay,T.
63	Padayachee,S.
---	Farie street
67	Aroonslav,R.K.
69	Mohamed,I.
71	Abrahams,E.
73	Johns,E.
75	Salie,O.
77	Muller,E.W.
93	Ho Chong,H.F.
---	Burness Street
---	Quoit Street
	LEFT
2	Naidoo,S.K.
4	Hendricks,J. Newton Hall. Methodist Church.
---	Pier Street
8	Frasler,S.
10	Parshotam,C.M.
10a	Parshotam,C.M.
12	Willis, W.
14	Williams, E.
16	Pillay, R.
16	Choice Grocers
18	Deysel, M.s.
20	Scheepers, A.E.
22	Trytsman, D.J.
---	Walmer Road
30	Naidoo, E.K.
30a	Naidoo, A.
30a	Wolf, a.

32	Pareria, H.	---	South Union Street		RANDALL STREET		
32	Prince, M.		Naomi Court		*RIGHT*		
34	Jackson, R.	---	Love Street	---	Walmer Road		
36	Sataar, H.I.	9	Muir, T.S.	1	Suanders,A.P.		
---	Rudolph Street	11	Narkedien, S.	3	Cherry,G.R.		
38	Coffie, M.	11a	Behr, D.G.	5	Erasmus,J.J.		
40	Pillay, J.B.	15	Nel, W.J.	7	Van Jaarsveld,J.P.		
40a	Moodley, A.M.	---	Gardner Street	---	Hoy Avenue		
42	Hill, N.	17	Frier, P.S.		Cunningham Primary School		
44	Moodliar, Dr. J.	---	Seymour Street		Child Welfare Society		
46	Hill, M.N.	19	Johannessen, D.	---	Duncan Avenue		
48	Abrahams, B.		Wesleyan Church	23	Dupie's Gen.		
90	Miller, P.C.	---	Mitchell Street		Blacksmith & Welding Works.		
90	Muller, E.W.	25	Battistoni, A.		Round Table Childhaven.		
90	Smith, Nurse J.M.	25	Bester, P.J.		South End Cemetry.		
90	Ho-Chong, A.F.	25	Styles, J.		*LEFT*		
----	Farie Street	25a	De Jager, H.W.	---	Frere Street		
	Mission of Good Shepherd	27	Dalton, D.J.	2	Van Rensburg,N.		
	South End Grey Sch.	27	Zeelie, E.J.	4	NcFie,J.		
	South End Coloured	29	Bouwer, D.L.	6	Ackerdien,D.		
	Sec. School	31	Dickson, J.H.	---	Sprigg Street		
----	Burness Street	33	Bouwer, D.L.	10	Gooseman,J.H.		
			South End Clinic	12	Jacobson,F.P.		
	NELSON LANE	---	Bullen Street	14	Cumberlege,M.M.		
1	Moodley, N.A.		*LEFT*	---	Emily Street		
3	Pathan, A.K.	---	South Union Street				
13	Povey, M.	4	Minnie, I.J.		ROCK LANE		
15	Adams, P.J.	4a	Moolow, M.	28	Viljoen,L.		
17	Reid, Miss J.	16a	Louw, J.C.				
19	Basson, H.	18	Williamson, A.		ROCK STREET		
2	Pillay, G.	20	May, P.		*RIGHT*		
4	Dullabh, M.	22	Vermaak, G.M.	---	Love Street		
6	Jacobs, S.	24	Tuohy, Mrs M.G.		St. Marys Cemetery		
8	Gillian, S.	26	Frost, R.A.		St. Peters Church		
8a	Bardien, Y.	28	Jacobs, H.		St. Peter's Rectory		
10	Felix, R.J.	---	Love Street	---	Gardner Street		
10	Peters, D.	30	Myburgh, L.D.	---	Hay Street		
10a	Langford, Mrs A.	---	Gardner Street	---	Seymour Street		
12	Sirkhotte, S.	32	Huntley, D.	3	Pillay Bros.		
		32	Du Toit, M.S.	5	Moodaley,V.R.		
	NELSON STREET	34	Pillay, N.a.	7	Mator, P.		
	RIGHT	36	Scheepers, H.	7a	Garage, S.E.		
----	Bullen Street	38	Van Huyssteen, J.J.	9	Potgieter, F.J.		
1	Hendricks, H.	40	Johnson, J.V.	11	Erasmus, H.		
1a	Boomgaard, M.	---	Seymour Street	11a	Grobellar, K.H.		
3	Bruintjies, T.	42	Gibson,D.C.	13	Dorasami, G.		
5	Governder, A.	44	Gibson,I.K.	15	Kahaar, H.M.		
7	Kow, M.	46	Swanepoel,P.J.	17	Van Loggenberg, J.M.		
----	Nelson Lane	48	Enslin,C.C.A.				
9	Van Antwerp, M.A.	50	Raga, C.D.	19	Fourie, ---		
11	De Villiers, J.C.	---	Mitchell Street	21	Gerber, M.M.		
13	Jappie, A.G.	52	Savahl,M.G.	23	Van Staden, M.P.		
15	George, J.W.	54	Nadasen,Mrs. C.	---	Alfred Road		
17	Rockman, J.	56	Jonker,N.B.	---	Love Street		
19	Wesley, A.J.M.	58	Hodge,R.N.	2	Coopoosamy, S.		
21	Wong, --.	60	Mackay,W.	4	Brown, J.		
----	Coode Street	62	Borrough,C.O.	4a	Brown, J.		
	LEFT	62	Brown,J.P.	6	Gibson, I.K.		
---	Coode Street	64	Becket,J.P.	8	Van Schalkwyk, E.D.		
8	Brown, A.	---	Bullen Street.	10	Delport, M.L.		
10	Van Rensburg, C.			12	Pillay, V.M. & Son		
12	Gerber, D.		QUIOT STREET	---	Gardner Street		
14	Whitefield, B.		*RIGHT*	14	Green, A.W.		
16	Chetty, S.M.	---	mitchell Street	18	Joubert, J.J.		
18	Jaffa, J.	1	Akom,L.	20	Apavoo, Dr. S.V.		
20	Pillay, J.	3	Pillay,R.R.	---	Seymour Street		
20	Ammorthan, C.	---	Bullen Street	22	Dorfling, H.J.		
22	Hercules, J.	9	Augustine,V.	24	Dudley, H.		
24	Kapp, M.E.	11	Pillay,N.	26	Chowles, F.S.		
26	Claasen, H.	11a	Sam,P.F.	28	Verwy, G.J.		
28	Ramjee, B.B.	---	Nelson Lane	30	Bosch, C.A.		
30	Ramjee, B.B.	23	De Vos,E.	32	Adams, Mrs A.		
32	Ramjee, B.B.	25	Joel,J.	32a	Worricker, G.S.		
34	Jacobs, C.	27	Alexander,C.	---	Mitchell Street		
36	Son, Kee, W.L.	29	Alexander,T.	34	Ward, A.W.		
---	Forest Hill Road	29	Alexander & Son,blgd contractors.	36	Chetty, P.		
		31	Khan,M.	36a	Chetty, P.		
	PIER STREET	---	Coode street	38	Pather, P.M.		
	(See also Upper Pier Street)		*LEFT*	40	Victor, J.J.		
	RIGHT	---	Mitchell Street				
---	South Beach Terrace		South End High School				
	Pier Street Mosque	---	Lea Place.				
3	Liebrandt, W.J.						

116

42	Thysse, J.P.
---	Bullen Street
44	Smith, A.D.
46	Lalla, G.
48	Hevia, A.R.
---	Blind End

RUDOLPH STREET
LEFT

---	South Beach Terrace
3	Salie, D.
5	Salie, G.
7-9	Narkedien, H.I.
11	Abdol, G.
13	Abdol, A.
---	Chase Street
15	Kee Son & Co.
19	Ahmed, A.
21	Marcus, A.
21a	Rademeyer, E.
25	Chetty, B.
27	Moodaley, V.
29	Moodaley, R.
	Commercial Fisheries
37	Hassim Sandan
39	Evans, c.H. & Sons
39	Cook, M.
---	South Union Street
45	Tong Wah
---	Thomas Street
53	Said, S.A.
53	Star Social Club
53/57	Malay Mosque
55	Pillay, P.M.
57	Pillay, R.
59	Davids, B.
	Ismaels Cash Store
---	Gardner Street
65	Ah Why
67	Hollywood Outfitters
67	Bhagattjee, S.A.
69	Jinnah, Y.
73	Daily Supply Store
75	Nagar, L.
75	Laloo, C.
81	Prince, Mrs M.
83	Thomas, G.
85	Snyman, W.N.
89	Economic Grocers
95	Karels, B.
99	Brown, G.
---	Seymour Street
101	Credrass, I.
103	Toyer, M. Supply Store
---	Mitchell Street
105	Ebrahim, --
109	Maynar, --
111	Nainar, T.
---	Bullen Street
115	Oxhide Boot & Shoe Repairing
115	Daya, K.
117	Prince, J.I.
119	George, A.
---	Coode Street
127	Naidoo, S.
127	Non-European Apostolic Church
---	Forest Hill Road

LEFT

---	South Beach Terrace
2	Hindu Primary School
2a	Naidoo, S.N.
6	Fleur, D.J.
8	Williams, M.A.
10	Frederick, J.
14	Meenachee, V.
18	Logardien
20	Moothoo, L.
24	Rademeyer, A.
---	Chase Street
26	Khaki, R.
---	South Union Street

28	Jaylarnie, M.
42	Kahn, A.
46	Abdulla, M.
48	Narotham, D.
48	Bansdas Bargin Store
52	Naidoo, P.
54	Potgieter, G.
54a	Abrahams, A.
---	Thomas Street
60	Kayster, D.K.
62	McDillion, D.
64	Kayster, D.K.
66	Heeneh, M.
68	Davids, A.
---	Gardner Street
74	Lala Jenna
76	Cassin, E.
76	Abrahams, K.
78	Lindstrom, B.E.
80	Pilley Kay Fruiterers
80	Bhagwan, P.
82	P.B. Stores (Pty)Ltd
82	Velloo Fruiterers
82	Bhagwan's Indian Records
---	Seymour Street
84	Brown, G.
88	Rockman, A.
88a	Simons, F.
90	Allen, J.
96	Chetty, S.M.
98	Dickerson, --
98	Abdullah, G.
---	Mitchell Street
100	Bonnesse, J.J.
100	Padayochee, V.V.
102	Abrahams, G.
106	Govindasamy, H.
108	Mallick, F.
110	De Maine, I.
112	Begg, M.H.
112a	Begg
114	Tayler, E.
114a	Moodaley, C.
116	Turner, J.
116a	Frieslaar, J.
118	STSimons, L.
120	Madatt, C.
134	Kader, I.
---	Bullen Street
---	Coode Street
	Bell, J.R.
	Union Church
---	Forest Hill Road

ST MARYS LANE

1	Benjamin, L.C.
1	Ross, C.
2	Phillips, E.
2	Rajappens, J.
3	Broyat, I.
4	Jamal, M.
5	Gradwell, J.

ST. MARYS STREET
RIGHT

---	South Union Street
1	Jones, w.J.
3	Van Rooyen, A. & Son (Pty) Ltd.
5	Merrit, K.F.

LEFT

2	Phillips, E.
4	Jamal, M.
---	South Union Street

SCOTT STREET
RIGHT

---	Pier Street
31	Commercial Fisheries
---	Walmer Road

LEFT

---	Pier Street

6	Muthayan, R.M.
8	Copper, G.
10	Vorster, A.L.
12	Titus, J.
14	Freeman, S.
18	Ital Steel Works (Pty)Ltd
---	Walmer Road.

SEYMOUR LANE

1	Diedricks, C.
1a	Wilson, R.A.
2	Pillay, V.S.
4	Loggenberg, G.

SEYMOUR STREET
RIGHT

---	Alfred Road
1	Harding, Miss M.
1a	Wilson, R.A.
5	Van Staden, A.J.
---	Donald Street
---	Rock Street
13	Pappas, M.
---	Pier Street
17	Bhana, N.
19	Davies, A.
21	Fourie, J.C.
23	Meyer, K.
25	Dorasamy, N.
---	Mitchell Lane
27	Weitsz, A.
29	Du Randt, F.L.
31	Swanepoel, P.
35	Williams, a.
35a	Williams, A.
37	Bardien, J.
39	Joel, A.
41	Mahomed, H.M.
43	Hendricks, I.
---	Walmer Road
47a	Moodley, N.
47b	Nathans Fresh Fish Supplies
---	Rudolph Street
51	Karels, A.
53	Brown, A.
57	Raban, A.
---	Carter's Lane
59	Coopysamy, S.
63	Ryneveld, I.
---	Farie Street

LEFT

---	Alfred Road
2	Padayachy, M.
4	Verral, A.E.
---	Donald Street
---	Rock Street
6	Myburgh, W.L.
6a	Spicer, Mrs G.
6a	Ellington, G.
---	Pier Street
8	Burger, A.N.
10	Gillbe, W.C.
12	Worthington, J.P.
14	Nel, I.T.
16	Murphy, W.
18	Smith, F.G.
---	Walmer Road
28	Williams, H.
28	Bansda, J.F.
30	Moodley, M.
32	Pillay, S.
34	Terblanche, G.
36	Gallant, F.
38	Soeker, S.
40	White, S.
---	Rudolph Street
48	Hendricks, W.S.
52	Pillay, B.
54	Lingham, M.
56	Jackson, D.
---	Farie Street.

SIMPSON STREET
RIGHT
--- Armstrong Street
1 Botha,J.H.
3 Coskey, Mrs.K.
5 Arendse,L.C.
7 Smith,S.S.
9 Vermaak,J.J.
--- Bridge Street
LEFT
--- Armstrong Street
2 Burmeister,H.
4 Canterbury,A.W.
4a Canterbury,A.W.
6a Smith,C.H.J.
8 Terblanche,P.
10 Swart,A.H.
12 Bezuidenhout,J.A.
14 Whitley,P.O.
--- Bridge Street

SOUTH BEACH TERRACE
RIGHT
--- Pier Street
1 Sanitas
15 Muthayan, V.
15a Muthayan Car Exchange
17 Cassim, A.
19 Padday, M.S.
21 Langford, A.
23 Mohamed, S.
25 Pillay, G.
25a Coopoosamy, C.M.
29 Jinnah, E.
39 Pillay, M.
--- Walmer Road
41 Freeman, J.H.
41a Loggenberg, M.
Muthayans Car Exchange
--- Stream Street
Hindu Primary School
--- Rudolph Street
LEFT
Satama (Pty)Ltd

SOUTH UNION STREET
RIGHT
--- Valley Road
13 Delbro Flats
13 M.V. Electrical
15 Fourie, W.P.
15 Sonop Vars Vrugte en Groente
15b Lang, Dr. N.
17 Makan Bhana
17 National Wholesalers
17a Makan's Bargain Store
--- St. Mary's Lane
19 Mankowitz, General Dealer
21 Esterhuizen, S.
23 Lingham, R.
25 Fakir, G.
25 Jamal's, Barber
25 Jamal's, Barber
27 Agherdien Tailors
29 S.E. Pharmacy
33 Olgas Fish & Chips
35 Everybody Stores
37 Rosenberg's Dress Shop
39 Rudolph'S Store
39a Koen,C.
--- Pier Street
41a Rautenbach,M.L.
41b Langford,A.
43 Springbok Cycle Bazaar
43 Premium Wholesalers (Pty) Ltd
45 Low Ah Kee
49 Roxy Milk Bar
51 Pamensky & Co

53a Palace Cinema
55 Economy Cleaners
55 Palace Fruiters
57 Favourite Cleaners
61 Du Plesis,C.J.
63 Algoa Timbers(Pty)Ltd
69 Eric's Goods Supply Store
71 Reject stores
75 Wong, P.N. General Dealer.
--- Walmer Raod
79 Union Butchery
79a Ganey,S.A.
81 Mahida's General Dealer
83 Ranchod,U.
87 Iswa Motors.
91 Midway Dealers Cafe
91a Davids,M.
93 Tong Wah
--- Rudolph Street
Friendly City Service Station
95 Pillay, D.
101 Humerail Service Station
--- Farie Street
LEFT
--- Baakens Street
6 Van Rensburg, L.J.
--- South Beach Terrace
22 Krost Bros. (Pty)Ltd
24 Botha, P.F.
24 Crafford & Marais
26 Coral Ann Products
28 Bring & Buy Agencies
30 Volpe's Drapery
32 Metro Outfitters
32 Raga, H.D.
34 Mackay, J.R.
36 Meyer, H.B.
36 M. & M. Upholsterers
36a Kee, Son & Co.
40 Greeff's Garage
--- Pier Street
52 Freeway Motors (Pty)Ltd
54 Union House
62 Greenbushes farmers' Dairy
64a Wiblin & co.
66 Baise, N., tailor
68 Tyrone Hotel
--- Walmer Road
74 Collins' Hotel
Braak Wine & Brandy Co. (Pty)Ltd
--- Stream Street
Evans & Sons, Showyard
--- Rudolph Street
--- Bowman Street

SPRIGG LANE
(Off Sprigg Street)
RIGHT
--- Forest Hill Road
1 David's D.
1 Van Rensburg, R.S.
3 Davids, M.T.
5 Jappie, A.
7 Rasdien, A.
~
9 Jappie, D.
11 Tobias, Mrs E.
13 Fitzgibbon, E.N.
13a Jenneker, F.C.
13b Malapermal, P.
15 Bagley, E.
17 Nordien, M.
19 Marriday, Mrs F.
--- Armstrong Street
21 Dolley, R.

23 Bowers, S.
25 Jardien, J.S.
27 Wolfraadt, G.S.
29 Mostert, N.W.
31 Van Onselen, R.W.
33 Ingram, J.
35 Sefedien, F.
37 Barth, Mrs J.L.
39 Botha, A.S.
41 Van Rensburg, P.
43 Kannemeyer, a.E.G.
Moslem School
63 Abrahams, M.
65 Bloew, C.
67 Agherdien, E.
69 Bekker, D.F.
--- Randall Street
LEFT
--- Forest Hill Road Playgrounds
--- Armstrong Stree:
22 Woolard, A.
24 Whitley, C.
26 Francis, A.
28 Nel, R.
30 Bezuidenhout, D.W.
30 William's Taxi Service
30a Bezuidenhout, H.
30b Le Roux, J.M.
22 Woolard, A.
24 Whitley, C.
26 Francis, A.
28 Nel, R.
30 Bezuidenhout, D.W.
30 William's Taxi Service
30a Bezuidenhout, H.
30b Le Roux, J.M.
32 Augustine, L.
32 Price, A.
32 Flynn, G.
32a Davis, J.
32b Ferreira, F.M.
34 Brink, J.
36 Polonia, F.A.
36a Vorster, L.F.
38 Essop, M.M.
38a Ccalvert, E.R.
40 Katzen, --
42 Adams, M.
42-44 Taljaard, J.J.Z.
44 Algoa Builders (Pty)Ltd
46 Du Preez, P.J.
46a Hendricks, L.P.
48 Padayachee, N.
48a Muthayan, K.
50 Michael, F.
52 Brown, A.H.
54 Scholtz, Mrs G.
56 Ludwig, A.L.
58 Smith, G.W.
60 Alfonso, Pl
68 Bruce, G.
70 Rockman, A.J.
72 Prince, M.
74 Prinsloo, H.
--- Randall Street

STREAM STREET
RIGHT
--- South Beach Terrace
5 David, F.
7 Kahaar, A.
15 Kleinveldt, T.
17 Booysen, K.
19 Marcus, L.
21 Nordien, H.J.
23 Pietersen, N.
25 September, A.
27 Connely, T.
29 Khan, A.I.

31	Kahn, E.A.
33	Babooo, N.
---	Chase Street
	LEFT
---	South Beach Terrace
2	Muthayan, U.
6	Uldimans, G.M.
6	Muthayan, R.N.
8	Cooper, G.
10	Vons
14	Sataar, R.
16	Sectaar, F.
18	assam, G.
20	Maude, General Dealer
24	Manon, H.A.
26	Abrahams, A.
---	South Union Street
28	Adams, A.K.
30	Cupp, C.

STROMBERG STREET
RIGHT

---	Wyndham Street
1	Du Plessis, C.J.
3	Van der Berg, J.
5	Thomson, N.A.
	LEFT
---	Wyndham Street
2	Daniel, E.L.
4	Watson, Mrs W.
6	Grobler, Mrs N.
6a	Nicholas, A.

THOMAS STREET
RIGHT

---	Walmer Road
1	Ah Kee, A.T.
3	Madhoo, M.
7	Naidoo, S.B.
9	Naidoo, S.R.
11	Lagerdien, A.M.
11a	Matthys, V.
13	Abrahams, R.
13	McBean, H.
19	Mallick, E.M.
23	Hendricks, P.
25	Pather, M.M.
	Pillay, N.
27	Abrahams, J.
---	Thomas Lane
	LEFT
---	Walmer Road
2	Samdam, A.
4	Padaychy, M.
4a	Moodaly, T.
6	Ramsamy, C.
8	Sam, a.
10	Ismail, H.
12	Ranchod, R.
20	Demaar, G.
---	Rudolph Street

UPPER PIER STREET
RIGHT

---	Bullen Street
	Clinic
39	Mare, F.
41	Pagel, E.R.
41a	Stevens, J.M
43	Verrall, W.F.
45	Thompson, G.
47	Barber, A.
49	Naidoo, C.P.
49a	Naidoo, T.R.
51	Adams, F.
51a	McTavish, Mrs K.
51b	Van Staten, H.B.
53	Rinters, S.M.
55	Rainier, L.C.
55a	Pieterse, C.J.
67	Abdullah, H.M.
69	Abdullah, K.

71	Smith, H.H.
73	Bentley, D.V.
73	Verwey, I.M.
75	Barriera, G.
77-79	Sacred Hearth Catholic School.
81	Hebler, H.
83	Van Jaarsveld, A.T.
---	Armstrong Street
85	Pohlman, R.
87	Marais, S.E.
89	Derbyshire, E.W.
91	Venter, H.T.
95	Phillis, --
97	South End Sheet Metal works.
99	Peters, H.P.
101	Yon Lee
103	Struwig, M.T.
105	Vassen, N.
---	Bridge Street,
	LEFT
---	Bullen Street
72	Plunket Hall Dutch Reform Church South End R.C. Primary School.
---	Kenny Street St.Monicas School Church
76	Rev Cole
76	Plunkett, B.O.
---	Bunn Street
78	Whalley, C.D.
80	Howarth, R.M.
82	Sutton, J.A.
84	Niemand, N.
86	Larsen, Mrs. F.
88	Koekemoer, D.
90	Wassman, H.N.
90a	Nawdish, E.D.
92	Vermaak, J.J.
92a	Howard, Mrs. J.
94	Meyer, H.
96	Lock, J.
98	Hanekom, G.
100	Meyer, C.P.
102	Mweyer, B.
102a	Kafaar, G.
104	Meyer, F.C.
106	Van Antwerpen, F.R.
108	Swart, C.C.B.
---	Armstrong Street
110	Hough, D.C.
112	Emanuel, E.J.
114	Johnson, C.P.
116	Hanekom, J.G.
118	Barkhuizen, D.
118a	Tee, F.M.
120	Murphy, D
122	Nel, R.R.
124	Groener, A.
128	Bester, P.J.
130	Juta, J.W.
130	Burgoyne, R.J.
132	Allison, W.
	Human, P.C.J.
---	Bridge Street

UPPER VALLEY ROAD
RIGHT

---	Valley Road Algoa Glassworks(Pty) Ltd. Stuttaford Storage and Van Lines. Alabaster Street
1	Associated Hemmers
---	Ellis Street
7	Claasen, J.H.
9	Low Ah Kee, J.
11	Indian Temple. Imperial Steam Laundry

15	Barnard P.J.
17	Chivers, R.S.
19	Zeelie, S.J.
21	Wilson, E.J.
---	Bridge Street Vacant Site
---	Barnes Street
29-39	Non European Baptist church
35	Hartel, T.r.
37	Slowitch, d.
41a	Eunson, B.
---	Alexander Terrace
71	Venter, J.J.
73	Van Rooyen, O.B.
75	Knighton, D.S.
77	Bagley, E.
81	Inch, H.W.
83	Dickson, A.
85	Green, w.
---	Webber Street
	LEFT
2	Talbot, B.
4	Impey, A.G.
6	Gill, F.
8	Bothma, --
8a	Victor, J.
10	Le Roux, A.J.
10a	Stroebel, S.F.
12	Diedricks, H.J.J.
16	Hechter, F.J. Emsley Cottages
1	Strydom, N.H.L.
2	Welgemoed, A.
3	Van As, N.
4	Keyser, B.
5	Van As, J.
18	Rautenbach, I.A.
20	Williamson, J.E.
22	Heaton, Mrs. L.C.
24	Le Grange, J.
26a	Ferreira, Mrs L.
28	Sneyd, M.I.
28a	Diedricks, J.J.
30	Gerber, A.L.
32	Stander, H.J.
---	Alabaster Street
34	Wallenstein, A.
36	Du Plessis, S.G.
38	Mullagen, L.
40	Kilian, H.J.
42	Katman, S.
44	Harmse, G.
46	Grobler, J.
---	Ellis Street
52	Oelofse, Ak.
54	Groenewald, M.C.
56	Burchell, G.
56	Cole, M.
56a	Dolley, A.M.
---	Bridge Street Abel Court, P.
62	Popular Fruiterers
62	Pillay, V.M.
66	Butler, R.
68	Arendse, A.P.
70	Gerber, H.H.
72	George, R.
74	George, G.
76	Gresham Steam Laundry
78	Layson, L.L.
80	Athiemoolan G. & Co.
84	Appasamy, S.S.
90	Knipp, E.
94	Black, J.W.
98	Bailey, F.L.
100	Black, R.G.
102	Crossland, J.W.
108	Aroguisamy, P.
---	Wyndham Road
120	Mentz, E.A. Victory Bottle Store
---	Webber Street

VALLEY ROAD
RIGHT

---	South Union Street
	Tram Sheds
	Cnr. Mangold
	Machina.Ltd.
---	Lower Valley Road.
5	Hattingh,W.
7	Bezuidenhout,B.
9	Neptune Chemicals.
21	Van Vuuren,P.J.J.
23	Erasmus,P.
25	Rupertsburg.
27	Niksch,D.
29	Nel,W.
31	Knight,W.
39	One Day Cleaners
41	Botha,J.H.
43	Stydom,G.P.
45	Beer,J.
47	Brown,C.J.E.
51	Vosloo,B.
55	Stander,H.J.
55a	Gerber.--
57	Stander Car Part's
---	Bridge over Baakens River.
	Continues as Bricmaker's Kloof.

LEFT

---	South Union street
---	Alfred Road
---	Upper Valley Road.
	Disca(pty) Ltd
---	Alabaster Street
16	S.A. Druggist.
---	Ellis Street
22	Stokes, O.
24	Swartz, C.P.
26	Posthumus, N.P.
28	Meiring, J.D.
30	Paton, P.
32	Greef, D.
34	Van Rensburg (Mrs L) 36 Kapp,W.C.
54	Butcher The
52	Oelofse,J.J. Butcher
78	Loyson,L.L.
80	Athiemmoolan,G.
	Shield Insurance Co Ltd
	Cape Coach Tours Co Ltd
	P.E.Passenger Transport Ltd.
	Baakens Passenger Transport Ltd

VICTORIA PARK DRIVE
RIGHT

---	Duncan Avenue
1	Van der Plaat, J.
3	Visser, C.J.
5	Fowlds, H.L.
7	Holton, R.C.
9	Hinde, M.
11	Dalton, F.E.
13	Carlton, M.L.
15	Adams, J.S.
17	Brewis, G.J.D.
17a	Wassman, E.N.
---	Hoy Avenue
19	Armstrong, L.J.
21	Naude, F.P.
23	Hardiman, E.
25	Claasen, B.J.
27	Wildman, S.
29	Rosling, E.M.
31	Alvarez, P.E.
33	Phelan, C.R.
35	Breytenbach, E.S.
37	Van de Venter, C.F.
---	Butters Avenue
41	Shepheard, W.G.

43	Gottschalk, J.M.
43	Stevenson, C.W.
43	Goldsmith, Mrs C.
43	York, J.
43a	Ward, A.J.
45	Werson, A.M.
45	Iverson, V.
47	Page, H.P.A.
49	Pohl, Miss J.
51	Dangers, E.
51	Lindstrom, A.M.
57	Morris, F.A.
---	Partridge Avenue
59	Kennedy, J.G.
61	Apartment House
63	O'donoghue, G.J.
65	Urton, N.
67	Barwood, D.R.
69	Alvarez, V.G.
71	Foxcroft, P.
71	Shaw, O.T.
73	Mayberry
75	Jonker, G.J.
77	Thorpe, J.S.
---	First Avenue, Walmer

LEFT

---	Duncan Avenue
	Victoria Park
	Victoria Park High School
---	First Avenue, Walmer

WALMER ROAD
(South End)
RIGHT

---	South Beach Terrace
1	Copoho, W.
3	Jobson, A.
3A	Boyce, F.
---	Scott Street
	Tyrone Bottle Store
---	South Union Street
7	Velkers, I.
9	Ginaud, G.
9a	Adams, A.
9a	Tifloen Tapie Safari Transport
11	Sing, For. W.O.
21	Apex Stores
21a	P.E. Bring & Buy Agencies
23	Francis, H.
23	Markedien, --
25	Johaar, E.
25	Andy's Taxi Service
27	Ransons Outfitters
29	Ranco Distributors
33	Appavoo, Dr. S.V.
---	Love Street
39	Davids Bros.
41	Donckerer, M.
	Web Recreation Club House, The
43	Standard Bank
43	Makan's building
45	Bhana, M.
---	Gardner Street
47	Bhanam M.
---	Seymour Street
49	Ideal Hairdressing Saloon
51	Spotless Dry Cleaners
51	Chozette, J.
53	Naidoo, R.G.
55	Ideal Fruiterers
---	Mitchell Street
63	Finro Enterprises
	Savahl, M.G.
67	Davis, Joe, hardware
67e	Entomological Services
67f	Litchfield Enterprises
	Kingdom Hall
---	Bullen Street
	Petra Hall
---	Kennedy Street

69	Parshotam, C.M. Shoe Repairs
71	Parshotam, S.
71	Ace Outfitters
71 XL	Fruit Depot
	Blessed Oliver Plunkett Parish
---	Bunn Street
	Andrade Building
85	Walmer Exchange Centre
85	Steyn, A.D.
87	Warwick's Radio
87	Atlas Cleaners and Dyers Ltd
87a	Eclipse Cleaners
89a	Villinger, R.A.
91	Daya, V.
91	Valla, D. & Son
95	Industrial Electrical Engnrs.
95	Mittechelli, S.
95a	Crugwagen, W.A.
97	Tyrone Bottle Store
99	Mooljee, M.
99	Popular Shoe Repairers
101	Channon, C.F.
103	South End Post Office
103	De Andrade, A.
105	Bailey, C.
107	Ferreira, A.
109	Meyer, N.P.
111	Davids, J.
113	Lee Ching & sons
115	Dowers, E.A.
---	Armstrong Street
117	Thomas, J.D.
119	Cape Magazine Co.
121	Herbst, A.P.
125a	Umleys, P.B., footwear specialists
127	Du Plessis, B.J.
129	Greeff, M.D.M.
131	Van der Walt, E.
133	Bosch, N.K.
137	Coopoo, S.
139	Moljee, M.
141	Scott, M.C.
143	Olivier, G.J.
145	Daya, P. & Sons
145a	Bosch, B.P.
---	Bridge Street
147	Imperial Butchery
147a	Daya, R.
---	Miller Street
151a	Ranchod, E.
151a	Emperor Cafe
153	Maken, M.
---	Kinsley Kloof
155	Black Mystery Packing Co.
155	Phillips, G.E.
155	Gerletts (Pty)Ltd
157	Marais, M.
159	Enslin, J.W.
161	Van Eck, G.
161a	Almanza, O.N.
163	Pohls Butchery
163	Calders Bottle Store
	Southern Court
165	Haggard, J.B.
167	Donaldson, A.F.
169	Ball, S.W.
171	Roux, D.J.
173	Robert, C.D,
173	Buyers and Sellers
175	Du Preez, J.T.
---	Webber Street
177	Niemand Bros. (Pty)Ltd
177	Triangle Service Station
179	Devitt, Mrs F.
181	Smith, J.
183	Renshaw, E.H.
185	Barkhuizen, F.

187	Nicholson, T.
189	Boyce, H.
191	Bereira, M.
193	Du Plessis, L.F.
195	Moens, H.E.
197	Joubert, J.J.
199	Watson, C.
201	Grobbelaar, F.
203	Morrison, H.G.
205	Candido, F.M.
207	Doyle, J.E.
209	Gerber, J.
211	Wittstock, O.E.
213	Loggenberg,E.R.
215	Bryden,W.
217	Boyce,R.E.
219	Bryoen,C.D.
221	Sampson,D.C.
223	Bradshaw,J.g.
225	Thompson,G.
227	Stokes, Mrs. D.E.
229	Scott, C.B.
231	Shell, O.
233	Nel, C.P.
235	Du Preez, C.J.
237	Rolyat Flats
243	Lindstroom, B.E.
---	Weetwood Road
	LEFT
---	South Beach Terrace
4	Dollie, A.
6	Anderson, T.
8	Naidoo, S.
8a	Mace, S.
10	Plaatjies, J.
10a	Dace, J.
12	Nunkar, D.
14	Naidoo, S.R.
18	Ricketts, J.
20	Francis, P.D.
30	Collins Hotel
---	South Union Street
32	Harmse, C.
32	Van Dayar, P.S.
36	Baboo, A.
40	Chetty, M., gen. dlr.
40	Barry, C.M.
42	Moodaley, S.R.
44	Madhoo, N., Shoe repr.
46	The Vanyagaw Vandayar
46	Moolow, J.
46	Imperial Social Club
---	Thomas Street
48	Low Ah Kee, A.T.
52	Du Preez, M.
56	La Continental Studio
58	Makans, I.P.
60	Makans Investments (Pty)Ltd
62	Hurst, J.
64	Smith, s.
72	Makan's footwear Specialist
74	Makan Bhana & Sons
76	Bhana, M.
78	Pillay, V. & Son
78	E.P. Rubber Stamp Co.
84	Prince of Wales Hotel
---	Gardner Street
92	Nisha, R.
92	Kim Sing, W.
98	Bhanas Outfitters
98	Rio Outfitters
---	Seymour Street
100	Algoa Cash Butchery
100	Mahomed Ishmail & Co.
102	Reddy, V.
102a	Davis, H.A.
104	Rio Outfitters
104a	Cummings, M.
106	Chetty, Mrs M.S.
106	Walmer Rd. Fresh Fish Supplies

109	Raga, D.a.
108	Toyer, M.
110	For Lee, gen. dlr.
110	For Lee
110	Andrews, J.H.
---	Mitchel Street
118	Ismail's Outfitting Store
118	Ebreham, I.
120	Jaftha, f.
120a	Excelsior Burchery
122a	Finro Enterprises
126	D. Khoosal & Sons
128	Chetty, A.
128	Remos, K.E.
128	Reddy's Cafe
132	Jack, Kee & Co., Y.C.
132	De Luxe Foods
---	Bullen Street Baptist Church
134	Henman, R.F.
136	Botha, C.L.
136	Eliates, R.K.
138	Heenen, M.
140	Kingon, F.O.
140	Carter, J.
142	Oxford Butchery
142a	Barcelence Store
144	Pinto, M.D.S.
144a	Hcdges, J.
146	Jones, E.
146	Nayacar, A.C.
148	Jack Kee
148	Escott, A.B.
148	Campbell, V.
---	Coode Street
150	Walmer Road Filling Station
---	Forest Hill Road
152	Pillay Bros.
152	Walmer Road fruit Store
154	Hansen, J.J.
156	Silver Lantern
156	Jorgensen Photographic Service
158	Jorgensen, A.A.
166	Du Plessis, I.V.0
166	Senekal, J.J.
160	Gouws, H.J.
160	Kasbah Restaurant,The.
164	Cooper, L.
168	Gouws, H.L.
170	Doyle, C.
172	Clarke, R.E.
174	Liebenberg, D.C.
176	Gouws, J.W.
178	Zaaiman, W.P.
---	Armstrong Street
184	Horman, A.
186	Cassin, M.
188	Brown, E.H.
188a	Isaacs, I.
190	Royal Butchery
192	Cassim, M.
194	Cassim & Son, M.
196	Minaar, P.
198	Salvador, M.
200	Olivier, F.T.J.
202	Rooikruis Tehuis vir Verswakte
202-204	Karoo estate Agents
204	Bonthuys, F.J.
206	Surf Shop, The
208	Doraswami, G.
208	Service Supply Store
208	Croft Cleaners & Steam Launderers
210	Welch, M.A.
212	Hurn, A.J.
214	Atlas Dry Cleaners
214	Good Hope Pool Services
214	Thelmyr Flats
214	Kwik Cleaners
214	Barksole Shoes
214	Goodhope Pharmacy

214b	Algoa Butchery
214a	Saker's Good Hope Pharmacy
216	Du Preez, C.D.
220	Chelsea Dairy
222	Barnard, C.J.
226	Ritz Restaurant
226	Ramasamy, M.M.
228	Robertson's Mineral Water Mnfrs.
228	Nel. V.
230	Fone, V.C.
232	A.L. Stores
234	On Hing
236	Gamieldien, M.
236	Banana Gardens
236	Gee Dee's Cafe
236a	Wellington Fruiterers
238a	Van Loggerenberg,W.H.
240	Ah Kun
244	Ah Kun
---	Randall Street
250	Evans, C.H. & Son
252	Evans & Son, C.H.
254	Gannakis, P.
254	Carton Barber, A.L.
254	Nel, S.M.
258	Elite Cafe
258	Elite Fruiters
260	Apartment House
260	Du Preez, F.G.
260	Atlas Cleaners & Dyers
260	Duthie, Mrs A.M.
260	Henry, E.
262	Smith, S.W.
262a	Concalves, --
264	Terblanche, H.P.
266	Erasmus, E.V.
268	Finlayson, --
268	Art Florist
270	Smith, A.D.
272	Young, M.S.
---	Butters Avenue
280	"Monte Carlo"
284	"Casino"
284a	Cantina
286	Bownes, W.
286	Bolleurs, J.M.
288	Liebach, W.
288	"Elite Court"
292	Vermaak, C.S.
294	Wells H.A.F.
296	Van De Weide, W.G.P.
---	Partridge Avenue
298	Lockhat, Mrs N.T.
300	Evans, S.J.
302	Kleingeld, J.H.
304	Longmore, H.C.
306	Teasdale, A.
308	Whitehead, C.W.
310	Bushby, A.
312	Panayioton, C.
314	Gustafsson, C.J.A.
316	Baptist Church
---	First Avenue, Walmer

WEBBER STREET
RIGHT

---	Walmer Road Alting's Garage Swanepoel, D.M. v.d.B.
1	Roe, K.f.
3	Mew, S.J.
3	Meyer, H.
5	Ward, E.M.
7	Bentley, B.M.
9	Danielson, H.P.
11	Roebert, A.D.
13	Grobler, G.E.
15	Le Roux, E.O.
---	Balfour Street
23	Sherborne, K.E.

27	Thyssen, V.C.		(South End)		39 VICTORIA PARK	
29	Howell, D.C.		*RIGHT*		DRIVE	
31	Marks, H.R.	---	Balfour Street	1	Jones, w.	
33	Van Antwerpen, M.J.	7	Bailey, H.W.	2	Roos, r.	
35	Sanders, C.H.	9	Cockroft, H.C.	3	Meyer, G.C.	
37	Shortland, D.	---	Stromberg Street	4	Brodie, M.E.	
39	Van der Westhuizen, L.E.	11	Wood, P.	5	Green, R.B.	
---	Anderson Street			6	Ledingham, D.	
43	Long, E.R.	13	Askew, E.J.	7	Laivort, J.	
45	Billett, G.M.	15	Anderholt, H.J.	8	Reynolds, B.O.	
45a	Van der Swanepoel, D.M.	---	Anderson Street			
47	Daniels, M.J.		*LEFT*		CANTINA	
49	Schaefer, P.	---	Kinsley Kloof		284A WALMER ROAD	
51	Marais, F.F.	6	Van Onselen, G.P.	1	Stevens, B.H.	
53	Langford, R.F.	6a	Cockcroft, R.C.	2	Fourie, N.L.	
55	Schierz-Cruscus, R.	8	Koetzee, J.P.Z.	3	Russell, E.L.	
55	Dibbins, W.	10	Jonson, S.G.	4	Whiteley, P.D.	
57	Doller, E.H.	12	Zaaiman, R.	5	Salazar, J.M.	
59	Henry, A.G.	14	Struwig, C.A.	6	Austin, N.	
61	Brent, L.P.	16	Geyer, Mrs A.E.	7	Durant, L.A.	
63	Geber, T.J.	8	Kotze, P.J.	8	van Breda, L.S.	
63	Venter, J.M.	20	Burger, W.P.			
65	Victory Delicatessen	22	Jonson, E.B.		CASINO	
65	Victory Bottle Store	24	Duthie, L.		284 WALMER ROAD	
65a	Daniel, N.	26	Bester, S.E.	1	Van der Berg,C.C.	
---	Upper Valley Road	28	Strydom, G.	1	Rodocamachi,G.	
69	Schafer, B.	---	Balfour Street	2	Chamen, J.B.	
71	Scheepers, C.E.	32	Kitching, J.W.	3	Chierichini, G.	
73	Scheepers, C.F.	34	Gerber, A.G.	5	Spies,P.B.	
---	Gladstone Street	36	Blewett, T.J.	6	Victor,K.R.	
75	Terblanche, F.	38	Martin, J.C.		CO0DE BUILDINGS	
75	McCartan, B.	40	Brown, H.M.		CORNER WALMER AND	
75	Carr, H.	42	Musgrave, C.B.		FOREST HILL ROAD	
75	Alting, P.	44	Gerber, F.J.	2	Ferreira, J.	
75	Webber Street	46	Paul, M.S.S.	3	Hastings, M.L.	
Supermarket		48	Barreira, J.	4	Roberts, A.O.	
75	Sharwoods (Pty)Ltd	48	Gerber, F.B.	5	De Villiers, J.	
75	Nick's Cafe	50	Hedderklick, R		Radio Paramount	
	Sharwood's Service Station	---	Anderson Street			
---	Weetwood Road	52	Brown, Mrs L.		ELITE COURT	
		52	Van der Berg, P.H.		292 WALMER ROAD	
WEETWOOD ROAD		54	Van der Berg, --	1	Roberts, R.V.	
	RIGHT	56	Channon, N.W.	3	Williams, S.	
	Victoria Park Grey	58	Stevens, M.C.	4	Meyers, S.	
	Junior School	58a	Parker, W.H.	5	Foxcroft, E.K.	
~		60	Forbes, H.A.	6	Gray, D.	
---	Walmer Road	62	Stevenson, A.F.	7	Shinley, L.F.	
	Altings Garage	64	Colley, B.M.	8	Williams, D.	
---	Webber Street	64	Watson, J.	9	Koen, G.E.	
	Sharwoods	66	Wright, P.M.	10	Woolard, E.K.	
3	Dempsey, Miss W.S.	68	De Jong, M.	11	Moss, W.H.	
5	Storan, T.	70	MacPherson, E.	12	Johannessen, C.J.	
7	Bruton, K.	72	Diedericks, N.D.			
9	Baldie, A.	74	Brown, M.L.		GABRY	
11	Buchanan, R.	---	Upper Valley Road		77 VICTORIA PARK	
15	Jeacocks, E.D.				DRIVE	
15a	Dyer, B.P.		ABEL COURT	1	Moorhouse, F.	
17	Pisanie, H.J.du.		*1 BRIDGE STREET*	2	McLagan, R.A.	
19	Zaaiman, J.H.	1	Du Plessis,g.		LIEBAND COURT	
23	Fowkes, S.J.	2	Swiegelaar,M.		61 VICTORIA PARK DRIVE	
25	De Wet, J.S.	2	Bester,E.	1	Hall,P.J.W.	
27	Bradley, W.S.	3	Adlam,D.J.	2	Deacon,S.M.	
29	Pienaar, --	4	Barnard, Mrs.J.	3	Sousa,Mrs M.L.	
31	Knysna Flats	5	Butler,K.F.	4	Evans,D.H.	
---	Baakens Valley	6	Hamilton,J.J.	5	Stephen,R.D.	
		7	Potgieter,T.I.	6	Coss,R.E.	
	WEBBERS ROAD	8	Lombard,B.L.	7	Swanepoel,H.B.	
		2	Mills Gift Shop	8	Wessels,H.J.	
1	Adams, H.			10	Lloyd,W.J.	
2	Pillay, M.N.		ANDRADE BUILDING	12	Dekker,J.H.	
3	Pond, T.		85 WALMER ROAD			
4	Bhana, N.		Ccropolis Cafe		LYCLO BUILDING	
8	Bhana, N.	1	Charles,---		Farie Street	
		2	Cefalco,J.		Watson Printing	
	WYNDHAM LANE	4	Villinger,R.A.		International Dresses (Pty) Ltd	
					The Times	
2	Muller, N.D.		BALFOUR COTTAGES		Menter's Refrigeration	
2	Dixon, G.		Balfour Street		Floray Clothing	
4	Hendricks, H.	1	Foce,J		Manufacturers.	
6	Damerell, C.	3	Godfrey,H.R.		Union Distributors.	
		4	Nortjie,C.J.			
					MAKAN'S BUILDING	
	WYNDHAM STREET		**BO PEEP FLATS**		CORNER WALMER ROAD	

AND GARDNER STREET
FIRST FLOOR
2 Hendricks, H.M.
Cape HERALD (Pty)Ltd
5 Assemblies of God (non European Section)
6 Davids, A.
SECOND FLOOR
14 Hendricks G.N.
Morkans

MON REPOS FLATS
BUTTERS AVENUE, VICTORIA PARK
1 Heunis, H.
2 Sliep, H.
3 Sponneck, P.E.
4 Barnard, Ck.J.
5 Morris, L.A.
6 Smith, A.L.
7 Roux, J.R.
8 Jute, R.J.
9 Bruton, K.A.
10 Cartwright, R.J.
11 Fodor, K.
12 Spies, P.B.

MONACO
280 WALMER ROAD
1 Pineda, C.
2 Doyle, T.B.
3 Bonthuys, W.B.
4 Nel, D.D.
5 Stols, G.H.
6 Van Rooyen, G.
7 Wilke, L.
8 Vazques, J.L.B.

MONTE CARLO FLATS
280 WALMER ROAD
1 Martch, H.
2 Boshoff, C.J.
3 Thompson, M.G.
4 Labuschagne, C.D.
5 Sinclair, J.B.
6 Van Schalkyk, T.N.
7 Elsley, C.R.
8 Van Rooyen, P.S

MONTE CHRISTO
59 VICTORIA PARK DRIVE
1 Roberts, J.W.
2 Blewett, T.J.
3 Bareira, R.K.
5 Whitnall, G.B.M.
6 Smith, N.H.
7 Baretti, G.L.
8 Lerm, J.J

NAOMI COURT
9 Pier Street
1 Bosch,J.B.
2 Blignaot,P.A.
3 Jordaan,P.
4 Van Staden,
5 Van Niekerk,H.S.
6 Koekemoer,N.
7 Thorsen,T.R.M.
8 Pople,C.E.
9 Gouws,Mrs J.F.
10 Westraat,J.H.A.
11 Watson,L.C.

PARK PLAZA
53-57VICTORIA PARK DRIVE

101 Ower, J.
102 Erasmus, J.N.
103 Naude, J.W.
104 Schafer, B.
105 Smith, R.A.
201 Watkins, E.

202 Faure, M.N.A.
203 Van Rooyen, L.
204 Bowen, K.
205 Kimpton, W.F.
301 Shepheard, A.J.
302 Francis, A.M.A.
303 Henning, P.T.
304 Van der Walt, J.J.
305 Petersen, O.H.
401 Cilliers, H.
402 Vaughan, N.R.
403 Beck, T.S.R.
404 Navmann, H.
405 Smith, M.S.
Portview
Balfour Street
1 Hiam,J.N.
2 gerber,D.A.
3 Roets,J.N.J.
4 Van Rensberg,C.M.
5 Gerber,R.G.
6 Van Eeden,J.J.
7 Savage,J.
8 Struwig,P.C.
9 Morris,T.M.
10 Emslie,G.
11 Moore,G.E.
12 Crous, Mrs. B.
14 Meyer,O.J.
15 Oberholzer,S.G.
16 Gerber,A.L.

ROCK COURT
2 Love Street
1 Mactavish, Mrs. K.
1 Scwart,J.
2 Olivier,C.
3 Smillie,A.S.
4 Shore,J.

ROLYAT
237 WALMER ROAD
1 Dippen,M.J.
2 Matthee,H.P.
3 Vermeulen,L
4 Will,R.G.
5 Comley,C.B.
6 Lawson,G.
7 Daniels,N.W.
8 Buchner,J.
9 Gracey,J.A.
10 Theron,M.J.
11 Comley,R.H.
12 Meyer,I.J.
12a Devenish,P.J.
14 Boscombe,M.
15 Van Loggerenberg,W.H.
16 Van den Berg Mrs,S.H.
17 Jarvis,D.F.
18 Wyatt,B.J.
19 Van der Merwe,D,J.
20 Evans, Mrs. S.
21 Rosling,G.V.
22 Hancock,E.C.
23 De Kock,A.M.
24 Jens,G.L.
25 Radwe,A.
26 Hardiman,E.A.
27 Armston,R.
28 Feggetter,G.
29 Baldwin,C.S.

SOUTH BANK
163 WALMER ROAD
1 Damerell,B.M.
2 Da Silva,J.A.
3 Dietz,H.A.
4 Barnard,J.
4 Best Friuters
5 Mace,T.
7 Munro,M.H.

SOUTHERN COURT
163 WALMER ROAD
1 Sulchze,J.
2 Pienaar,D.
3 Erasmus,B.
4 Barnard,J.
5 Maree,J.L.
6 Du Preez,D.R.
7 Jack,D.A.

TEEMA FLATS
2 Harris Street
1 Bosch,V.
2 Dorkin,T.A.
3 Gradwell,G.R.
4 Taljaart,P.A.
5 Papoulias,G.
6 Sutton,M.A.
7 Hammerschmidt,M.
8 Robertson,K.
9 Fakas,A.
10 Elliot,W.H.R.
12 Slabbert,D.S.
13 Odendaal,D.M.
14 Oosthuizen,L.B.F.

THELMYR FLATS
214 WALMER ROAD
1 Ferreira,W.M.
2 Victor,S.D.
3 Williams,J.

UNION NOUSE
54 SOUTH UNION STREET
1 Botha B.
3 Oosthuizen,J.S.

VALLEY ROAD FLATS
57 VALLEY ROAD
1 Gerber,L.A.
4 Foskett, A.G.
5 Hulsman, R.
6 Rasmussen, T.
7 Meier, H.
8 Savador, A.D.C.

BIBLIOGRAPHY

A. PRIMARY SOURCES

NATIONAL ARCHIVES OF SOUTH AFRICA , De Villiers Street, North End, Port Elizabeth.

1. CITY ENGINEERS FILES
    1.1   Act and Ordinances- The Group Areas Act.
    1.2   Correspondence Files 2/4 Volume 1-4, 1951-1958.
    1.3   File No's 41/0/9 Volume 1, 1965-1966.

2. SCHOOL BOARD FILES

2.1   Minute Books
    2.1.1 Volume (3-9), 1899-1909
    2.1.2. Volume (25-30), 1924-1927.
    2.1.3. Volume (61-71), 1949-1957.
    2.1.4. Volume (78-83), 1960-1963.
    2.1.5. Volume (85-89), 1965-1969.

3. PRESS LIBRARY, TIMES MEDIA

3. 1 Press clippings from:
    3.1.1 Eastern Province Herald, 1950 to the present.
    3.1.2 Evening Post and Weekend Post, 1950 to the present.

4. AFRICANA COLLECTION, PORT ELIZABETH PUBLIC LIBRARY.

    4.1 South End, Voters' Roll of 1905/1906
    4.2 South End , Street Address of 1964/65
    4.3 South End, Bussiness Directory of 1916

5. INTERVIEWS

These are mainly former residents of South End in the field of education, religion and sports

1   Mr G. Abrahams, Religious and sports administrator, 14 January 1996
2   Mr Anthony, ex-Pincipal of Lea Place Primary, 1996
3   Mr D Barth, community and youth Leader, 18 July 1996.
4   Mr A Beaton, community leader, 18 January 1996.
5   Professor AJ Christopher, Head of Department, University of Port Elizabeth, 26 February 1997 and 4 March 1997.
6 Mr P. Clarke, sports administrator and Press Reporter, 12 May 1996.
7 Mrs E. Dantu, ex-pupil of St Monicas and St Thomas,
8 Mr E. De Kock, sportsman and sports administrator, 12 May 1996.
9   Mr R. Doraswami, former teacher at South End High School, sportsman and sports administrator, and later principal of Arcadia High School,
10 Mrs S George, former teacher at Hindu Primary School,
11 D Govinjee, former pupil of South End High School, sportsman and sports adminstrator, later

lecturer at Dower Training College, 12 November 1995.

12 Mrs M Harridene, librarian, Africana Collection, Port Elizabeth Public Library, 12 april 1996.

13 Mr A Jobson, sportsman and community leader, 4 December 1995.

14 Mrs E Marks, former teacher at Lea Place Primary School.

15 Mr S Pillay, community leader and businessman in South End, 23 April 1996.

16 Mr E. Such, former teacher at Hindu Primary School,

17 Mr R Uren, former teacher South End High school, sportsman, sports administrator and later principal of Bethelsdorp High School.

18 Mr and Mrs Williams, former teachers at St Monica's Primary School and parishioners of Blessed Oliver Plunkett Roman Catholic Church, 12 January 1996.

19 Mr E Yon, former teacher at Hindu Primary School, sportsman and sports administrator, 18 January1996.

20 Mr S Abrahams, sportsman and sports administrator, 3 April 1997.

21 Mr L Bruiners, school teacher at Gelvandale High, sportsman and sport administrator, 3 April 1997.

22 Mrs M Van Staden, former pupil and teacher of Sacred Heart School.

23 Mr S Abrahams, sportsman and sports administrator, 7 April 1997.

24 Mr K March, sportsman and sports administrator, 7 May 1997.

25 Mrs R. Parbhoo, sportswoman, 17 May 1997.

B. SECONDARY SOURCES

1.   BOOKS , BROCHURES, MAGAZINES, PAPERS

a.   Abrahams, A. (ed) *Muslim Heritage and Ancestry Port Elizabeth and Uitenhage*, (n.d.)

b   Du Pre,. R.H., *Separate but Unequal: The `Coloured' People of South Africa; A Political History*. Johannesburg: Jonathan Ball, 1994.

c   Du Preez, I.F. and R.H.du Pre, *A Century of Good Hope: A History of the Good Hope Conference, its Educational Institutions and Early Workers, 1893 - 1993*. East London: Western Research Group, 1995

d.   Durham, B. *A brief History of the church of St Mark and St John the Evangelist..* Parkside, 1989.

e   Harridene, M., *Port Elizabeth, A Social Chronicle to the end of 1945,* Port Elizabeth: EH Walton and Sons, 1997

f.   Harris, K. `Accepting the Group, but not the Area: The South African Chinese and the Group Areas Act.' Paper presented at the South African Historical Society Conference, Pretoria (6-9 July 1997.

g.   Historical Society - History of Port Elizabeth Indians.

h   Human,L.,*The Chinese people of South Africa:Freewheeling on the fringes.* Pretoria: University of South Africa, 1984.

i   Kenhall, H. *By taking Heed: The History of the Baptist Church in Southern Africa 1820-1977.*

j   Redgrave,J.J.*Port Elizabeth in Bygone days*, Rustica Press, Wynberg, 1947.

k   Smedley,L.N. *The Chinese Community in South Africa.* Pretoria: Human Science Research Council,1984.

l.   Union Congregational Church, *Port Elizabeth; 150thAnniversary brochure, 1830-1980.* Port Elizabeth, 1980.

m.   *Victoria Park High School, A brief history 1940-1990.* Port Elizabeth, 1990.

n.   Victoria Park Grey Primary School, School Magazine, Vol 7, 1995, Port Elizabeth.

o.   *Walmer Road Baptist Church, Port Elizabeth, 75th Jubilee 1888-1963.* Port Elizabeth, 1963

2 THESES AND DISSERTATIONS

a   Abrahams,C.C. `A pedagogical evaluation of the role played by inter alia various churches in the education of the Coloured child in Port Elizabeth area between 1803 and 1940', M.Ed dissertation, University of Port Elizabeth, 1989.

b   George, A.C., `The London Missionary Society, A study of the Eastern Cape to 1852', M.Ed dissertation, University of Rhodes, Grahamstown, 1983.

c.   Hendricks, S., `Arthur Nortje: A Biography of the South African Years, 1942-1965.' B.A. Honours Extended Essay, Vista University, 1996.

d.   Nel, J.G., `Die geografiese inpak van die Wet op Groepsgebiede en verwante Wetgewing op Port Elizabeth' M.A dissertation, University of Port Elizabeth, 1987.

e   Terblanche,H.O., `Die Nederduitse Gereformeerde Kerk in Port Elizabeth, 'n Historiese oorsig van die eerste halfeeu (1907-1957)', M.A. dissertation, University of Port Elizabeth, 1973.

3   NEWSPAPER ARTICLES

a   Du Plessis, C. `The hill of History', Weekend Argus, 7 May 1983.

b   Michaels,J. `The last days of South End', .

c   Oliver,E. `South End as I knew it', Magazine, Weekend Post, 18 July 1987.

d   Van Wyk, Linda, `Golden days in old South End', Family Post, 25 July 1987.

4. PHOTOGRAPHS.

a   Bob Binnell Collection.
b   Times Media Library.
c   Africana Collection.
d   Mr T. Abrahams
e   Mr S. Abrahams
f   Mrs S. Samuels
g   Mrs R. Peterson
h   Mrs F. Hendricks
I   Mrs S. Sataar
j   Mr Simon

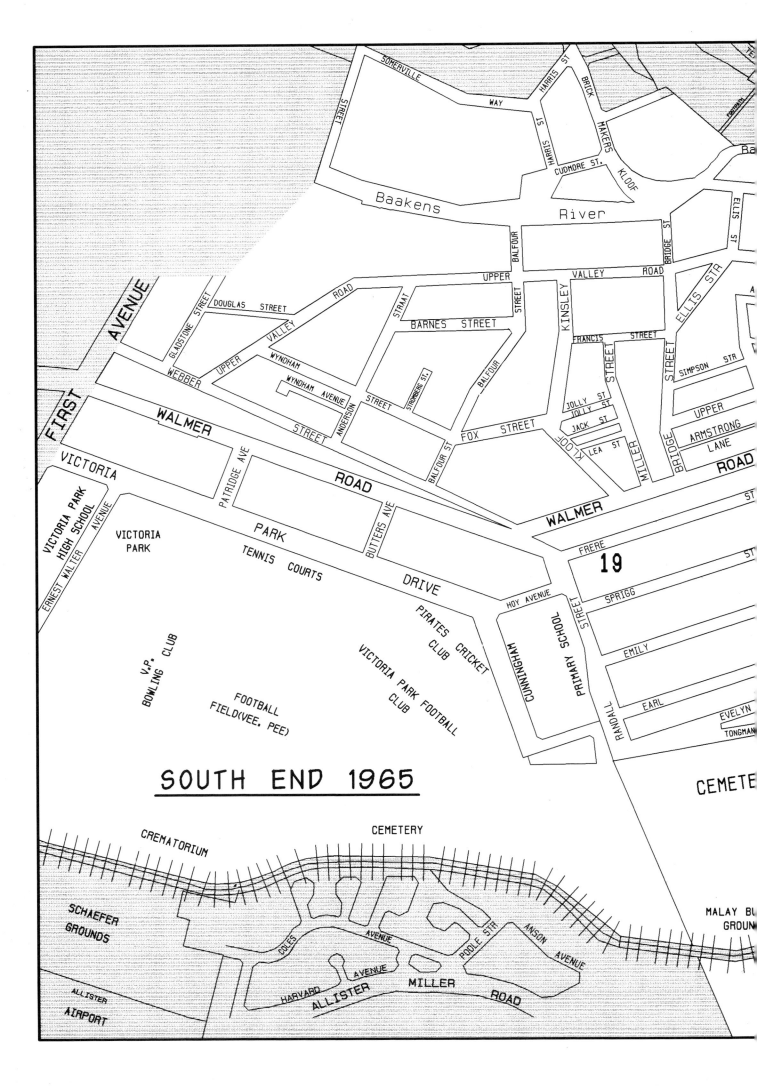

SOMERVILLE STREET
WAY
HARRIS ST
HARRIS ST
BRICK
MAKERS
KLOOF
CUDMORE ST.
ELLIS ST
ELLIS STR
Ba

Baakens River

BALFOUR
BRIDGE ST
UPPER ROAD
VALLEY ROAD
KINSLEY
STREET
FRANCIS STREET
ELLIS STREET
SIMPSON STR

FIRST AVENUE
GLADSTONE STREET
DOUGLAS STREET
VALLEY ROAD
STRAAT
BARNES STREET
STREET
WYNDHAM
WEBBER
UPPER
WYNDHAM AVENUE
STROMBERG ST.
ANDERSON STREET
STREET
BALFOUR
JOLLY ST
JOLLY ST
JACK ST
UPPER
ARMSTRONG LANE

WALMER STREET
STREET
FOX STREET
BALFOUR ST
KLOOF
LEA ST
MILLER
BRIDGE
ROAD

VICTORIA
PATRIDGE AVE
ROAD
BUTTERS AVE
WALMER
ST
STr

VICTORIA PARK HIGH SCHOOL
ERNEST WALTER AVENUE
VICTORIA PARK
PARK
TENNIS COURTS
DRIVE
HOY AVENUE
FRERE
19
St

SPRIGG
CUNNINGHAM STREET
PRIMARY SCHOOL

V.P. BOWLING CLUB
FOOTBALL FIELD(VEE, PEE)
PIRATES CRICKET CLUB
VICTORIA PARK FOOTBALL CLUB
EMILY
EARL
EVELYN
RANDALL
TONGMAN

SOUTH END 1965

CEMETE

CREMATORIUM
CEMETERY

SCHAEFER GROUNDS
MALAY BU
GROUN
COLES AVENUE
POOLE STR
ANSON AVENUE
ALLISTER AIRPORT
HARVARD AVENUE
ALLISTER MILLER ROAD